# Defense policies of East-Central European countries after 1989

MANCHESTER
1824

Manchester University Press

# Defense policies of East-Central European countries after 1989

Creating stability in a time of uncertainty

**JAMES W. PETERSON AND JACEK LUBECKI**

Manchester University Press

Published by Manchester University Press
Altrincham Street, Manchester M1 7JA, UK
www.manchesteruniversitypress.co.uk

*British Library Cataloguing-in-Publication Data is available*

ISBN 978 1 5261 1042 8 hardback
ISBN 978 1 5261 1043 5 paperback

First published by Manchester University Press in hardback 2019

This edition published 2020

Typeset by Servis Filmsetting Ltd, Stockport, Cheshire

# Contents

# Tables

# Acknowledgements

It is important to acknowledge the political courage of those leaders and societies who accomplished the 1989 changes that led to the adoption of liberal-democratic systems in the Czech Republic, Hungary, Poland, and Slovakia. Those transformations enabled the preparation of national defense policies that served to protect their states as well as contributing to the important regional and global missions of NATO and the EU.

The editorial staff at Manchester University Press have provided unwavering support for the project and the authors are thankful for that. Jim Peterson also acknowledges the mutual respect that he and his co-author Jacek Lubecki have for each other, a reality without which this book would not have been a possibility. Finally, Jim would like to thank his wife Bonnie for her strong support for this and all of his projects.

Jacek Lubecki would like to extend his thanks first and foremost to Jim Peterson, without whom the book would not have happened, and to his Hungarian consultant, Professor András Rácz of Péter Pázmány Catholic University in Budapest, without whom the Hungarian chapter could not have been written. He is also grateful to the publishers of *The Polish Review*, who allowed him to use selections from his article "Poland in Iraq" (2005) in chapter 6 of the book. His thanks go to his fiancée Christine Barsky, who inspired him during the writing, his daughter Francesca Lubecki-Wilde, who helped him with editing, and to his mother Kazimiera Lubecka, for her assistance with the research.

# Abbreviations and acronyms

| | |
|---|---|
| AfD | Alternative for Germany |
| CFSP | Common Foreign and Security Policy (EU) |
| CSDP | Common Security and Defense Policy (EU) |
| EEAS | European External Action Service |
| ENP | European Neighborhood Policy |
| ESDP | European Security and Defense Policy (EU) |
| EUAM | EU Advisory Mission (Iraq) |
| EUFOR | EU Force |
| EULEX | EU Role of Law Mission |
| GDP | Gross Domestic Product |
| HDF | Hungarian Defense Forces |
| KFOR | Kosovo Force |
| MON | Ministry of National Defense (Poland) |
| NATO | North Atlantic Treaty Organization |
| OSCE | Organization for Security and Cooperation in Europe |
| PESCO | Permanent Structured Cooperation on Security and Defense (EU) |
| PfP | Partnership for Peace (NATO) |
| PiS | Law and Justice Party (Poland) |
| PO | Citizens' Platform Party (Poland) |
| PRT | Provincial Reconstruction Team (Afghanistan) |
| V4 | Visegrád Four (Czech Republic, Hungary, Poland, Slovakia) |
| WTO | Warsaw Treaty Organization (or Warsaw Pact) |

# Introduction and overview

## Theoretical framework

Chapter 1 develops theoretical constructs that will guide the analysis in ensuing chapters. Its central argument is that post-communist convergence between the Visegrád Four (V4) defense policies is best understood as a result of the universal adoption of liberal-democratic political systems and ideologies by the countries in question. However, the chapter argues, post-communist divergence in the respective countries' defense policies, made especially visible by their post-2014 differential reactions to the Russo-Ukrainian Crisis and its fallout, cannot be understood within the framework of liberalism as both a political system and a theory of international relations. Different schools and concepts of realism and constructivism are therefore evoked as necessary for illuminating the noted divergence between Poland, which responded robustly and in militaristic fashion to the perception of a Russian threat, and the rest of the Visegrád countries, with their lukewarm responses. Within realism, the chapter draws attention to Poland's distinctive geopolitical position. Within constructivism, the chapter considers the notions of 'role theory' and 'strategic cultures' as a key for understanding the countries' diverging polices.

## Pre-1945 historical and political experiences

Chapter 2 focuses on the deep regional and historical contexts that were characteristic of the period leading up to the imposition of communist controls in the late 1940s. There is differentiation between the long era leading up to nation-state formation after the First World War and the interwar/Second World War era.

Prior to 1918, there was much historical variation in the political experiences of the four geographic units spread across the East-Central European region.

Czechs fell under Austrian control after their defeat at the Battle of

White Mountain in 1620, and so three centuries under the control of Vienna became their destiny but also the source of deep resentment against control by an outside power. However, Bohemian experiences prior to the defeat by Austria became a kind of basis for national pride and even democratic expression in later decades. The memory of King Wenceslaus in the tenth century animated artists and musical composers in the late nineteenth century. Contributions of King Charles IV in the fourteenth century reminded later Czechs of the importance of his reign as well as practical results such as the creation of the second oldest university in Europe, construction of the famous bridge across the Vltava River, and initial work on what later became known as Prague Castle. A century later, Jan Hus inspired a movement that challenged domination from Rome and the detailed strictures of the Catholic Church. As such, the Hussite battles animated later aspirations for popular participation within the Austrian Empire and beyond.

For Poles, the key memory was loss of their geographic, territorial, and political homeland, which had been a large multinational empire, between the partitions by the three large empires in the 1790s and recreation of their own state after the First World War. Just like in the Czech case, the memories of pre-foreign colonization glories animated Polish nationalism of the nineteenth century. Indeed, early nineteenth-century dreams of its recreation led Romantic poets such as Mickiewicz to compare Poland's situation to that of the crucified Christ. According to Mickiewicz, Poland's intense religiosity and loyalty to Rome would somehow bring about a national resurrection, which in turn would usher in a universal liberation of all peoples of Europe. In more concrete terms, Poles continued their military and political struggles for independence under Napoleon and in a series of national uprisings (1830, 1846, 1848, 1863, 1905), mostly aimed against Russia. It was also in a war against Soviet Russia that Poland solidified its independence in the 1918–20 period.

In contrast, Budapest was in charge of a large empire that included Romanians, Serbs, Ukrainians, Slovaks, and others. It shared center stage with the more powerful Austrian Empire to the northeast, but still its leaders had plenty of room for self-confidence, in contrast to the Poles and Czechs. Merging of the two Central European Empires into the Dual Monarchy in 1867 provided a location and status for Hungary that the envious Czechs never received.

The Slovak situation was quite different, in part because of its smaller size in comparison to the other three units that eventually became nations in the Visegrád Group. Lack of attention from Budapest left the Slovaks in need of much development after becoming part of Czechoslovakia in 1918. It may be that their intense Catholic religiosity was also a substitute for the lack of political clout. Joining with the more developed Austrian-dominated Bohemia after the First World War may have led to a sense of dissonance, as the Czechs clearly dominated the newly created Czechoslovakia, and many Slovaks felt that they substituted one form of subordination for another.

Between 1918 and 1945, transitions were more similar in the region under consideration. All developed democratic political forms to fit into their new nation-states under heavy pressure from the West after the end of the Great War. After all, President Woodrow Wilson had taken the US into the war to make the world safe for democracy. However, by the end of the 1920s, only Czechoslovakia retained those democratic forms in the manner in which they had been created. Hungary's six-month experiment with communist rule in 1919 led to a military crackdown, while Marshall Piłsudski had risen to power in Poland by the late 1920s. The emergent authoritarian patterns of the late 1920s and early 1930s multiplied and morphed into profoundly different totalitarian rule once Hitler's conquests commenced in the mid-to-late 1930s. Concentrated rule from Berlin was the sharpest possible contrast to the quiet democratic hopes of 1918. Rule by outside invaders, establishment of concentration camps, and efforts to eradicate the large Jewish population in the region stimulated common fears and enormous tragedies within the whole of Central Europe.

The legacies from this long historical period for the region after 1989 are many and, as to be expected, point to divergence among the four. A legacy of democratic expression may be most characteristic of the Czechs. The Hussite revolts against control by Rome in the fifteenth century, political and cultural expressions of resistance to Vienna in the late nineteenth century, and a relatively successful experiment with democracy in the 1920s, put a stamp on their activities after the fall of communism. In contrast, Slovak legacies centered on smoking resentment at their subordination to outside powers with little chance for their own national autonomy. First Budapest and then Prague after 1918 became authority symbols that seemed to demonstrate continuing insensitivity to Slovak needs and distinctiveness. Thus, it is not too surprising that they created their own nation-state in 1993, merely four years after the overthrow of the Czech-dominated communist system. For Poles, a resistant and undying devotion to their territorial state and the looming Russian threat was a lesson from past history, and so it is understandable why their leaders after 1989 sought to play a critical and central role in the narrowly defined region, as well as within the wider framework of EU and NATO. Hungary had become used to a larger state and the dominant role within it in the period prior to 1918. The Treaty of Trianon sharply cut back on its size and provoked a strong nationalist reaction. A legacy that carried over into post-communist times was an intense desire to protect those Hungarians who ended up outside the nation. Under Prime Minister Viktor Orbán after 2010, this kind of self-defensiveness and protectiveness appeared to many observers to be extreme and part of the ultra-nationalist European movements that took out their frustrations on migrant groups that had ended up in their nation. Hungary's negative reaction to the huge inflow of migrants from Syria and elsewhere in September 2015 was a powerful expression of this outburst of extreme nationalism.

The theme of political development also looms large in considering the preparedness for effective self-rule within a democratic political framework after 1989. In so many ways, the historical and political transitions converged. Certainly, the experience of each of the newly freed states after 1989 had been with state-centered varieties of political development. Subordination to imperial rule was a common pre-1918 political pattern for all four post-communist states, and was also the dominant reality of the 1945–89 period. Even though the imperial controls had been characteristic of the distant past, historical memories of them continued to percolate throughout the cultures. German and Soviet occupations again took away any traditions of self-rule and democracy that had germinated in the 1920s, as subordination to a massive, centralized, terroristic state became the hallmark for nearly a decade.

The democratic components of political development were not exactly out of sight but were harder to delineate as important features of their national experiences. Each of the three post-First World War East-Central European states set up democratic (or, semi-democratic, in the Hungarian case) systems under considerable Western pressure. Their situation paralleled that of the defeated German state with its Weimar Republic. However, in all of these European cases (with the partial exception of Czechoslovakia), the participant political culture that must underpin democratic institutions and governance was shaky. They had all been in the habit of following political directions from the imperial capitals, and so the fuel that would power the practice of democracy was at a very low level.

## The communist era, 1945–89

Chapter 3 centers on the important key points that may have figured in security policy formation after 1989. Interestingly, each of the three nations in communist times revolted against the combined force of their own local communist regimes and Moscow. In 1956, Poland challenged the presence of Soviet personnel in their own political system and emerged with limited autonomy after successfully defying and pacifying the Soviets, after Khrushchev flew the Politburo into Poland in a show of force. During the same year, the Hungarians developed a broad based program of reform under Nagy that anticipated a multiparty political system as well as the growth of representative interest groups. Departure from the newly created Warsaw Treaty Organization (WTO) was also part of the program. Invasion by the troops of the Soviet military brought a quick halt to the reforms and led to an outflow of refugees. The Prague Spring Reforms of 1968 in Czechoslovakia were equally broad based but also included a significant demand for greater protection of freedom of expression. Invasion by Warsaw Pact forces in August of the reform year replaced the Spring with a deadening Winter. The Polish challenge continued to resonate in future decades, with significant demands expressed in 1970, 1976, and 1980. The Solidarity challenge of 1980–81 was rooted in considerable popular support and spread like wild fire throughout the nation. Surprisingly, a crackdown by the Polish military, rather than outside forces, brought it to an end. Significantly, only Poland avoided Soviet invasion, which, the book claims, is an important part of explaining post-1989 long-term divergence between Poland and the other Visegrád countries.

However, the larger picture in all three East-Central European nations was the uniformity of rule by communist elites through institutions inherited from the Soviet model. National leaders emerged through the mystery of inside politics within the respective Politburos, and policy ratification occurred through the Central Committee sessions that regularly occurred throughout the year. Every five years, Party Congresses took center stage, with accompanying newspaper issues often printed in the characteristic "red." Recentralization of controls in Moscow was the normal pattern after the repression of the local reform movements, and the rebellions seemed to be the exception rather than the rule.

All of the above-described events and patterns have national security implications and thereby influenced defense thinking and paradigms after 1989. In terms of actual legacies, the three nations in communist times each challenged Soviet controls in somewhat different ways. Thus, the lessons that they extracted from each episode would probably have been different, and so divergence of conclusions may have been likely. In addition, each of them had been part of the Warsaw Pact but also victims of it. That experience may have carried over after 1989 in terms of their differing expectations about becoming part of Western security organizations such as NATO and EU. They joined the Western alliance voluntarily, but still they may have inherited a kind of ambivalence about following dutifully each proposal and project that came from Brussels.

In terms of political development, the lack of attention in communist times to anything connected with democracy may have produced convergence of experiences and expectations for all of the Visegrád players. Now, after a quarter of a century of democratic practices in the four countries, it is clear that it takes a long time to develop the strong roots of a stable democracy in a short period of time. Political parties have come and gone, while national leaders have risen to power quickly but have fallen from grace just as fast due to inexperience, corruption, or the tendency to become wrapped up in causes that have no staying power. In spite of that reality, democratic development has proceeded apace, and it may be that the apparent shallowness of the political roots of democracy is related to the common and converging experience of wanting never to repeat the excessively statist solutions of the communist era.

## Country studies

Each of the four nations will receive attention in a separate chapter dealing with the high points of national defense and security policy considerations after 1989. Some experiences are held in common. For example, each of the Visegrád nations joined NATO in the 1999–2004 period. Each contributed troops and experienced casualties through participation in alliance projects. Their military involvement in Bosnia after the 1995 Dayton Agreement and in Kosovo after NATO engagement in 1999 made sense in terms of overall alliance goals. Part of the reason for offering membership to East-Central European nations was to have full-fledged regional partners who could contribute to nearby areas of conflict. For Hungary, especially, pacification of the Western Balkans contributed directly to the country's security. The Visegrád countries' contribution to the American-led operations in Afghanistan and Iraq, likewise, revealed the countries' common desire to show loyalty to NATO and its hegemon.

However, dramatically different rates at which the countries contributed to multilateral operations also showcased the growing divergence in their respective defense policies and capacities. As our analysis shows, Poland stood out in its continuous emphasis on military capacity and, therefore, in the desire and ability to contribute to multilateral missions. This was a result of a combincation of internal and external factors, the former conditioned by the country's political culture, and the latter by the perception and reality of Russian threat. Conversely, the other

V4 countries had cultures which de-emphasized military spending, and developed threat perceptions in which Russia did not feature in any prominent way. Reasons for this divergence are given below.

## Return to the theoretical framework

Chapter 8 pulls together the emergent data from the four country security studies in light of the initial theoretical components. What legacies from the pre-1989 period gave each of their security policies such a distinctive flavor and contributed to divergence within the Visegrád defense community? How did their own political development after 1989 generate convergence among them on questions of national security? In answering these questions, the book contributes to the building of theory on the matter of East-Central European security questions. In light of the Ukrainian/Crimean Crisis and resurgent Russian policy ambitions, these are questions of considerable importance.

# I

# Theoretical framework: liberalism, realism, and constructivism

## Divergences and convergences after 1989

In the first years after the seismic events of 1989, there was a widely shared belief that the V4 collective adoption of liberal internationalist ideology would translate into congruent foreign and defense policies in each country. This would arise through the implementation of a democracy, and assumptions of "democratic peace" theory which suggested the dissolution of the Soviet Union would make the world a safer place because emerging democracies are disinclined to fight one another. The relatively quick replacement of the WTO with NATO confirmed these strong hopes. Nations strove to join both NATO and the EU, willingly implementing domestic democratic practices in order to pass the various checkpoints set up by these international organizations. As the Czech Republic, Hungary, Poland, and Slovakia all constructed liberal polities domestically, and adjusted their foreign and defense policies to liberal internationalist frameworks, there is no question a policy convergence occurred among the V4 post-1989 which persists to this day.

However, not until the Ukrainian Crisis exploded in 2014 were V4 countries exposed to a security threat, the geographical proximity of which highlighted their truly divergent foreign and defense policies, which had been manifest practically in these countries since before communism. Though all V4 countries continue to operate within a liberal internationalist framework, Poland in particular has differentiated itself with a more proactive military presence than any of the other V4 countries.

Poland has consistently spent a significantly greater amount of its budget on military buildup and operations than the other V4 countries since the fall of communism. In fact, since joining NATO, Hungary, Slovakia, and the Czech Republic have distinguished themselves by a growing neglect of their militaries in budgetary allocations. Conversely, Poland's dimensionally greater concern with the continual threat posed by Russia has been visible since the 1990s. However, it is thrown into relief especially today, in the wake of the Ukrainian Crisis. Poland's accelerated military buildup since 2014 – as contrary to the other V4 leaders' lukewarm reactions and even expressed sympathy towards Putin – reveals a profound divergence that should be examined.

To understand the post-communist foreign and defense policies of the Visegrád Group, their Communist and pre-communist political histories must be analyzed. Though Poland's current foreign and defense policies provide the most distinct point of contrast within the V4, it is essential to understand the nuanced historical legacies and geopolitical circumstances of each of the four East-Central European countries in order to contextualize Poland's status. Why is Poland an outlier? And why are the other V4 countries so unconcerned about their defense against a once-more looming Russian threat?

## Liberalism, realism, and constructivism

In order to answer these highly relevant questions, a theoretical framework must be established for analyses of these countries, past and present. It comes as little surprise that liberalism, and its derivative liberal internationalism, is the group of international relations theories which most compellingly explain defense policy convergence in post-1989 East-Central Europe. Liberalism is a second-level-of-analysis international relations framework which views the type of domestic political system a country implements as the decisive factor in understanding that country's foreign and defense policy choices. Specifically, the long-standing practice and ideology of liberal democracy are seen as decisively modifying foreign policy behavior. Famously, as expressed in the "liberal peace theory," liberal democracies do not go to war against each other. Liberal democracies also tend to create international institutions that project and protect liberal democratic principles such as rule of law. Liberal democracies tend to cooperate in a sphere of international interaction in a pattern called liberal internationalism (Doyle 1986).

The establishment and consolidation of liberal democracies in the V4, their desire to join NATO and the EU, and their behavior as loyal members of these two powerful institutions is best explained by liberalism. The successful political development of East-Central European countries as liberal democracies since 1991, and their resulting convergent foreign and defense policies, will, therefore, be approached here through a liberal theortical framework. However, this framework will only serve to understand V4 foreign and defense policy convergence. Another theory must be utilized to understand the simultaneous V4 divergence and Polish exceptionalism that can be observed most notably since the 2014 Ukrainian Crisis.

To understand foreign and defense policy divergence in the V4, two theoretical frameworks present themselves. First, realism. Realist theories assume that states pursue power (classical realism) or survival (neo-realism), and, under conditions of security dilemma, they inevitably threaten and wage war. Accordingly, realist scholars expected post-Cold War Europe to revert to multi-polar conditions characterized by wars and threats of war. For example, John Mearsheimer predicted a conflict between Hungary and Romania over the Hungarian minority in northern Transylvania (Mearsheimer 1990). Though this did not occur, realists can still explain the persistence of relative peace in Europe with the presence of US hegemony. Realists argue an unstable and insecure world would naturally follow a withdrawal of US security commitment to Europe – a prospect which both the Obama and Trump presidencies brought closer to the fore.

A form of "soft" realism based on a notion that states balance against any concentration of power also applies to some realities of post-communist Europe. It can be used to explain why all peripheral European countries ("the New Europe") aligned with the US in the run-up to the Iraq Crisis of 2003 (balancing against the Franco-German tandem) and why all Visegrád countries today are likewise pushing against the EU core states, showing a predilection towards Atlanticism (Michta 2006). Similarly, CSDP can be interpreted as a form of soft-balancing against the US, or a security guarantee in expectation of US withdrawal from NATO/Europe (Merlingen 2012). The fact that diplomatic rather than military relations are the foundation for this "soft" realist conceptualization of V4 policy, though, makes this framework less important for the book, which discusses military defense policies.

Still, realism remains a seemingly compelling framework for explaining "Polish exceptionalism" in terms of Poland's perception of a Russian threat. Poland's geographical proximity to Russia, specifically the Kaliningrad oblast', as well as Poland's size as compared to the Czech Republic, Hungary, and Slovakia, seems to confirm realism's relevance to the discussion of V4 divergence. As a medium-sized power, Poland has both greater security interests and a greater ability to react to perceived threats than the other, smaller, V4 countries, which do not border Russia directly.

The tendency of small states to be "policy takers" and simply adjust to given power realities is a well-known concept in realist international relations theory. However, the concept of the "small state" is also inherently problematic as a descriptor of an objective rather than a subjective reality (Hey 2003, 3–4). Israel, which is smaller in terms of territory and population than Slovakia, Hungary, or the Czech Republic, is certainly not perceived as, nor does it act as, a "small state." Likewise, interwar Hungary, smaller in population and virtually identical in boundaries to today's Hungary, pursued policies of aggressive territorial revisionism against its neighbors, which could not be more different from the country's liberal internationalist policies pursued today. In this case, virtually identical structural circumstances did not result in the same outcomes. Clearly, countries' strategic interests are not a simple reflection of their structural circumstances, such as geography and size, but are results of structural circumstances as processed by particular perceptual lenses.

Perceptual realities point out us in the direction of constructivist frameworks and concepts such as "strategic culture" and "role theory" as more compelling explanations of the patterns of defense policy behavior that we see among the V4 countries. Indeed, constructivist frameworks, which focus on countries' self-perception based on the lessons of the past ("strategic cultures")[1] or the constructed and assumed roles the countries play in international organizations ("role theory")[2] offer indispensable theoretical lenses to examine V4 divergence, as well as clarify the convergence, of post-communist defense policies in Hungary, Poland, Slovakia, and the Czech Republic (Gray 1999, Aggestam 2004).

The "strategic cultures" framework asks us to examine a nation's history and culture in order to understand its defense policies. Through this lens, we are compelled to set aside an objective understanding of a country's place in a geopolitical order for a moment, and instead examine how the recent and remote perceptions a nation has of itself have formed a strategic culture within the country in question. When we take the time to understand elite and popular perceptions of defense and foreign relations within each respective V4 country, the domestic values of the people of Poland, Hungary, Slovakia, and the Czech Republic and their subsequent conceptualization of future threats, the findings are quite surprising. The common perception that the communist past has had a lasting legacy of extreme uniformity among the V4 is debunked and replaced with the conclusion that communism was a surprisingly powerful period in provoking diverging strategic defense cultures, particularly in Poland, whose military buildup contrasts decisively against the relative demilitarization of Hungary, Slovakia, and the Czech Republic since 1999.

Role theory coupled to strategic cultures, in turn, is indispensable for examining the still notable V4 convergence that occurred during the periods prior to and immediately after joining NATO, encompassed roughly by the period 1999–2011. The successful applications of Poland, the Czech Republic, and Hungary to be admitted to NATO in the first (1999) tranche of Eastern European applicants was clearly predicated on their ability to project themselves as useful potential alliance members to Western perceptions – security creators, not just security takers. As we will see, military spending in these countries spiked briefly during alliance accession, then declined precipitously among all of them except Poland. After joining NATO, all V4 countries played the role of "loyal members" of the alliance, with an emphasis on participation in the alliance's multilateral missions in the former Yugoslavia and Afghanistan. Similarly, all of the V4 countries embraced and played the role of "loyal members" of the CSDP framework. The countries' Atlanticist orientation, in turn, compelled all V4 countries to play the role of loyal ally to the US in Iraq.

However, this "loyalty game" was played consistently with dramatically different levels of commitment: the difference between Polish brigade-size (over 2,000 troops), combat-oriented, long-lasting deployments to Afghanistan and Iraq, as compared to typically company size (150–300 troops), typically non-combat, brief and reluctant deployments by Hungary, Czech Republic, and Slovakia, cannot simply be explained by Poland's greater size and capability, as the Polish commitment was not just quantitatively but qualitatively, greater. The "loyal ally" role was thus played by all, but the embodiment of that role was manifest quite differently. Differences in respective strategic cultures, and different perceptions of the Russian threat were decisive in explaining the most recent variance observable in the V4. The countries of the region that truly fear Russia have given money and lives to display their commitment to multilateral missions in the hopes that, if necessary, their Western allies would show the same alliance loyalty.

The discussion of concepts provided by constructivist fameworks brings us to a broader reflection on the future of the region. Unlike structuralist frameworks, such as realism (with its unrelenting pessimism) or liberalism (with its optimistic determinism, at least when coupled to a naïve understanding of Fukuyama's "end of history" thesis),[3] constructivism is non-deterministic and envisions a wide spectrum of "worlds that we make" (Onuf 1989). According to this framework there is nothing inevitable about the persistence of a liberal internationalist world that was joined and co-constructed by the countries of East-Central Europe after 1989. At the same time, and with all of the detected divergencies, if we discover that the core commitment to liberal frameworks in foreign and defense policies is by and large unchallenged, even in the case of the ideologically self-proclaimed "illiberal democracy" constructed by Orbán in Hungary, there might be reasons to expect that structures that support liberal order in East-Central Europe have a staying power that goes beyond vagaries of electoral politics and theatrics projected by loud nationalist populist leaders who seem to not really offer alternatives to liberalism in foreign policy The investigation concludes by conjecturing how much the rise of nationalist populism will change the pre-existing realities of East-Central European defense policies.

## Notes

1 Gray gives us a working definition of strategic culture: "the persisting (though not eternal) socially transmitted idea, attitudes, traditions and habits of mind, and preferred methods of operation that are more or less specific to a particular geographically based security community that has had a necessarily unique historical experience [...]. Furthemore, strategic culture can change over time, as new experience is absorbed, coded and culturally translated. Culture, however changes slowly" (Gray 1999, 51–2).
2 Aggestam states that "a role reflects norms and ideas about the purpose and orientation of a the state as an entity and as an actor in the international system" (Aggestam 2004, 8).
3 Fukuyama's 1989 "The End of History" article published in the *National Interest* was never properly understood and remains misunderstood, even by its own author. A notion of a long-term normative triumph of liberalism does not predict its unchallenged existence, or deny a possibility of illiberal challengers that might appear to prevail. For the text of the celebrated essay, see www.wesjones.com/eoh.htm, accessed July 31, 2017.

# 2

## Empires and peripheries: security and defense realities of East-Central Europe

### Pre-history: East-Central Europe prior to the nineteenth century and the emergence of modern empires – Poland's partitions

By around 1000 AD, the medieval entities of Bohemia/Moravia, Poland, and Hungary (but not Slovakia) emerged from the chaos of the early Middle Ages as Western (Latin) Christian states. For all three, their ethnic centers happened to correspond roughly to where the respective countries are situated today, but their nature and actual political boundaries varied widely, with volatile fates of their ruling strata. As the Middle Ages progressed, all three of them found themselves defined by the geopolitical space between the mostly Germanic Holy Roman Empire to the West, and Christian Orthodox or, later, Muslim entities to the East and Southeast. By 1500 the two most important of these Eastern entities became the Tsardom of Muscovy and the Ottoman Empire. Lovers of geopolitics and of "civilizational" logic can point out that the countries in question are today still defined by being situated between transnational entities in the West (NATO and the EU), and countries of mostly Orthodox (Russia and Ukraine, Romania, Serbia) or Muslim (Turkey) cultural heritage to the East.

The differences between the political developments of the East-Central European entities in question are as important as their similarities. Most importantly, Slovaks, or the Slavic population of roughly contemporary Slovakia did not develop a culturally distinct ruling strata of their own, and thus evolved as an "a-historical" people ruled by Hungarian/Magyar nobility until the emergence of modern national consciousness in the eighteenth to nineteenth centuries. Thus, the Slovak sense of "marginalization" or being "the periphery of periphery" has its roots in the inability of the Slavic population of Slovakia to develop its own forms of medieval statehood (Kirschbaum 1995). Conversely Bohemia-Moravia, Poland, and Hungary developed their native aristocratic strata and therefore became proto nation-states. However, in the modern/early modern period all three of them at one point or another became subject to foreign imperial entities, and, then, with modernity, re-emerged as nation-states. The timing and nature of this subordination and re-emergence varied. These processes, in turn, rooted the respective national political and strategic cultures, boundaries, and geopolitical positions in the modern age.

Hungarians or Magyars evolved from their conquest empire to a feudal imperial state spread around the Carpathian basin, becoming, among others, the ruling class of today's Slovak territories, where the nobility (of whichever ethnic origins) became Magyar or Magyarized (Makkai 1990a, 1990b, 1990c). The medieval Hungarian Kingdom flourished under the rule of the French Anjou, Germanic Luxemburg, and, finally, the indigenous Hunyadi dynasties in the fourteenth and fifteenth centuries (Bak 1990). Under this last dynasty, King Matthias Corvinus created an empire backed by a model mercenary professional army (the so-called "Black Army," or *Fekete Sereg*), which was unbeatable (Gyula 1982). However, the Ottomans ended the Hungarian medieval-renaissance state and its then ruling (Polish-Lithuanian) Jagiellonian dynasty at the battle of Mohács in 1526 (Wandycz 1974). From then until the early eighteenth century the bulk of Hungarian territories were to be divided and contested between the Ottoman and Austrian Habsburg Empires, while an autonomous, multicultural principality of Transylvania played on a balance of power between the two imperial sides. However, the loss of Hungarian sovereignty did not mean the end of Hungarian autonomous institutions or consciousness among the Magyar nobility and middle classes, which were spread all over the former lands of the Hungarian Kingdom.[1] Later, led by their indigenous elites, Magyars fought for a modern Hungarian nation-state against the Habsburgs in the eighteenth and nineteenth centuries.

The 300-year-long disappearance of Hungary as a significant sovereign entity fed a strategic culture marked by a sense of insecurity and fear of subjugation by outside forces. This culture was reinforced by the country's twentieth-century history, marked by the partition by the Treaty of Trianon (1920), subjugation by the German-Nazi (1944) and Soviet (1945–89) empires and, then, a revival of independence as a part of the Western European world since 1989. This independence, in the minds of more nationalistically minded Hungarians, has masked another form of imperial subjection.

The Czech lands (or Bohemia and Moravia), just like Hungary, developed a native nobility, together with their own political entity, the Duchy and later (since 1198) hereditary Kingdom of Bohemia, ruled by princes and kings of various dynasties – the native Přemislid, Luxemburg, Jagiellonian and Habsburg. This entity, almost since its beginning, was a part of the Holy Roman Empire and thus an intrinsic participant in politics of this mostly Germanic confederation. The Kingdom's development was also marked by a fair degree of Germanization, either directly by German-speaking settlers or through Germanic cultural influence on the native upper classes.

Characterized by an unusually high level of prosperity and urbanization, the medieval Bohemian Kingdom reached its peak in the fourteenth century. The fifteenth century was marked by Hussite wars, whereby the non-Germanized urban and rural native Czech and Moravian population fought back against Germanic forces using the Hussite heresy and revolutionary military tactics as ideological and material vehicles for success (Luetzow 1914). While the Hussites were never defeated in battle, they split into moderate and radical factions, with the latter being eliminated, and the former reaching a compromise which re-integrated the Bohemian Kingdom into the Holy Roman Empire. However, in the sixteenth and seventeenth centuries the Protestant upper strata of the Bohemian Kingdom resented imperial Habsburg rule, which resulted in in the rebellion of 1618, and the rebels' catastrophic defeat at the battle of White Mountain in 1620. This defeat was the Czech Mohács – as Bohemia and Moravia were reabsorbed by the Habsburgs; the native nobility and ruling urban elite were either exiled or subjugated, and the country re-Catholicized and further Germanized (Wedgewood 1961 [1938]).

With the battle of White Mountain the Czechs and Moravians largely lost their national agency until the emergence of modern nationalism in the eighteenth and nineteenth centuries and the creation of the Czechoslovak state in 1918. This triumph was short-lived, as the trauma of subjugation by outside forces was reinforced by the Western betrayal at Munich (1938), and German (1939–45), and Soviet (1948–89) takeovers. A similarity to the Hungarian case is uncanny. However, there is also a difference. With a progressive disappearance of identifiably Czech nobility after 1620, Czech consciousness was relegated to the lower social strata, especially the modern intelligentsia and bourgeoisie in the eighteenth and nineteenth centuries. Thus, when Czechoslovakia was created in 1918 its dominant Czech nationality carried a distinctly middle-class/bourgeois, liberal, democratic, and anti-imperial political culture, quite distinct from Hungarian aristocratic and imperial heritage. Also, there was no Czech equivalent to ethnic Hungarians being spread all over the Carpathian basin, Czechs being a compact nation with no significant post-imperial heritage of dispersion around former imperial space.

If the key dates in Hungarian and Czech early national traumas are 1526 (the battle of Mohács) and 1620 (the battle of the White Mountain), the Polish equivalent trauma was the Third Partition of Poland in 1795, which marked a disappearance of the sovereign Polish state from the map of Europe. The differences in timing mattered here. The Polish Kingdom's disappearance came relatively late (some 200 years after the Czech, and 300 years after Hungarian analogous events), on the brink of the modern political age, and after a long imperial existence as the Polish-Lithuanian Union or Commonwealth (1386–1795).

The origins of the Polish-Lithuanian Commonwealth date back to the Middle Ages, when in 1386 the Lithuanian Grand Duke Jogaila accepted the crown of the Polish Kingdom and thus merged the two countries in a dynastic union, creating the largest state in Christendom. The state continued as a dynastic union until the Union of Lublin of 1572 which created a single federal Commonwealth, ruled by its nobility and by an elected King through a proto-liberal representative constitutional system. This robust entity had its "golden age" in the sixteenth and early seventeenth centuries, reaching the maximum size of 1.2 million square km and some 11 million people, and occupying (roughly) the territories of today's Baltic states (Estonia, Latvia, and Lithuania), Poland, Belarus, and Ukraine (Davies 1982; Lukowski & Zawadzki 2006).

The Commonwealth was hugely diverse and multicultural, but united by its noble class (*szlachta*) which was spread all over the state, represented some 10–15% of its population, had a common political consciousness, and nominally ruled the country. Thus, as the Commonwealth faltered and shrunk due to external (chiefly Muscovy-Russian, Ottoman, and Swedish) and internal (progressive weakening of the central government) challenges, it left behind, all over its former territories, a distinctly Polish or Polonized populations, especially in what is today Lithuania, Belarus, and Ukraine. This post-imperial dispersion very much resembled the Hungarian case, and represented a national reality very dissimilar from the Czech compactness.

The final demise of the Commonwealth came when its ruling strata tried to strengthen and modernize the state, which the neighboring absolutist empires of Russia (under Empress Katherine the 2nd) Austria, and Prussia saw as a potential threat. While Hohenzollern Prussia and Habsburg Austria were eager to seize Polish territory, the chief agent and coercive enforcer of the partitions of Poland was imperial Russia. This reinforced a strategic theme of mutual hostility, fear and mistrust in the Polish-Russian relations, a theme that has persisted largely unchanged for the last 500 years.

The disappearance of early modern Poland came relatively late, on the brink of modernity, while the country had a politically conscious and nationalistically mobilized ruling strata. This meant that the partitioning empires had to deal with an almost constant Polish nationalistic resistance throughout the nineteenth century. Most importantly, Russia, which absorbed the bulk of the Polish population and territory, had to put down Polish armed uprisings in 1830–31, 1863–64, and 1905–7 (the latter a hybrid event which united features of a national uprising and a social revolution). Austria, in turn, confronted Polish national uprisings in 1846 and 1848, and Prussia confronted Polish armed resistance in 1848. Initially led by the Polish nobility and its middle-class descendants, and by a relatively small urban middle class, the Polish nationalist resistance against foreign occupations sought to involve Polish-speaking peasantry, which represented the vast majority of ethnic Poles. While militarily defeated, Polish defensive anti-foreign nationalism of the nineteenth century flourished, animated by memories of past glories of the Commonwealth,[2] and a desire to rebuild a Polish state. Due to this persistent nationalism the Polish state was revived in 1918, when all three of the partitioning empires were defeated in the First World War and collapsed from within.

Polish history featured themes very similar to the Bohemian and Hungarian past, including subjugation to external entities and a dramatic resistance against them, thus creating similarities in the countries' strategic cultures: a sense of geopolitical fragility, fear of subjugation, and defensive nationalism. Just like Hungarians, and unlike the Czechs, the Polish modern nation emerged as a post-imperial entity in the sense that the Polish population was spread all over the former Commonwealth, especially in territories of today's Belarus and Ukraine. Just like in the other countries under consideration, the 1939–89 Polish developments were to reinforce pre-existing themes of its strategic culture: a sense of fragility (the country was conquered by Nazi Germany and communist Soviet Union), a fear of betrayal (in the Polish perception, the country was betrayed by the West in 1939 and 1944), and a fear of subjugation (by Nazi Germany in 1939–45, and by the Soviet Union in 1945–89).

After 1989 Poland and its Central European neighbors, animated by hostility towards an imperial Soviet Union, rejoined the Western world eagerly, but there were themes of their political and strategic cultures that were conducive to potential anti-Western feelings – a fear of betrayal or of subjugation most importantly. At the same time, a fear of and hostility towards Russia has been present in Polish strategic culture to a degree several times greater than in the Czech Republic, Hungary, and Slovakia. The Polish geopolitical position (directly adjacent to Russia, specifically the Kaliningrad oblast') and Poland's size (demographically and territorially three to four times larger than either of the other three Visegrád countries) mattered, but the weight of the

500-year-long history of Polish-Russian confrontation was a factor of undeniable importance. The Russian hostility to Poland has been reciprocally deep – it is for this reason that in 2005 Putin established Russian National Unity Day on November 4, an anniversary of Russian expulsion of a Polish garrison from Moscow in November 1612, after two years of Polish occupation.[3] It mattered that the only foreign invader that successfully occupied Moscow for any extended period of time in the last 400 years were Poles.

## The nature of the Austro-Hungarian Empire and the emergence of the Czechs

In the millennium prior to the creation of Czechoslovakia in 1918, there were key events and developments of transcendent importance in configuring the security position and needs of the new state in its first century between 1918 and 2018. Particularly important among these were: the Hussite military and political accomplishments of the fifteenth century; the defeat of their army by the Habsburgs at the Battle of White Mountain in 1620; the outburst of nationalism during the 1848 Revolutions; the vacillation between Vienna's crack-down and reforms in ensuing decades; and resentment at the equal treatment provided to Hungary during the creation of the Dual Monarchy or *Ausgleich* in 1867.

During the fourteenth century, the Czech Lands marched to a high pedestal in the region under Charles IV, who served as their King as well as Holy Roman Emperor. During his rule, the second oldest university in Europe emerged, as a Catholic Church institution committed to the training of Jesuit priests. Bearing the emperor's name, it still stands today as the prestigious Charles University. He also commissioned the building of the Charles Bridge across the Vltava and thereby established a linkage between the area around the future castle and the commercial areas of the city. Furthermore, he began work on the Prague Castle, a task that would consume the efforts of several future generations. All these institutions still stand as reminders of the glories of the Czech past. Charles also visited Krakov, Poland, where he made important agreements and came to significant understandings with his Polish counterpart King Kazimierz the Great.

Nearly a century later, the leaders of these rejuvenated Czech Lands stood up to Rome and other regional leaders under the leadership of Jan Hus, the Rector of Prague University, later Charles University. A century before Martin Luther in Germany, he challenged the material claims of the church on peoples across the realm of Catholicism. Church leaders brought him to Geneva for a confession of his sins: his refusal to do so lead to his execution in 1415. His followers built an army that engaged in combat with the foreign leaders, in particular the Hungarian King Sigismund, who at one point occupied Prague Castle. Eventually, the Hussite Army in 1421 defeated the Hungarians at the famous Battle of Vitkov Hill, an accomplishment celebrated in Czech music through the twenty-first century. Memories of that victory heartened Czech nationalists in the late nineteenth century and were symbolically linked to the victories of the Czech Legion at Zborov in July 1917.

However, all this glory came to naught during the loss to the Habsburgs at the Battle of White Mountain in 1620, nearly two centuries after the heartening victory at Vitkov Hill. The battle was precipitated in part by the refusal of the Bohemian Diet to elect a new Habsburg as King in 1618. In fact, the Bohemian cavalry reached as far as Vienna, but their nobility would not make the sacrifices necessary for a victory over the Habsburgs. Thus, the loss at White Mountain provided the Czechs with the same subordinate status as the Germans, and only the Hungarians continued to possess semi-autonomous status (Taylor 1970, 15–17).

In the long run, the Czechs were subjected for the next two centuries to absolutist control by Vienna, whose controls resembled those of a "bureaucratic machine" (Taylor 1970, 44). Finally, in the 1840s, the Czechs became restive and formally began to tug at the corners of the Austrian blanket. In 1840, the Bohemian Diet made the formal decision that it had the right to reject political proposals that emanated from the Habsburgs. Then, six years later, they argued for restoration of rights to pre-White Mountain status. Pressures were brewing throughout the region and, in March 1848, the Bohemian Diet demanded a series of liberal reforms. There was a widespread basis to the political challenges from the Czech Lands, for the peasantry was activated in hopes of getting rid of the hated tax called the robot (Taylor 1970, 56–66). Burgeoning Czech and Moravian nationalists became engaged in the revolution, and the famed intellectual and nationalist František Palacký called for transformation of the Austrian Empire into a "federation of peoples" in his letter of April 11. In early June, discussion at a Pan-Slav Congress in Prague centered in part on discussions of reconstructing the Empire according to federal lines, within which the Czech nationality would be evident and respected (May 1951, 25). On June 12, the Whitsuntide Riots broke out in Prague, and the Czech Lands (Bohemia and Moravia) succumbed to the Habsburg military. Compromise was in the air, and many of the main players met at the Kroměříž Conference in southern Moravia to work out the details (Taylor 1970, 74–87).

During the 1850s, Vienna resumed a centralist approach through what became known as the Bach period (1849–59). Minister Bach dissolved the Kroměříž Assembly and called for the return of the Habsburg Empire into a "revived German Confederation" (Taylor 1970, 94). Czechs benefitted somewhat from the October Diploma announced in 1860, for the Habsburgs agreed to require cooperation between the Reichsrat and the provincial councils (Taylor 1970, 109, 124). However, in the early 1860s, the Austrian Minister Schmerling returned to the principles of Bach and reinforced the German's paramount role. Overall, in terms of security arrangements, the Habsburg state rested its controls on the bureaucracy, army, police, rural gendarmie, and Catholic Church (Agnew 2004, 126). Such arrangements subverted the spirit of the 1848 revolutionaries and postponed serious security changes for Czechs until much later.

The 1867 arrangement between Vienna and Budapest was, in addition, destabilizing to Czech security dreams. The arrangement was particularly unsettling, for the back and forth of reform movements had left the Czechs subtly subordinate to the Germans in several ways. For example, in the more relaxed period of the 1860s, Czechs still were underrepresented in their towns in comparison with the Germans. Czech deputies in the Imperial Parliament represented 12,000 inhabitants and the Germans only 10,000, and this gave the advantage to the Germans (Taylor 1970, 115). In 1867 the *Ausgleich* granted special status to the Hungarians, again at the expense of the Czechs. As a result, 80 Bohemian deputies boycotted meetings of the Reichsrat, and demanded the same equal rights status that Austria had just granted Hungary (Taylor 1970, 153–4).

The *Ausgleich* also led to the emergence of tábory, gatherings that evoked the memory of the Hussite period of the fifteenth century. Similarly named organizations were part of the protests by those Czech reformers against a similar pattern of central rule in the earlier period. An important milestone in the development of Czech nationalism was the decision to build a National Theater in Prague. Ordinary people from all over the realm contributed money to an institution that would be committed to presenting works of art in Czech rather than in German. Many gathered at the location for the Theater in 1868 in order to lay its cornerstone, and Czech protests against Vienna broke out on that occasion (Agnew 2004, 133). Additional activities by Czechs in reaction to the creation of the Dual Monarchy included a boycott of the Emperor Franz Joseph's visit to Prague as well as well as more demonstrations on the anniversary of Hus. There was also a military component to the Czech resistance, for Czech military conscripts declared that they would fight for neither Austria nor Hungary (May 1951, 51–2). Thereby, the spirit of the 1848 Revolution lived on.

The Taaffe Foreign Ministry (1879–93) set off another period of assertiveness by Czechs, who were able to establish a university in Prague that taught courses in Czech, while the outer service began to permit use of either Czech or German in administrative contacts with the public (Taylor 1970, 169–70). This language ordinance further required that all legal actions be done in the language of the petitioner (May 1951, 195). During the Badeni period of the 1890s, the Austrians granted the 1897 Ordinance, a striking document that permitted both Czech and German to be used for the inner service within the bureaucracy itself. Given the expected result that Czechs would have more jobs than Germans in the bureaucracy, German protests forced both the resignation of Badeni and cancellation of the plan (Taylor 1970, 196–211). In 1905, the Moravian Compromise carved up the region into national districts, each of which had the power to determine its own dominant language (Taylor 1970, 214). That Pact also called for universal suffrage without respect to nationality (Agnew 2004, 152).

In conclusion, Czechs fought difficult battles prior to creation of the state, although they were mainly political and less often military. However, it is true that that military and security issues often formulated the action plan for the political challenges. Memories of the Hussite victory at Vitkov Hill in 1421 encouraged nineteenth and twentieth century nationalists to endeavor to recreate that heroism in later times. In a very different way, the defeat at the Battle of White Mountain resonated through the next three centuries. Political challenges to the Habsburgs in the 1848 Revolutions aimed at repairing that earlier devastation. Unwillingness to accept the wavering Austrian signals about Czech rights in the decades after 1848 also reflected in part the continued humiliation of the results of White Mountain.

## Hungarian Empire, 1848–1918

The emergence of modern Hungarian, Czech, Slovak, and Polish nations and nation-states all followed the standard developmental route. Spurred by forces of cultural, economic, military, and political modernization, and factors such as the spread of literacy, a sense of cultural and political commonality emerged between groups previously divided by social status but united by factors such as common language and religion. These culturally defined groups, in turn, developed a sense of common political destiny in search of a nation-state. Indeed, the two processes – cultural and political – often emerged at the same time. Thus, for instance, Polish peasants (prior to the late eighteenth/early nineteenth century seen by Polish nobility as aliens to be held in serfdom) and Polish nobility or middle classes developed a sense of cultural and political commonality to create a modern, independent Polish nation. For all four nations under consideration, which were all under a form of foreign domination, it was relatively easy to define oneself in opposition to this domination, and in search of one's full national sovereignty. This goal, for all nations under consideration except Slovakia, was accomplished by 1918, but with important differences that have a bearing on the emergence of the respective strategic cultures and national boundaries.

Historically, the key moments in the emergence of nationalisms Europe-wide were first the Enlightenment, which celebrated national ("folk") languages, then, romantic nationalism which celebrated "folk" cultures and came mostly with a liberal (democratic, egalitarian, anti-authoritarian) political-ideological tinge. By the second half of the nineteenth century, nationalisms became increasingly intolerant, imperialist, authoritarian, and socially Darwinist, without fully subsuming the earlier liberal impulse. This evolution was present in all cases under consideration, but most fully in Hungary. Nationalist political development took the most liberal direction in Bohemia-Moravia, and the most "defensive" form in Slovakia (Wandycz 2001: 135–65). Poland, as we shall see, featured a "hybrid" form of nationalism, split between liberal and anti-liberal impulses.

The high point of Hungarian liberal nationalism was the Revolution/ War of Independence of 1848–49 when the country's Magyar gentry, intelligentsia, urban middle classes, and some peasantry fought for independence of the traditional territories of the Hungarian Kingdom from the Austrian Habsburg Empire. The dominant and most widely proclaimed ideological strain of the Revolution was national-liberal: besides national independence the Revolution proclaimed a republican form of government with a widespread array of liberal-democratic reforms (Deák 1990). However, as the Austrian Empire fought back, non-Magyars of the Hungarian Kingdom (mostly Croats, Serbs, and Romanians, plus some Czechs and Slovaks) were all too willing to fight for the Habsburgs. While the Revolution was only defeated by a massive Russian intervention, mutual hostilities between Hungarians and non-Magyar nationalities of the Hungarian Kingdom intensified.

By a twist of historical irony, after a dramatic defeat in the war against Prussia in 1866 the Austrian Empire turned to the Hungarian elite to rescue the failing state. This was accomplished by offering a form of limited national sovereignty to the Hungarian Kingdom within a framework of a confederate "Dual Monarchy." As a result the Hungarian part of the Dual Monarchy became the largest and most powerful, be it semi-sovereign, modern Hungarian state which existed between 1868 and 1918 (Tibor 1990). By the late nineteenth century, animated by a sense of Hungarian nationalism, the Hungarian state elite launched policies of Magyarization, an attempt to make all people of the country Magyar in culture and political consciousness. Helped by socio-economic modernization Magyarization was fairly successful. In the territories of the Hungarian Kingdom, by 1910 the percentage of the population reporting Hungarian as its mother tongue grew from 46.6% in 1880 to 54.5% in 1910, but the process was largely limited to urban middle classes, and left non-Magyar ethnic rural peripheries intact or irresponsive (Jeszenszky 1990). In the meantime, Serbia and Romania rose as nation-states, and Russia started pursuing a vigorous policy of pan-Slavism, stimulating and helping Czech, Slovak, and Ruthenian (Rusyn) nationalisms against the Austro-Hungarian Empire. With Serbian, Croat, Slovak, Romanian, and Rusyn minorities within its borders, the Hungarian Kingdom found itself challenged from within and without.

Hungarian foreign and defense policy prior to, during and shortly after the First World War attempted to square the circle of its strategic dilemma: a desire to maintain autonomy and survival within the Dual Empire, and the fear of encirclement and destruction by irredentist neighbors and potentially hostile national minorities. The latter concern required unity with Austria and an aggressive policy of deterrence or confrontation with Russia, Serbia, and Romania. The former consideration saw a potential war with neighbors with apprehension: even if successful, it meant an addition of extra national minorities to the Hungarian Kingdom, thus diluting its barely achieved Magyar majority. An unsuccessful war could lead to a total destruction of the Empire and the Kingdom (Jeszenszky 1990).

Between 1914 and 1918, Hungarian elites pursued varied and contradictory foreign policy courses. Initially, Austro-Hungarian Hungarian Prime Minister István Tisza was opposed to the war in 1914. By late 1914 and 1915, this was followed by Hungarian behind-the-scenes attempts to secede from Austro-Hungary and conclude a separate peace with the Entente in exchange for guarantees of Hungary's borders. This option was pursued, among others, by Hungarian liberal politician Mihály Károlyi. As the Central Powers' strategic fortunes improved with the defeat of Serbia (1915), Romania (1916), and Russia (1917), Hungarian annexationist nationalism grew and Hungary took over parts of Romania (May 1918, Treaty of Bucharest) and wanted to annex Bosnia, Dalmatia, and parts of Serbia (Fried 2014). However, as the entire Austro-Hungarian Empire faltered, Emperor Charles pursued secret separatist negotiations with the Entente trying to save the Empire. Likewise, the last Austro-Hungarian Prime Minister, Mihály Karolyi, promised a liberal order and nearly total autonomy to national minorities of the Hungarian Kingdom in an attempt to save it. This was too little and too late (Piahanau 2014).

The structure of the Hungarian military under the Dual Monarchy corresponded to Hungary's strategic dilemma. The Austro-Hungarian military consisted of three parts: the joint forces, with its army (Gemeindene Armee) large and underfunded, and separate forces of Hungarian (Honvédség) and Austrian (Landswehr) parts of the empire (Rothenberg 1981). The Honvédség was arguably the best funded of the empire's land forces, as the nationalistically minded Hungarian parliament lavished far more funds on its military than the liberally minded Austrian parliament (Rothenberg 1981). In 1914, prior to mobilization the Honvédség standing strength consisted of 9 infantry divisions (out of the total 48 divisions in the A-H Army) plus many independent formations, for the total of around 100,000 troops. The military's doctrine, training, and so on were subordinate to Vienna and reflected the European-wide orthodoxy which envisioned a short, sharp war of movement similar to the Franco-Prussian war. In the brutal war of attrition that followed, the Hungarian part of the empire ended up mobilizing 3,000,000–4,000,000 soldiers (Jeszenszky 1990). This was by far the largest military force that the country ever put into field during wartime, dwarfing in size the Royal Hungary military in the Second World War or the country's Armed Forces under communism.

The fall of Austria-Hungary unleashed radical forces opposed to the conservative and aristocratic system that ruled Hungary prior to 1918. A liberal republic under Károlyi proclaimed a wide array of freedoms and practically abolished the country's military, which made it helpless as armies of Romania and the nascent Czechoslovakia invaded Hungary. Then, a radical Hungarian Soviet Republic was proclaimed in 1919 under Belá Kun, who preached the gospel of class warfare and armed struggle against imperialist foreign powers in the name of a global proletarian revolution. Kun's regime of violence and radicalism unleashed equally brutal domestic reaction, which, eventually, led by former Austro-Hungarian Admiral Miklós Horthy and working in conjunction with invading armies of neighboring Romania and Czechoslovakia, destroyed the Hungarian Soviet Republic (Hajdu & Nagy 1990).

Horthy's restauration of the traditional social order in alliance with foreign invaders also meant that he was helpless when the Trianon peace Treaty of 1920 took away two thirds of pre-war Hungarian territory and 70% of its population, thus cutting Hungary to its bare ethnic core of around 7,600,000 inhabitants, and leaving some 3,000,000 Hungarians as ethnic minorities in neighboring countries, mostly in Czechoslovakia, Romania, and Yugoslavia. The 1918–20 defeat and disintegration of Austria-Hungary thus became the worst geopolitical catastrophe that the country had suffered since the battle of Mohács in 1526. As a result interwar Hungary was established as a reactionary "Kingdom of Hungary" under Regent Horthy, a revisionist country, pining for restauration of pre-1918 territories. The country's military and defense policies was bound to be defined by Hungarian revisionism (Ormos 1990).

In terms of Hungarian strategic culture, it is important to notice that Hungarians might be inclined to see the catastrophe of 1918–20 as result of an absence of full strategic autonomy under a supra-national imperial entity: the Austro-Hungarian Empire. On the other hand, Károlyi's republican episode showcased the weakness of pacifist liberalism and of Hungarian reliance on ideological sympathy of Western powers. Hatred of Marxist revolutionism (together with a fair dose of anti-Semitism, communism being perceived as "Jewish") was certainly instilled by the Belà Kun episode. However, most importantly, to the extent that Western Entente powers (chiefly France), together with ethnic neighbors, imposed the Trianon Treaty on Hungary, twentieth-century Hungarian nationalists were bound to see Trianon's makers as the chief national enemies. Elements of this resentment, coupled to a sense of betrayal by the West in 1956, are still alive in the country today, and partially explain the rise of modern Hungarian nationalist populism embodied by Prime Minister Viktor Orbán's and his FIDESZ party program tinged with resentment of the West.

## Special features of the Hungarian Empire and emergence of the Slovaks

In some ways, the subordinate role of the Slovaks in the Hungarian Empire shadowed Czech experiences under Austrian rule. At the same time, there were major differences in the treatment that each received from their imperial overlords. In addition, there were few connections between Czechs and Slovaks during the centuries of subordination, and this reality constituted warning signs for the eventual nation-state that included both ethnic groups.

While Czechs have been able to point to a rich experience during the Bohemian Kingdom, with great leaders such as King Wenceslaus, Charles IV, and John Hus, it has been more difficult for Slovaks to cite parallel historical periods of greatness. However, there was a Great Moravian

Empire until the tenth century, and it was a Slavic state that included both Morava and Nitra. Unfortunately for the Slovaks, the Magyars defeated the entity in 907, and the pattern of domination by Hungary would continue until the twentieth century. In 1526, the Ottomans defeated the Magyars at Mohacs, and this ended up ironically providing Slovaks with more administrative power and experience. Budapest moved the main administrative, cultural, and religious institutions to the Slovak areas to protect their overall position against the Ottoman rulers. By the eighteenth century, Hungary itself came more under the sway of Habsburg power, and Slovak linkages were firmly with Budapest from that time until 1918 (Kirschbaum 1995, 23–87).

Before and after the 1848 Revolutions, Slovak nationalism grew in important ways. For instance, from the 1780s on, there was considerable attention given to development of the Slovak language. Early on there was development of key principles of the literary language, and this enabled publication of inspiring folksongs in Slovak in the 1830s. Thus, Slovaks were prepared to participate in the national awakening that took place across Europe and came to a head in the 1848 Revolutions. In September leaders set up the Slovak National Council, which constituted the "first modern Slovak political institution" (Kirschbaum 1995, 113–19). Slovak nationalists even went so far as to issue the Myjava Declaration of Independence from Hungary, but Budapest reacted with a crack-down and punishment for those who were responsible (Kirschbaum 1995, 119).

Slovaks took a bold and definitive step forward in nation-building through their 1861 Memorandum, which followed an important meeting at Turčiansky Sväty Martin. This Memorandum called for equality between Hungarians and Slovaks within the imperial setting, but the Hungarian Diet refused to receive it. That interaction paralleled the Czech experience within the Habsburg Empire between 1620 and 1918. In the Slovak case, dissolution of the Hungarian Diet enabled the Slovaks to use their Memorandum to pass the Nationalities Act of 1868. In the 1860s, education in Slovak expanded considerably, and the opening of Matica Slovenska in 1863 was a great help in that regard. Inevitably, that organization became the "hub of Slovak cultural and literary endeavors" (Kirschbaum 1995, 133–5).

Although the *Ausgleich* of 1867 was primarily an arrangement between Vienna and Budapest, it did have an impact on Slovak nationality. Prior to that arrangement, there had been some efforts to create a Czecho-Slovak language that would bring these two peoples closer together. However, the arrangement between the two larger powers stopped that movement and further separated Czechs from Slovaks (Taylor

1970, 202). Furthermore, the Austrian-Hungarian agreement did not include any pressure on Hungary to recognize its various nationalities (Kirschbaum 1995, 128).

During the late nineteenth century, centralizing moves by Budapest had the result of pushing Slovaks closer to a solution that would engage the Czechs. In 1875, the Magyars closed the Matica Slovenska; the response of the Slovak National Party nearly a decade later was insistence on passivity in light of Hungarian pressure. In spite of the fact that the 1895 Nationalities Congress called on Hungary to become a multi-national state, the inevitable result was continued Magyarization. This step seems to have firmed up Czech and Slovak unifying moves, for a year later the Československá Jednota was founded in Prague with the intention of linking the two groups more closely. Czech-Slovak budding connections moved even further after the 1907 Černová Massacre, at which the deaths of nine Slovaks occurred.

It is clear that Slavic connections proceeded apace during the nationalist thrust of the nineteenth century. Developments occurred in growth of the official Slovak language, the uprising of nationalist feelings in 1848, and new organizational embodiments. The unabated pressure for conformity and Magyarization from Budapest ironically led the Slovaks to explore further connections with the Czechs, a very similar ethnic group from which the centuries had separated them. All of these developments prepared the soil for the Slovak gamble of joining Czechs in a federated nation-state in 1918.

### Establishing Czecho-Slovak connections, 1914–18

Habsburg crack-downs characterized the early period of the First World War, and were initially responses to public demonstrations by the Czechs. For example, there were disturbances at the time of the 60th anniversary of the Emperor Franz Josef's coronation: the monarchy responded by imposing twelve days of martial law (May 1951, 425). Based on Article 14 of the 1867 Constitution, the Emperor commenced rule by decree, created a War Supervisory Office, shut down several publications of Czech political parties, and imposed censorship on theater performances and books (Rees 1992, 14–15; Harna 2009, 383; Paces 2009, 76).

One response by Czechs during the war was to create and build their own political institutions, each of which pointed to the demand for the construction of a new nation-state. First, in the early years of the war, their eventual first President Tomáš G. Masaryk was based in Geneva, Switzerland, where he formed, in 1915, a Czech Maffia. Participants included Young Czechs, realists, States' Rights Progressives, Social

Democrats, and the Sokol Movement (Nosek 1926, 196; Paces 2009, 76). In particular, the Maffia kept up strong communications ties with the émigré community, a disparate set of groups that was offering considerable assistance in fulfilling the dreams of a state (Rees 1992, 17–18). Second, Czechs who remained in Prague set up a National Committee to plan the transition to a state for themselves (Harna 2009, 385). It was an inclusive organization that brought in members of most of the key Czech political parties. Third, many Czechs had moved to Paris during the war, and they put together the critically important Czech National Council in November 1916. Importantly, the Czech leaders Masaryk and Beneš included the Slovak leader Rostislav Štefánik at the top of its organizational structure (Bažant et al. 2010, 241). Significantly, with an eye on a future combined state, the Paris organization underwent a name change to Czech-Slovak National Council (Harna 2009, 384. The implications of that name change were positive for the possibilities of a nation-state that could incorporate both Czechs and Slovaks.

Masaryk left Switzerland and traveled to key nations to build support for nation-building efforts. In England in 1915, he outlined how there was commonality between Czech hopes and British legal norms as well as their focus on individual rights (Taylor 1970, 257). In addition, he endeavored to convince the British that Austria-Hungary was a serious enemy, as some there tended to look at them as benign in comparison with the more hostile Germans (Nosek 1926, 203). Two years later the eventual Czech President visited Russia at the time of their two revolutions. His goal was to connect with the Czech Legion that was in Siberia at the time. These were soldiers who had defected from the Habsburg military and joined the Russian Army at the end of the tsarist period. Their role became a complicated one after the November Revolution by the Leninists. Masaryk also traveled to America to talk with émigrés who had moved there. His conversations included not only Czechs but also Slovaks and Ruthenians. All those groups were enthusiastic about the potential for a new state and energized those working for similar goals in Europe (Taylor 1970, 265).

The impetus for a combined state flowed from the Slovaks and their leaders as well. For example, Hlinka as the newly chosen leader of the Slovak People's Party in 1917 called upon the Czechs and Slovaks to unite and sever the links to Hungary (Kirschbaum 1995, 146). In the same year, Masaryk made it clear that the group of military members fighting in Russia was the Czecho-Slovak Legion; it included 40,000 soldiers by the end of 1917 (Kirschbaum 1995, 150). Later, Slovaks continued to articulate their needs on the day after the founding of the state. On October 29 1918, they crafted a resolution that demanded "an unlimited right of self-determination on the basis of independence" (Nedelsky 2009, 66–73). Both their Martin Declaration of October 30 and Slovak National Council were instrumental in accomplishing the merger with the Czechs (Taylor 1970, 269). Slovaks also brought somewhat different attitudes and experiences to the early nation-building process. While members of the Slovak elite often took on attitudes that were similar to the Magyar nobility that they were now replacing, many Slovaks were impoverished, politically powerless, and more traditional than their new Czech partners (Beneš 1973, 44–6). In sum, the Slovaks were generally positive about joining the Czechs in a new state but somewhat unaware of what their actual status would be within it.

Key events in the year 1918 prefigured the actual creation of the state on October 28, 1918. In January of that year, Czechs in the Reichsrat called for their own sovereign state and lobbied the allies that they were a genuine non-Bolshevik alternative to the Habsburgs (Taylor 1970, 264). In May the Slovak Šrobar responded to Masaryk's overtures by asserting that there should be a union of Czechs and Slovaks (Kirschbaum 1995, 150). During the same month, Masaryk signed the significant Pittsburgh Agreement, which provided the legal basis for the new state. One immediate and concrete consequence of that document was the decision of the National Committee in Prague to halt train deliveries of coal and grain to Vienna, the hope being economic paralysis that might lead to major political concessions (Harna 2009, 390–391). On October 18, Masaryk from the US issued the Washington Declaration, and that completed the long process of declaring the independence of Czechoslovakia (Harna 2009, 391). Finally, on October 28, the Czechoslovak National Committee in Prague proclaimed officially way that Czechoslovak independence was an accomplished fact. At last, it was done.

### The interwar period, 1918–38: Czechs and Slovaks

During the period between the two world wars, there was growing Slovak concern and even anxiety about their role in the new federated state. To Slovaks, the Czechs took a more centralist approach than expected, while Czech experience in administration provided them with the most attractive governmental jobs. While Czechs tended to take a secularist approach to key issues, Slovaks felt a certain threat as the Catholic faith played a major role in their own decision-making processes. Even in the agricultural sector, Slovak farms were smaller than those in Bohemia and Moravia. This situation contributed to making the Slovak level of economic development lower than that of the Czechs. Some of these tensions came to a head during a key symbolic event in 1925. Czechs held commemorations of the 510th anniversary of the death of Jan Hus. In response, the Papal Nuncio left the country and headed back to Rome. Slovaks felt betrayed by the Hus celebration, while Czechs drew parallels between Slovak devotion to the Catholic faith and similar positions held within the hated Habsburg Empire (Seton-Watson 1962, 175–82). In 1928, the occasion of the 10th anniversary of the founding of the nation-state generated another expression of Slovak discontent. The Slovak People's Party published "Vacuum Juris," which contended that Slovaks had somehow put a secret clause into the original agreement that set up the state. In that secret clause was an assertion that the first ten years would be a probationary period, after which the Slovaks could call for renegotiating its terms. Czechs were shocked, and jailed the article's author Vojtech Tuka (Rothschild 1974, 115). Certainly, these tensions weakened the state and its leaders for the confrontations that would emerge in the next decade.

Of course, that threat entailed the rise of Nazi power in Germany and eventually surrounding nations. In the 1931 elections, an ominous sign was the improved positions of Nazis and communists (Rothschild 1974, 123). In the 1935 elections, the Agrarians finished first, but a new German Party under Konrad Henlein was next in the electoral results. At the same time, there was a balance in the decade, for Czechoslovakia remained the only East European state that preserved its democratic procedures for a full two decades after the end of the war. The Founder President Masaryk stood up for democratic traditions against the Nazi threat through his resignation in 1935 and until his death in 1937 (Seton-Watson 1962, 183–5).

In some ways, Czechoslovakia in 1938 was more prepared than surrounding political systems to resist a Nazi invasion. The mountains on all sides provided some protection but, more importantly, its industrialization processes were advanced and vital to the economic development of the region. By the 1930s, its industries produced half the steel and pig iron in East-Central Europe. Its war industry was actually larger than that of Italy (Rothschild 1974, 87). Although the global Depression did take its toll, the impact was less severe than in surrounding nations. In late May of that year, the Czech military demonstrated its capabilities through an impressive mobilization (Rothschild 1974, 131). However, the worst happened, as a combination of allied passivity and Czech reluctance left an open path for the Nazi invasion. Importantly, the Munich Crisis and the experiences that followed became symbols of appeasement for many decades to follow.

## The emergence and destruction of the Polish Second Republic, 1918–45

There was no modern Polish state prior to 1918, but this does not mean that the partition period did not influence Polish strategic thought, culture, and defense policies of the twentieth century. Inasmuch as Polish society fought for independence between 1795 and 1918, it had to create an accompanying body of strategic, political, and military thought and practice. Prior to 1864 liberal nationalism was dominant, and its focus was dual: to enlarge the scope of the Polish nation by incorporating the Polish peasantry/lower classes and ethnically non-Polish minorities into the sphere of Polish national consciousness; and to find an effective way of defeating vast conventional military powers of partitioning empires. The former consideration led to various civic- (non-ethnically exclusive) and class-conscious forms of Polish national-ism, which often sought to recreate the former Commonwealth based on liberal, democratic, and egalitarian principles. The latter led to a body of military-political thought and practice that marked the cutting edge of European nineteenth- and early twentieth-century doctrines of non-conventional warfare (the so-called "Polish school") (Wandycz 2001; Laqueur 1997).[4]

Just like in the Hungarian case, the late nineteenth century saw the emergence of an ethnically exclusive form of Polish nationalism which sought to define Polishness in narrow ethnic and religious terms, essen-tially defining the Polish nation as Polish-speaking Catholics only. This form of nationalism also saw the Polish nation as engaged in a Darwinian struggle for existence against "aliens" – most importantly, Germans and Jews (Porter-Szucs 2002). The chief exponent of this ideology eventually became a Polish political movement calling itself "national democracy" (in Polish *Narodowa Democracja* or ND, hence the Polish term *endecja*), led by its intellectual and political leader Roman Dmowski (1864–1939). Dmowski not only rejected Polish liberal civic nationalism, but also its military component. Dmowski's hard-headed realism led him to believe that Poland's existence was strategically defined by its two super-power neighbors, Germany and Russia, and that between the two, Poland's hope for independence lay in alliance with Russia and opposition to the much more threatening Germany. Dmowski was convinced that Russia would be compelled to support Polish national aspirations motivated by an increasing German threat, and Poland would re-emerge thanks to smart geopolitical maneuvering and a conventional armed struggle in alliance with Russia and with its allies in the West (Wandycz 1990; Dmowski 1991 [1908]; Dmowski 2009 [1925]).

Dmowski's and *endecja*'s thought and politics found a counterweight in Józef Piłsudski (1867–1935), who continued legacies of Polish liberal nationalism in its political, strategic, and military dimensions. Piłsudski was a leader of the Polish Socialist Party (*Polska Partia Socialistyczna* or PPS) which waged political and armed (non-conventional) struggle against Russia prior to and during the Revolution of 1905–7. In Piłsudski's strategic thought Russia was Poland's chief enemy, and a defeat/containment of Russia the key to Poland's independence. Crucially, Piłsudski took into account the multi-national nature of the Russian empire that, according to him, could be defeated and contained by nationalisms of its non-Russian ethnicities. Accordingly, in Russia's western borderland Piłsudski envisioned a re-creation of a modern (federated) form of the Polish-Lithuanian Commonwealth which would contain Belarussian, Ukrainian, and possibly Baltic nations, united together to contain Russia. After 1909 Piłsudski embraced a nationalist-centrist political orientation and started organizing Polish conventional Armed Forces under Austro-Hungarian auspices; during the First World War he led these forces to fight against Russia. When Central Powers proved that they did not intend to restore Polish sovereignty, Piłsudski led his forces to mutiny against Germany and Austria-Hungary. Piłsduski's military, together with Polish armies raised in France and Russia under *endecja* auspices, became the core of sovereign Polish military in 1918, with Piłsudski as its head as the head of state (Hetherington 2012).

Piłsudski's strategic vision was implemented between 1919 and 1920 when he led Polish armies into areas of the former Commonwealth, seeking to recreate it as a liberal confederation. When the Red Army counter-attacked, attempting to create a "Polish Soviet Republic" in 1920, Piłsudski defeated the Bolsheviks at the battle of Warsaw, and thus preserved freshly won Polish independence. Today, the anniversary of this victory on August 15 is the Armed Forces Day, the most important military holiday in Poland, thus clearly defining modern Poland's greatest military achievement and its most important enemy. However, Piłsudski's attempt to recreate a modern version of the Commonwealth failed, as the Polish-Soviet war ended in a draw and division of Belarus and Ukraine between Poland and the Soviet Union. Simultaneously, it became obvious that dominant forms of modern Ukrainian and Lithuanian (and, to a lesser extent, Belarussian) nationalisms aspired to ultimately create their own states independent of either Polish or Russian influence. The multi-national interwar Polish state thus could not claim the loyalty of its most important non-Polish minorities, which became a strategic liability. The idea of a confederated Commonwealth strong enough to stand up to either the Soviet Union or Germany was dead.

Sandwiched between two hostile potential superpowers, interwar Poland[5] could not escape, in the long term, the geopolitical reality diagnosed earlier by Dmowski. However, in the 1920s, both the Soviet Union and Germany were weak, and Poland could find reassurances in an anti-German treaty alliance with France (signed in 1921 and renewed in 1939), and in various strategic – mostly bilateral – relationships with Eastern and Central European neighbors, including an anti-Soviet treaty alliance with Romania (first signed in 1921, and renewed in 1927). Poland also unsuccessfully tried to create a multilateral system of alliances of all East-Central European countries: the Baltic countries, Czechoslovakia, Romania, Hungary, Yugoslavia, and Bulgaria, in the so-called (in Latin) *Intermarium* ("between the seas") or, in Polish, *Międzymorze* concept (the seas in question being the Baltic and the Black Sea) idea. This concepts failed on mutual hostilities or suspicion between the countries in question (Okulewicz 2001; Levy 2006; Chodakiewicz 2012).[6]

All of Poland's alliances were to prove either irrelevant or insufficient to save the country from nearly simultaneous Nazi and Soviet aggression in 1939, which amounted to a fourth partition of Poland and ended Polish independence. Especially the French guarantees (backed by the UK in 1939) proved to be false. While France and the UK did declare war on Nazi Germany in 1939, Western allies' subsequent military inaction (the so-called "phony war," or in French, "funny war" *drôle de guerre*) amounted to abandonment of Poland to German and Soviet conquests. Today we know that France and the UK never had the material capacity or intention to materially help Poland in the first place. Whether the lack of substantial military help to Poland in 1939 amounted to a "betrayal" of Poland by Western allies, has been a subject of a protracted historical and public debate in Poland, with obvious contemporary overtones.[7]

The Polish interwar ruling elite was aware of insufficiency of the country's bilateral alliance system, and the country made strenuous efforts to build up its military power. While at the peak of the country's mobilization during the Polish-Soviet war the Polish effectives amounted to nearly 1,000,000 soldiers, its normal military manpower after demobilization was reduced to around 300,000, which in the 1920s represented the fifth largest military in Europe (after the Soviet Union, France, Italy, and Spain). Under Marshall Piłsudski (who took power in a military coup in 1926) the Polish military became a state-of-the art force, and foundations were laid for an indigenous military industry (Wyszczelski 2005). However, in the 1930s, dramatic armament and modernization efforts of first the Soviet Union and, then, Nazi Germany, quickly rendered the Polish military relatively weak and obsolete, and Poland vulnerable (Zgórniak 1993, 231; Lubecki 2011). Polish efforts at military modernization, hampered by the country's relative poverty and backwardness, came too little and too late. While the country managed to, again, mobilize nearly 1,000,000 soldiers in September 1939, the 1,500,000-strong Wehrmacht and nearly 600,000-strong Soviet Armed Forces which invaded Poland were larger, more modernized, and more capable. What followed were long and bloody German-Soviet (1939–41), German (1941–44), and then Soviet (1945–89) occupations and domination, which Western powers allied to Poland (France, the UK, and then the US) were unable or unwilling to prevent.

For the Polish strategic memory and culture, the lessons of 1939 (German and Soviet invasions) and 1944 (the Soviet takeover, legitimized by Western powers at the Yalta conference) were decisive. The Polish people and elites learned to mistrust paper guarantees of security unbacked by specific commitments of sufficient material force. Poland also needed to find an escape from the strategic dilemma of encirclement by Germany and Russia/the Soviet Union. We will see how Poland's current security and defense policy and doctrine are defined by these lessons of the mid-twentieth century. While the "taming" of Germany through the country's transformation into a peaceful member of the Western community of nations removed the encirclement dilemma, Poland is still confronting a potentially hostile Russia. With respect to this threat, Poland's inclination is to trust the material military power and troops of the US, and not paper guarantees of NATO or West Europeans, still associated with the betrayal of 1939. Also, given the potential Russian threat, a modified form of Piłsudski's strategy is still valid. Poland's security clearly lies in enlarging the sphere of independence of all non-Russian states and nationalities of the post-Soviet space, especially, of Russia's Western neighbors (the Baltics, Belarus, and Ukraine). This strategy puts Poland squarely on a collision course with Russia, interested in maintaining influence in countries on its western periphery. Likewise, the interwar idea of a "between the seas" block of countries gained a new viability, as these countries are today mostly friendly and cooperative with each other. The existence and continuing viability of the V4 alliance of Poland, the Czech Republic, Slovakia, and Hungary illustrate this concept. Finally, without any illusions about Poland's strategic self-sufficiency, Poland's policy is to maintain a conventional military force strong and modern enough to be a credible alliance partner with the US and NATO, and to initially resist and provide a minimal deterrent against a potential Russian aggression.

## Interwar Hungary, 1918–41

In many ways, Hungary's fate after the First World War was the exact opposite of Poland's and more like Germany's, which became Hungary's chief ally during the Second World War. Hungary's policies and fortune during the Second World War, in turn, became a replay of the First World War. Just like then, the country tried and failed to maintain its strategic autonomy vis-à-vis its Germanic ally, and ended up on the losing side after exhausting all of Hungary's resources (Tilkovszky 1990). Just like Poland, though, Hungary was ultimately incorporated into the Soviet Empire, albeit explicitly as a defeated Axis country (Kenez 2006). Conversely, Poland and Czechoslovakia were treated formally as winners of the Second World War, and the countries gained territory at the expense of Germany after the end of the war. Hungary, in turn, was cut back to Trianon borders, but this time could not blame the West for this fate. The notion of Western betrayal, though, was revived in Hungary as the result of the failed Revolution of 1956.

Just like Germany, interwar Hungary was a revisionist country pining for reversal of Trianon, hemmed in by a hostile alliance of the Little Entente of Czechoslovakia, Yugoslavia, and Romania, and chafing at restrictions on its military power. This policy was supported by the country's semi-authoritarian regime, led by Regent Horthy and supported by a reactionary alliance of landed, industrial, and cultural (the Catholic Church) elites, which allowed for limited, albeit lively, liberal political institutions and life (Ormos 1990; Tilkovszky 1990; Hanebrink 2005). The crumbling of the Versailles order in the early 1930s allowed for Hungary's rearmament, which kicked into high gear in 1938, when under Prime Minister Kálmán Darányi a gigantic military procurement program was enacted. The program was aimed at the creation of a 107,000-strong standing army and a 250,000-strong mobilized army, which was to be a fast, modern motorized force modeled on German and Italian examples, geared towards a quick war of (re)conquest. The reality fell far short of this goal – Hungary's limited workforce and industrial resources could simply never create a force comparable to or capable of standing up to state-of-the art militaries. However, the Hungarian military did fight and defeat Slovak and Yugoslav militaries in short border conflicts.

Aided by Western abandonment and subsequent partitioning of Czechoslovakia in 1938, and supported by Germany and Italy, Hungary demanded and obtained ethnically Hungarian parts of Slovakia and Trans-Carpathia in the "First Vienna Award."[8] These gains were magnified during the fall of Czechoslovakia in March 1939, when Hungary occupied the entire Trans-Carpathia and, after a brief border war with Slovakia (the so-called "little war" or *Malá vojna* in Slovak), took more formerly Slovak territories. In 1940, again, thanks to German pressure, Romania was forced to cede Northern Transylvania to Hungary as the result of "the Second Vienna Award," and in March–April 1941, Hungary first allowed for and then joined the German aggression against Yugoslavia and took ethnically Hungarian territories in Vojvodina (Braham 2000).[9] The policy of reversing Trianon triumphed, but at the cost of surrendering Hungarian strategic autonomy to Germany. Indeed, by the end of 1940, Hungary signed and joined a multilateral Tripartite Pact involving most German allies in a treaty aimed against the US. More ominously, after an apparent initial reluctance, Hungary joined Germany and its allies in the attack against the Soviet Union on June 26, 1941.[10] By December 1941 Hungary found itself at war with the UK, while the US declared war on Hungary in June 1942 (Tilkovszky 1990).

## Czechs and Slovaks in the Second World War

Additionally, the Munich Pact influenced Czech attitudes about their regional position after the end of the wartime hostilities. President Beneš concluded that Czechs were in the middle and would need to balance the West against the Soviet Union. Particular alliances could prove to be unreliable, and there needed to be a tight linkage between Czech security and "the stability and security of the continent as a whole" (Leff 1997, 42).

Czechs and Slovaks were separated into two distinct territorial units under German control during the war. For Czechs, there was the Protectorate of Bohemia and Moravia, in which the Germans controlled defense and foreign affairs. The central controls imposed serious restrictions such as closure of all Czech universities and colleges. At the same time, the German military relied on Czech industry for a good share of its war material. In September 1941, the Germans sent Reich Protector Richard Heydrich to rule, who took the step of imposing martial law (Agnew 2004, 208–12). he was assassinated by the Czech resistance, and the Germans then destroyed the Czech town of Lidice as punishment. Slovaks lived in the newly created Slovak Republic under Tiso for a full six years, and the Germans compelled the Slovak Army to fight with them (Agnew 2004, 216–17). Obviously, this dual solution exacerbated the growing tension of the previous two decades between Czechs and Slovaks. Importantly, there was a government in exile as a third force in the equation. President Beneš moved to London during the war, then went to Moscow two months before the war's end in order to establish a National Front back on home territory after the war (Agnew 2004, 221). Czechs and Slovaks were also present in a number of other countries. A Czech and Slovak Legion was active in Poland until its capture by the Soviet Union during the period of the Molotov-Ribbentrop Pact. There were two Czech regiments that fought in France, while the Czechoslovak Armoured Brigade was active in England and helped to blockade German forces in the Battle of Dunkirk. Importantly, the First Czechoslovak Army Group fought in the Carpathians and later joined in the liberation of Czechoslovakia at the end of the war (Agnew 2004, 219).

In both territories there were underground movements as well as major acts of heroism that led to brutal German retaliation. In May–June 1942, the Czechs assassinated Heydrich, a move that led to eradication of the entire city of Lidice as well as the re-imposition of martial law (Agnew 2004, 212). In 1944, the Slovak Uprising took place, which took the Germans two months to end (Agnew 2004, 218). Perhaps the two spectacular acts of resistance made some amends for the Munich submission, but they also provided a kind of common ground for Czechs and Slovaks to reknit their territories after the end of the war.

It all came to an end with the liberation in May by the Soviet and American armies. The American Army entered from the west and freed up much of Bohemia up to the city of Prague, while the Red Army entered from the east and liberated Prague. There was symbolism in this dual liberation process, as one lesson of Munich had been that there would be a need for Czechoslovakia to balance both regions in the future. Prophetically, looking ahead, there was a continuous need to balance both pressures and opportunities from the two. For over forty years Czechoslovakia would be a member of the Warsaw Pact and in the Soviet orbit. For three years after the war and again after 1948, connections to the West were paramount. Perhaps the lessons of history entailed a surprising reversal of the Munich experience. Post-war experiences taught the lesson that the East let the Czechs and Slovaks down while the West once again opened the door to hope!

### Poland and Hungary in the Second World War

Unlike Hungary, Poland was supposed to be a nominal victor of the Second World War. While the country was occupied by Germans and Soviets in 1939, a Polish government-in-exile was formed in France, backed by a significant military force of soldiers, sailors, and airmen, who continued to fight alongside Great Britain after the defeat of France (Kochanski 2012). In the meantime Polish territories were brutalized by simultaneous Soviet and Nazi occupations between 1939 and 1941. Between the two, the Soviet regime and occupation was, if anything, more genocidal and criminal during the 1939–41 period, deporting around 320,000 Polish citizens, and engaging in mass killing of some 150,000 (Gross 1988; Synder 2010). The most notorious of these massacres was a spring 1940 series of secret mass killings of some 22,000 Polish military officers captured by the Red Army in 1939 (Allen 2010). Known as "the Katyn crime" (in Polish *zbrodnia katyńska*: Katyn, near Smolensk, was the best known of the mass execution sites), the massacres were to play a dramatic role in the subsequent development of Polish-Soviet and Polish-Russian relations.

With the June 22, 1941 German attack on the Soviet Union, and the subsequent UK alliance with the USSR, the Polish government in exile under General Sikorski was pressured to reach out to Stalin with an offer of political and military alliance against Germany. A series of accommodations and agreements were indeed signed in late 1941, leading, among other things, to the creation of a 40,000-strong Polish military force led by General Władyslaw Anders in the USSR. However, it very quickly became obvious that many officers who were supposed to run the force were missing, and nowhere to be found. While the Soviets were giving evasive or misleading answers, the Germans, who took over the execution site in Katyn, announced their discovery of mass graves to the world in April 1943 and blamed the Soviets for the crime. When Sikorski demanded an impartial investigation, the Soviets, claiming that Germans committed the massacre, broke diplomatic relations with the Polish government-in-exile. In the meantime, Anders' army left the USSR in the spring of 1942 to transfer, via Iran and Palestine, to North Africa and Italy, where it fought as the Polish Second Corps, most importantly in the Battle of Monte Cassino.

The break of diplomatic relations and the exit of Anders' army from the USSR allowed Stalin to create a Polish government and military force faithful to the Soviets. In this respect, the Soviet leader could count on a small group of ideologically dedicated Polish communists, and a larger group of Poles who were willing to serve the Soviets out of pragmatic or even patriotic considerations. In this last respect, Stalin's cause of creating a Poland subordinated to the Soviet Union was helped by Dmowski's realist pragmatism and its confirmation in the catastrophe of 1939. It seemed to be manifest that Poland's survival between two hostile superpowers depended on choosing the lesser evil, and, between the two, Russia, be it even in its Soviet permutation, was the one to be preferred. Thus, among masses of Poles who formed a Soviet allied Polish Division in the spring of 1943, a Corps in summer 1943 and the

First Army in 1944, there were some interwar military leaders including the Army's commander, General Zygmut Berling. Still, the shortage of Polish officers was so acute that more than 50% of those serving in the Polish military were Soviet.

By summer 1944 the Soviet Army entered the areas of interwar Poland and a Soviet-allied Polish government was created, backed by growing Polish Soviet-allied military formations and the full weight of the Soviet Army, which immediately moved to dismantle and repress any signs of anti-Soviet resistance. In a last desperate attempt to preserve Polish sovereignty, the Polish government in exile in London launched operation "Storm" (*Burza* in Polish), which was an attempt by the Polish underground military formations of Home Army (*Armia Krajowa*, AK) to capture territory from the Germans in front of advancing Soviets, and thus create a *fait accompli* of liberated and sovereign Polish territories. This action failed, as the Soviet forces dismantled and destroyed Polish AK formations, arresting and killing their leaders and soldiers and transferring men to Soviet-allied formations (Kochanski 2012: 384–434). In the final and supreme act of resistance, the AK launched and sustained an anti-German uprising in Warsaw between August 1 and October 3, 1944. The Warsaw uprising was put down by Germans, who razed the city and killed some 150,000 civilians in the process. While the Soviet forces came up to the eastern shore of river Vistula dividing the city (most of Warsaw is on the western shore of the river) in mid-September 1944, they refused to help the uprising on the West bank in any substantial way. The Western allies supplied the insurgents from the air, but could not or would not change Stalin's position of letting Warsaw be slaughtered (Davies 2005).

By early 1945 a Soviet-backed government of Poland had at its disposal two armies, with some 370,000 soldiers,[11] albeit around 50–60% of their officers were Soviet (Kajetanowicz 2013; Smoliński 2016). These armies participated in the final defeat of Germany in 1945, fighting, among others, in the battle of Berlin. In July 1945, Western allies took away their official recognition of the Polish government-in-exile in London. Instead, they recognized the Polish communist government in Warsaw, after this government incorporated some political forces and representatives previously active in the Polish government-in-exile. Western allies eventually dismantled the Polish Armed Forces in the West, some half of whom (mostly lower ranks) returned to communist Poland (Smoliński 2016). The communist Poland and its substantial military power were thus born out of the maelstrom of the Second World War.

The Second World War brought dramatic changes to Polish boundaries and geopolitics. Most importantly, interwar Polish territories in the East, which represented the legacy of the old Commonwealth were detached from Poland and transferred to Soviet Belarussian, Ukrainian, and Lithuanian Republics. In compensation, Poland was given ex-German territories in East Prussia, Silesia, and Pomerania, and Poland's western boundary was moved to the Oder-Neisse line. The German population of these areas either fled or was expelled, while the Polish population in the east moved to newly established Poland, flocking especially to the ex-German territories (portrayed in Polish propaganda as ancestral Polish territories from the early Middle Ages, or "recovered territories"). Unlike Hungary, post-Second World War Poland thus emerged with no substantial Polish minorities abroad, but, just like Hungary, Poland became an ethnically homogenous state. This was especially the case when the most substantial remaining national minority in the new communist Poland – Ukrainians living in the southeastern corner of the country – were either resettled and dispersed into the "recovered territories" or expelled to the Soviet Union. This happened mostly between 1945 and 1948 in the course of brutal and successful counter-insurgency/ethnic cleansing campaigns against Ukrainian armed resistance and population (Pałka 2008; Misiło 2013).[12] Thus, the *endecja* nationalist dream of ethnically "pure" Poland free of its chief enemies Germans, Jews, and Ukrainians, was achieved by communist Poland.

Lessons of the Second World War are ambiguous in Polish strategic culture and continue to be debated today. Besides the previously discussed question of Western "betrayal" in 1939, there is the question of specifically US "betrayal" at the allied conferences in Teheran in 1943, Yalta in 1944, and Potsdam in 1945, where the US either conceded to Soviet territorial or political demands with regard to Poland, or trusted Soviet assurances about Polish sovereignty that proved to be hollow. While questions of historical fact continue to be endlessly debated by Polish, Russian, and Western historians, Polish public opinion, both educated and popular, does not seem to dwell too much on the supposed US Second World War culpability, which is balanced against US support of the cause of Polish democracy and independence throughout the entire Cold War and afterwards (Lubecki 2005; Domber 2014).

On the other hand, the wisdom and strategic lessons of operation "Storm" and the Warsaw Uprising of 1944 continue to be debated. Essentially, defenders of the course of action that the Polish government-in-exile undertook in 1943–45 see it as either a noble or rationally defensible last-ditch attempt to defend Polish sovereignty under impossible odds, while the opponents see these same actions as foolish and misguided romanticism (Zychowicz 2013). Neither side seems to offer a real, as opposed to fanciful, solution to the impossible strategic dilemma in which Poland found itself in 1945. In this last respect, a neo-*endecja* notion that the communist option in 1945 guaranteed a form of Polish national survival and sovereignty are not be lightly dismissed. On the other hand, a recently evoked idea that Poland should have allied with Nazi Germany against the Soviets in 1939 met with a storm of opposition and controversy (Zychowicz 2012). Still, the overall drift of the most recent (post-2010) and the most popular Polish indigenous literature and opinion on lessons of the Second World War seem to be right-wing, anti-Western, and autarkic-nationalistic, as opposed to either the pragmatism or post-nationalism which dominated between 1989 and 2010 (Porter-Szucs 2014).

Between 1941 and 1944 Hungary's limited military resources were mostly used in support of Germany on the Eastern Front. There, Hungary suffered its single greatest battlefield defeat in modern history, when the 200,000-strong Hungarian 2nd Army was destroyed in a series of battles on the River Don in January 1943 (Denes & Kliment 2015). The defeat illustrated the woeful inadequacy of Hungarian military modernization efforts. Hungarian industry could not create a modernized military force regardless of its strenuous efforts, and a large part of the country's military production (for instance, most of its modern aircraft production) was supplied to Germany (Szabo 2001, Jaszay et al. 2009).

As the Soviet Army continued its string of victories and the Western allies invaded North Africa and Sicily, Hungary launched a desperate effort to distance itself from Nazi Germany and conclude a separate peace with the Western allies – but not with the Soviet Union. Indeed, in repetition of the pattern established in the First World War, Hungary attempted to maintain a strategic autonomy vis-à-vis its German ally throughout the entire war: as early as 1942 the government of Prime Minister Milklós Kállay tried to conclude a separate peace with Hungary's neighbors and Western allies. These efforts continued into 1943, but failed on border issues, as Western allies and Hungary's neighbors made the return to Trianon boundaries a pre-condition for any serious peace talks (Tilkovszky 1990). In the meantime, rightly mistrustful of Hungary's intentions, Germany occupied Hungary in March 1944, but Hungarian nominal state sovereignty and machinery was preserved and continued to serve the Germans (Wiesel 1982; Braham 2000).[13] Indeed, the bulk of Royal Hungarian Armed Forces stayed faithful to the German allies to the end, and participated in the defense of the Carpathian mountain passes, a dramatic fight against the Soviets (and their newly found Romanian allies[14]) on the plains of East Hungary in the fall of 1944, and, in the last desperate defenses of Budapest and western Hungary in the winter of 1944 and spring of 1945 (Kenez 2006; Ungváry 2006; Bernad & Kliment 2015).

A broadly based anti-German Hungarian resistance movement, which included parties ranging from monarchists to communists formed in May 1944 under the name Hungarian Front. In the meantime, Horthy finally reached out to the Soviets with an offer of an armistice, which was agreed upon on October 11, 1944. Horthy consented to give up Hungary's territorial gains since 1937 and to declare war on Germany. However, his regime's attempt to switch sides on October 15 1944 was easily quashed by Germany and its Hungarian allies led by the head of the Hungarian fascist Arrow Cross Party, Ferenc Szálasi, who continued to lead a firmly pro-Nazi and criminal[15] Hungarian regime to the end (Tilkovszky 1990; Braham 2000; Bernad & Kliment 2015). In the end, just like after the First World War, post-Second World War Hungary emerged devastated, defeated, and stripped back down to Trianon territories (by the Paris Treaty of 1947). The long night of Soviet subjugation was to follow.

In terms of formation of Hungarian strategic culture, one would presume that dreams of pre-Trianon "greater Hungary" were finally exorcized by the demonic war, which led Horthy himself to give up all the territorial gains of 1938–41. However, unlike in the Polish case, the Second World War did not lead to the disappearance of Hungarian minorities abroad. These still exist, constantly reminding Magyars of Hungary's territorial losses at Trianon and the need to defend Hungarian national rights in neighboring countries. Still, nationalistic and irredentist Hungarian militarism largely disappeared as a result of the Second World War to be seemingly replaced by a full embracing of democracy and liberalism.[16] This, indeed, was the direction that Hungary took during the brief and ambiguous transitional 1945–48 period, which was followed by an imposition of a full-blown repressive Soviet-style regime that ruled the country between 1948 and 1988 (Kenez 2006).

## Notes

1 Indeed, one of Hungary's greatest military leaders and thinkers, Hungarian-Croatian Count Miklós Zrinyi (1620–64) lived during that period.
2 Spread especially in popular novels by nineteenth-century writer Henryk Sienkiewicz, who to this day is the most widely read Polish writer.
3 The other reason was the holiday's proximity to the traditional October (1917) Revolution celebration.
4 The (today) thoroughly forgotten ideas of the "Polish" (and "Italian") schools of insurgency warfare, in turn, prefigured the major themes of

twentieth- and twenty-first-century guerrilla and non-conventional warfare classics, including Mao's, Che Guevara's, al-Qaeda's and ISIS theories and practice.

5 Known as the "Second Republic," the "first Republic" being the Polish-Lithuanian Commonwealth of 1572–1795.

6 Especially Polish-Lithuanian and Polish-Czechoslovak relations, and were hostile and involved armed border conflicts. Polish armed forces clashed with Lithuanian military between 1919 and 1922, and Polish pressure forced Lithuania to establish a diplomatic relationship with Poland in 1938. Likewise, Poland and Czechoslovakia fought a brief border war over Tschetschen Silesia in 1919, and Poland forced Czechoslovakia to cede the entire Tschechen Silesia and other disputed Czechoslovak border territories to Poland in 1938. In September 1939, resentful over the loss of some Slovak territories, the Slovak government of Fr. Jozef Tiso joined the Nazi German invasion of Poland with a force of around 50,000 soldiers and airmen, and recovered the lost Slovak territories (Baka 2006).

7 For a tiny sample of this debate today, see, Leszek Pietrzak, "Wrześniowa zdrada aliantów" (Allies' September Betrayal), in *Uwazam rze*, online edition, www.uwazamrze.pl/artykul/1043566/wrzesniowa-zdrada-alian tow, accessed March 14, 2017 (a nationalist view, which fully embraces the notion of "Western betrayal"), and compare to Artur Hajnicza, "Zdrada Zachodu – fakt czy obsesja?" (Western Betrayal – Fact or Obsession?), in *Gazeta Wyborcza*, January 30–31, 1999 (a liberal view that rejects the notion of "Western betrayal"). See also Zychowicz 2012.

8 Today Trans-Carpathia is known as "Trans-Carpathian Ukraine," as it was incorporated into Ukrainian SSR by Stalin in 1946.

9 It was also in Vojvodina where Hungarian forces committed their most significant war crime of the Second World War, the so-called "Novi Sad (Újvidék) massacre" of January 1942, involving mass killing of around 5,000 mostly Serbs and Yugoslavian Jews. It is significant that perpetrators of this crime were to be tried in in Hungary in 1943, as the country attempted to distance itself from indigenous fascists and Nazi Germany.

10 The pretext for the war was the supposed Soviet bombing of the city of Kassa (Slovak Košice, currently in Slovakia). Today's evidence (still inconclusive) indicates that the bombing was either a Hungarian, German, or Romanian false-flag operation. See Dreisziger 1972.

11 In comparison, the Polish government in exile in London had armed forces of 186,000 at the end of the war, and 250,000 by December 1945.

12 Significantly, the key ethnic cleansing/counter-insurgency operation "Wisła" ("Vistula") in 1947 was planned and executed by General Stefan Mossor, an outstanding staff officer of Polish interwar military, who became the deputy Chief of General Staff of Polish (communist) military in 1946. Mossor was also the author of the Polish plan of war against Germany in 1938, and the chief author of Polish military doctrine and war plans in the 1946–50 period. He was arrested in 1950 and freed and rehabilitated in

1956. Mossor's figure symbolizes continuities between pre- and post-Second World War Polish militaries, security establishments, and policies.

13 This included rounding up some 500,000 Hungarian Jews outside of Budapest. Most were sent to the gas chambers of Auschwitz. See Wiesel 1982.

14 Unlike Hungary's attempt to switch sides, Romania's effort had full support from most of the country's military.

15 The party members and militias killed 10,000–15,000 Hungarian Jews, and deported around 80,000, many of whom perished.

16 In the 2014 parliamentary elections the *Jobbik Magyarországért Mozgalom* (Jobbik, Movement for Better Hungary) ultra-nationalist party received around 20% of party-list votes, making it the third most popular party in Hungary. The party hints at Hungarian irredentism, and created the (now disbanded) paramilitary group *Magyar Gárda* (Hungarian Guard).

# 3

## Communism and late communism: from forced convergence to divergence

### The foundation of communist defense policies: Stalinism and post-Stalinism

All four countries under discussion (three considering the unified Czechoslovak state until 1993) were incorporated into the Soviet Empire at the end of the Second World War. After a period of limited liberalism between 1945 and 1948, they were subjected to uniform processes of Sovietization and Stalinization. The military and defense policies differed across the countries in the 1945–48 time frame, but uniformity was enforced during the period of high Stalinism between 1948 and 1953. Popular revolts in Poland and Hungary in 1956 created a trend towards divergence, accelerated by the Czechoslovak Revolution of 1968 and Polish revolts of 1968, 1970, 1976, and 1980. However, a level of Soviet-enforced strategic uniformity still prevailed in the respective countries' military and defense policies all the way until the breakdown of the Soviet Empire in 1989. Because communism, especially "late" communism, represents the immediate background to the countries' current military and defense policies, it is important to discuss this period in some detail. As we will see, there are important and surprising continuities in the respective countries' military and defense policies between communist and post-communist periods.

The initial conditions of the respective countries' military and defense policies corresponded to their very divergent fates during the Second World War. Communist Poland emerged with the most substantial military resources of some 440,000 soldiers by fall 1945. These forces were used against the Polish and Ukrainian anti-communist and nationalist resistance. They were then selectively demobilized, leaving Poland with a 140,000-strong standing military by 1948. According to the country's military doctrine, this force was supposed to be used, in firm alliance with the Soviet Union and Czechoslovakia ("the Slavic bloc"), against the presumed threat of German revanchism, backed by the UK and the US ("the Germanic bloc").[1] Czechoslovakian initial post-war policy was very similar to Poland's. Hungary, however, as a defeated country, was completely disarmed, and later its military forces were formally limited by the 1947 Paris Treaty to 70,000 soldiers.[2]

During the initial Stalinist period (1948–53), the military-industrial complexes of all three countries were transformed into copies of the Soviet equivalent in a process akin to institutional cloning – that is, in a mechanical reproduction of structures without regard to complementarity among the three nations (Jowitt 1993). Everything, down to details of uniform, the Commissar system of political officers, and the military doctrine, was slavishly copied from the Soviets. Instead of clear and multilateral institutional mechanisms of coordination, Moscow's and Stalin's domination of the empire was maintained through bilateral treaties, opaque forms of personal subordination, and incorporation of Soviet military officers directly into the Armed Forces of "allied" countries. This last phenomenon was prevalent especially in Poland, where a Soviet Marshall Konstantin Rokossovsky (albeit of Polish ethnic origin) became the Polish Minister of Defense and head of the Armed Forces. The terrorising and repression of real or perceived "enemies of the people" was prevalent – in another imitation of the Soviet pattern, both communist parties and the military personnel of the respective countries were bloodily purged and purged again. This affected, in particular, military officers with a non-communist past, but also communist officers with suspect loyalties (Kovrig 2006).[3] Military professionalism suffered and was replaced by ideological loyalty to the regime.

In contrast to the 1946–48 period of demobilization, high Stalinism was characterized both by a very high level of militarization and military spending, and by development of heavy industry geared towards military production. At the peak of their defense capacities around 1952, Poland, Hungary, and Czechoslovakia reached levels both of military spending and of peace-time militaries larger than ever in their modern history. These gigantic establishments[4] were to fight alongside the Soviets in expected wars against the West and/or against the "heretic" communist Yugoslavia (Lunák 2006: 75; Jaszay et al. 2009; Kajetanowicz 2013). The economic costs of this huge military effort resulted in dramatic economic dislocations and imbalances, exploitation of industrial and agricultural labor, and a fall in living standards in economies that had barely recovered from the Second World War. The misery and poverty created by Stalinist militarization was eventually one of the key causes of popular revolts in Poland and Hungary in 1956.

The death of Stalin in 1953 led to "silent destalinization," which included changes in top personnel and policies. The hated and extremely repressive Communist Party head Mátyás Rákosi in Hungary was replaced by his rival Imgre Nagy as head of the government (Prime Minister), while the power of Rákosi's Polish equivalent Bolesław Bierut was also cut down to size and replaced by a system of "collective leadership." The fortuitous death of Czechoslovak Communist Party leader Klement Gottwald in 1953 was followed by similar political changes in Czechoslovakia. Most importantly, repression was selectively suspended, while militarization was scaled down to more sustainable levels. However, a combination of popular resistance, misery, and hatred of the communist system led to mass popular revolts in the communist empire: first in Berlin/East Germany in 1953; second in Poland in June 1956; and third, in Hungary in October–November 1956. This last event was the bloodiest and most significant of the "revolutions," and is still an important event in the development of current Hungarian strategic and political culture.

## WTO defense framework

"Normalization" of communism after the peak of Stalinism was accomplished through several developments. One was the creation of the Warsaw Pact in 1955, which, besides the propaganda value, tried to legitimize Soviet domination through the creation of more collective institutional channels of control and cooperation. The result of the Polish Crisis of 1956 was the creation of a precedent as well as of a promised "national road to socialism" in terms of Soviet tolerance for a limited degree of autonomy for countries in the empire. Hungary tested these limits in 1956, and Czechoslovakia in 1968. They triggered a unilateral Soviet invasion (Hungary, 1956) and a multilateral Warsaw Pact invasion (Czechoslovakia 1968), to which the countries' militaries offered little to no resistance. After 1956, Hungary used its autonomy to create a relatively prosperous pseudo-market economy, while the country was conspicuous for its neglect of the military sector. Poland and Czechoslovakia, in turn, developed and modernized their militaries with justifications that focused on the threat of a revanchist Germany. The Polish military and defense policies, just like the militaries in all of the subject countries, remained fully subordinate to the Soviet policy, but a Polish public perception of the military as a patriotic force to be distinguished from the communist regime persisted. This myth continued, even when the Polish military and its head, General Wojciech Jaruzelski, took power in 1981 and crushed the "Solidarity" movement, thus terminating the Polish liberalization episode of 1980–81. However, the crisis started in the Soviet Empire by the Polish Solidarity movement proved to be fatal. After a short neo-Stalinist revival under Yurii

Andropov (1982–84), the Soviet imperial system started liberalizing under Mikhail Gorbachev, and, instead of reviving, died.

The May 1955 Treaty of Friendship, Co-operation, and Mutual Assistance was signed in Warsaw (hence the "Warsaw Pact") between the Soviet Union and its seven Eastern European allies, partially as a response to the 1955 US/NATO decision to remilitarize West Germany, but partially also as an attempt to provide at least a façade of regular, multilateral and institutionalized coordination between the Soviet Union and its Eastern European communist clients (Mastny & Byrne 2005). Nominally, the purpose of the alliance was collective security against external aggression (article 4) by any country or group of countries. The alliance members also subscribed to the principles of independent sovereignty and mutual non-interference in their respective internal decisions (article 8).[5] Institutions that were supposed to embody these principles included the ruling Political Consultative Committee (article 6), a Committee of Ministers of Defense in charge of coordination of Armed Forces, and the Technical Committee that controlled military equipment, procurement, and modernization issues – this last committee was matched with a Military Industrial Cooperative Standing Commission in charge of military-industrial cooperation within the Council for Mutual Economic Assistance (the Soviet bloc multilateral economic organization) (Germuska 2015). There was also a unified joint military command structure (article 5), but only for peacetime – during the war, the allied forces were to be fully subordinate to Soviet command structures (Ross Johnson 1977).

The Warsaw Pact loudly proclaimed principles of non-intervention that somehow did not prevent the Soviet unilateral military intervention in Hungary in 1956. The Soviet-led intervention in Czechoslovakia in 1968 (operation "Danube"), in turn, was a multilateral Warsaw Pact affair, albeit commanded by Soviet General Pavlovski. This military operation, which involved around 500,000, mostly Soviet, but also Polish, Bulgarian, and Hungarian troops, was the largest Soviet-led invasion and the only one that the Warsaw Pact ever conducted. It further exposed the Warsaw Pact's hollowness as a multilateral collective defense treaty as well as a fig leaf for Moscow's repressive control over the "allies." Nevertheless, the changing realities of Soviet-Eastern European relations did result in some autonomy for the Soviet clients. The outcome of the Polish October 1956 crisis illustrated this phenomenon.

## 1956 and its outcomes in Poland and Hungary

Poland, just like Hungary, experienced "silent" de-Stalinization after 1953, but the popular rage at lingering economic exploitation, oppression, and misery created by the communist regime could not be contained: that anger resulted in a bloody popular uprising, followed by a savage repression in Poznań in June 1956. Just like in Hungary, the uprising was a catalyst for a reformist/nationalist communist leader, Władysław Gomułka, to ascend to power in October 1956, an event that apparently happened without Moscow's consent. Moscow's rage at this act of insubordination resulted in a Soviet reaction similar to the one in Hungary's case – a movement of Soviet and Polish (Soviet-officered, or otherwise loyal) military units towards Warsaw and a threat of military intervention. In response (at least in popular perception) the Polish Internal Security Corps mobilized its own troops.[6] An armed clash and a potential bloodbath were prevented by direct negotiations between the Polish communist leadership, led by Gomułka, and a Soviet delegation led by Khrushchev, with the latter apparently being impressed by a possibility of Polish armed resistance, and reassured by Gomułka's firm commitment to a strategic relationship with the Soviet Union. The resulting compromise allowed for a measure of Polish domestic autonomy, including de-Russification of the military, rehabilitation of many of the older/non-communist military officers, and freedom for the Polish Armed Forces[7] to develop their own military doctrine, structure of forces, and equipment.[8] This trend was followed in the rest of the Soviet Bloc. While the Soviet control was maintained, both through formal and informal means,[9] cruder forms of subjugation were terminated after 1956, and the members of the Warsaw Pact operated within limited autonomy (Ross Johnson 1977; Jones 1981; Lewis 1982; Mastny & Byrne 2005).

What mattered for the development of Polish strategic culture as a result of the 1956, and, later, of the 1980–81 (more about this later) crises in Poland, is that in both cases the country escaped a direct Soviet military intervention (unlike Czechoslovakia in 1968 and Hungary in 1956), thus avoiding either a moral and material destruction (Hungary) or utter demoralization (Czechoslovakia) of its military. Moreover, even though the Polish communist-controlled Armed Forces were used by the regime (in 1970 and 1981–82) for internal repression, a persistent public perception in Poland was that country's military was actually a patriotic force, reluctant to be used as a force of repression and potentially willing to defend the country against external enemies, be it revanchist Germany or even the Soviet Union. This perception mattered, for in the national culture in which a sovereign military force and armed struggle for independency were all-important, communist Armed Forces were still held in high regard, maintained their coherence and professionalism, and transitioned relatively easily into a post-communist reality. The situation was diametrically different in Czechoslovakia and Hungary, where communist-era militaries were more compromised and demoralized than in the Polish case, and where the post-communist period brought about relatively quick de-militarization, which, in the Hungarian case, actually continued the trend that began in 1956.

In Hungary, when Rákosi tried to return to full power and removed Nagy in 1955, neither the Hungarian people (for whom Nagy, a heretofore loyal communist, became an unlikely hero), nor Moscow were happy. By 1956, Khrushchev was in power, and denounced Stalin in the not so secret "secret speech" in February 1956. Khrushchev also forced Rákosi to resign again in July 1956 but replaced him with Ernő Gerő, Rákosi's clone, who was equally hated in Hungary. Spurred by news of the Polish events in October 1956, where the Polish people and Communist Party successfully defied the Soviets, the Hungarian people revolted. Nagy was returned as head of the government, while János Kádár became the head of the Communist Party.

In the course of the Revolution, in late October 1956, armed Hungarian insurgents, joined by elements of the country's military, defeated an initial Soviet attempt to intervene on the streets of Budapest. With the country in a full revolt, and the Hungarian military in disarray, Nagy decided to throw in his fate with the Revolution, proclaimed the country's neutrality and withdrawal from the Warsaw Pact, and asked Soviet troops to leave Hungary. The Soviet leaders feigned negotiations and withdrawal, but intervened again with a force of 30,000 during the November 1–19 operation *Vikhr* (or Whirlwind). They brutally[10] put down the sometimes formidable resistance by mostly irregular forces of insurgents and the Hungarian National Guard (Kiraly 2003).[11] In the meantime, most of Hungary's regular military, a still substantial force of some 120,000, stood down. As a result, when the fighting was over and the inevitable reaction and repression took place under János Kádár, the Hungarian Armed Forces were seen as unreliable and dramatically cut in size, emerging with only 38% of their pre-existing personnel (Germuska 2015). The job of repression was taken on by the Soviet Union and the newly formed Hungarian internal security troops ("Kádar's Hussars"), which were made up of regime loyalists.

While the Hungarian communist military was later rebuilt (in the 1960s) under Kádar, the country became conspicuous for its demilitarization (Barany 1993). The percentage of military spending of the country's GDP was indeed below 2% around 1960, and fluctuated to 2.5 % of GDP in the period of late communism in the 1970s and 1980s, as compared to Poland's 3–4% and Czechoslovak 5% median figures for the same period (Crane 1987: 43). Instead of military spending, the Kádar regime emphasized economic growth and limited market reforms, the result being that it turned Hungary into a fairly consumer-oriented "happiest barracks" in the Soviet Bloc.

While the Soviet Union's continuous mistrust of the Hungarian military might be a factor explaining Hungary's relative de-militarization after 1956, the pattern clearly had more to do with internal considerations, for it continued after the fall of communism. Indeed, later on, in the 2000s, Hungary generally spent less than 1% of its GDP on the military.[12] The combined effects of Hungary's defeats in the First World War, the Second World War, and 1956 clearly established a long-standing cultural and institutional pattern of demilitarization that was analogous, perhaps, to similar transformations in Germany and Japan. For the Hungarian people and their government, the military was clearly not a priority, either before or after the fall of communism, and, today, national heroes of the Revolution and war of independence in 1956 – the last war that the country fought – remain irregular insurgents.

Another theme that emerged in Hungarian strategic culture from the Revolution of 1956, besides a solidification of the hatred of Russia/the Soviet Union, and of communism, was a notion of "Western betrayal." Indeed, while the West and the US in particular were cautious with their official diplomatic pronouncements during the Revolution, offering diplomatic support but no promises of armed intervention against the Soviets, the Hungarian section of CIA-created Radio Free Europe cheered on the armed resistance against the Soviets. In some cases, they gave implicit promises of Western armed intervention on behalf of the insurgents.[13] The perception created among Hungarians was that the US encouraged armed resistance in Hungary, only to betray it later. Hungarian nationalist anti-US and anti-Western narratives, increasingly popular as the memory of communism faded, could only benefit from this notion.

### Special case: the invasion of Czechoslovakia by the Warsaw Pact in 1968 and the controversial roles of WTO partners

It is vital to look at the picture that the Brezhnev Regime had of East-Central Europe during the mid-1960s, for the invasion of Czechoslovakia was accomplished against that backdrop. Leonid Brezhnev had replaced Nikita Khrushchev as First Secretary of the Communist Party in 1964, and it was not certain what his position would be on key issues within the bloc. As early as 1966, the Soviet leader asked Czechoslovak First Secretary Antonín Novotný to consider dispatch of troops to the border of his nation. There were Soviet troops on the borders of both Poland and Hungary, but there was a gap with regards to the eastern border of Czechoslovakia (Petrov 2004, 145–6). From the vantage point of the WTO, this was a powerful indicator of alliance weakness and vulnerability.

In May 1968, Soviet military officers arrived in Czechoslovakia, ostensibly to celebrate the anniversary of the end of the Scond World War. However, their ulterior motive was to assess Czechoslovak military units and examine the whole situation. Also, Soviet officers were interested in exploring prospects for crossing the Czechoslovak border during an invasion (Latysh 2010, 4). Soon, extended war games and military maneuvers under the label Šumava took place on Czechoslovak territory. By July, the Soviet leadership was debating the merits of continuation of the exercises or escalation to an invasion (Ouimet 2010, 23).

There was intense discussion among WTO partners during the week prior to the August 20 invasion. From their vantage point, failure to invade could lead to either a civil war in Czechoslovakia or the total loss of a socialist ally. The top Soviet military leaders Grechko and Zacharov struck upbeat poses about the prospects for WTO victory. Brezhnev was insistent that the invasion be a multilateral one, after the lone wolf experience in 1956 with the Soviet invasion of Hungary. Combat soldiers from Poland, Hungary, and Bulgaria would participate along with Soviet troops, while a liaison unit from East Germany would also be engaged. There was uncertainty within the leadership about possible political consequences of the invasion, but these were not strong enough to prevent it (Kramer 2010, 47–8).

The Soviet leader enunciated the Brezhnev Doctrine in order both to justify the invasion and to provide a foundation for future military activities within the bloc. This doctrine simply posited that the interests of the socialist commonwealth outflanked the national interests of the individual members of the WTO (Petrov 2010, 155). How that went down with the populations within the fellow socialist states remained an open question. The invading forces entered Czechoslovakia at 11 pm on August 20, 1968. They met no armed resistance, as the Czech and Slovak soldiers remained within their barracks. A military force of 450,000–500,000 troops easily took over airfields, government buildings, and both transportation and communication networks. The occupying forces arrested all top Czechoslovak leaders, while the Presidium of the Czechoslovak Communist Party condemned the invasion by a 7–4 vote (Kramer 2010, 48–9). In order to further control the flow of intelligence, the Soviet KGB established offices in both Prague and Bratislava. It remained unclear what kind of commonwealth the Soviet leadership had in mind in fulfilling the spirit of the Brezhnev Doctrine.

An open question was the length of stay by invading troops and whether a long-term occupation would result. In October, the answer was clarified through the signing of a treaty that called for the permanent stationing of troops in the land (Ruggenthaler and Knoll 2010, 182). No doubt, part of the reason for this decision was the need to fill the gap in Soviet control of East-Central Europe, but part of the motivation was also fear of continued dissent and opposition from not only the Czechoslovak population but also from its ruling Communist Party. Ironically, the Brezhnev Regime permitted the Czechoslovak leader Dubček to remain in power until April 1969. Partly, this was based on the Moscow Protocol signed in August after four days of talks by both Communist Party leaderships on Soviet soil (Kramer 2010, 51). In the end the occupying troops would remain until the 1989 Revolution that toppled the Czechoslovak Communist Party leaders from power.

A significant part of the military operation was the participation in planning by four WTO members, in addition to the leaders from the Soviet Union. Initially, the announcement outlined a planned role for troops from Poland, East Germany, Bulgaria, and Hungary. However, decades later, archive openings revealed that Brezhnev had held the East German troops back, and so they never did cross the border and take part in the operation.

The Polish role in the operation was a visible one, as their dispatch of 25,000 troops made them the second largest army in the invasion. The capabilities that they brought with them included 647 tanks, 566 armored personnel carriers (APCs), 371 cannons, and 36 helicopters. They blockaded garrisons, conducted patrol services, engaged in propaganda, and knocked out radio stations. Their withdrawal came at the end of October (Kamínski 2010, 104). In spite of the wholehearted involvement by the Polish military, there was considerable internal anguish about that role within the Polish population. There were concerns uttered about possible retaliation by the US, and some feared the economically stringent conditions that might affect Polish citizens. In addition, there were questions about whether the invasion was compatible with or even permitted by Warsaw Pact Statutes (Kamínski 2010, 107–11). More than a decade later, there were serious observers who wondered if the 1968 invasion was a precursor to the crackdown in

1981 on the Polish Solidarity movement (Wróbel 2010, 135). Thus, the Polish regime and popular perceptions about the invasion were profoundly different.

The East German Army included a considerable force of 120,000 troops and officers. With the nickname of "Red Prussians," they played a full part in planning for the upcoming operation Danube. The combined force mobilized along their southern border included tens of thousands of Soviet soldiers, 2,000 Soviet tanks, 2,000 APCs, 16,500 East German soldiers, and 500 East German tanks. Preparations brought in two specific East German units with assigned responsibilities. The Dresden-based 7th Armored Division included 7,500 troops, 1,500 vehicles, and 300 tanks. Their blueprint included a movement across the Czechoslovak border into Litoměřice, Mimoń, and Děčín. Their second unit was the Halle-based 11th Motorized Rifle Division and was scheduled to enter Plzeň with 9,000 troops and 1,700 vehicles. The assumption after the invasion was that all of this had taken place, and different stories did not emerge until the archives opened up after 1989. Apparently, Brezhnev was in touch with Czechoslovak communist opponents of Dubček, and they had convinced him of the unwisdom of the inclusion of the East German units (Wenzke 2010, 148–55). Memories of the German role in the Second World War were too strong and acted as a powerful deterrent on the Soviet leadership. It is surprising that no participants in the invading forces or elements of the target population were aware of or spoke about this important feature of the invasion.

Bulgarian Communist Party First Secretary Zhivkov was a forceful advocate of the need for an invasion. In fact, the Bulgarian Council of Ministers ratified Decree # 39 that legitimized participation by Bulgarian troops in the invasion. The size of the Bulgarian military contingent was smaller than either the Polish or the planned East German units. Their 12th Artillery Regiment from Elchovo Garrison sent 1,200 soldiers across the Black Sea into the Ukrainian Republic near the Czechoslovak border. They entered Slovakia at Matóvce, met considerable Slovak resistance, and eventually took over barracks, police stations, the post office, and the newspaper *SME* in Banská Bystrica. Further, the 22nd Artillery Regiment from Charmanli Garrison consisted of 962 men who arrived in the Ukrainian Republic at Kolomyja Airport. Soviet troops eventually gave them control over both Ruzyně and Vodochody Airports. In fact, both units were firmly incorporated into the Soviet military structure. While the Bulgarian troops unexpectedly received hatred instead of flowers from the Czechoslovak citizens, they received a reception hero's reception at every Bulgarian town during their October return (Skálová 2010, 183–8).

Hungarian Communist Party Chieftain Janos Kadar was reluctant to endorse the invasion, as he had, just that year, introduced his New Economic Plan, which brought a number of capitalist principles into economic planning. Even though he had been the leader who had expelled the reformer Imre Nagy from power in 1956, with considerable help from the Soviet military, he had come to understand the need for substantial modifications in communist-style planning. However, he did meet in Yalta with Brezhnev five days before the invasion and agreed to be part of it. In contrast to the Soviet leadership, his focus was on long-term political considerations and compromises rather than on an abrupt and unthinking military occupation (Békés 2010, 217–20). Therefore, the Hungarian role in the invasion was more halting and tentative than that of the other WTO participants.

In conclusion, the Warsaw Pact invasion caught the world by surprise. However, it made an indelible impression on the military forces of the three East-Central European players. While Czechoslovakia was the target of the attack, both Poland and Hungary became part of the invading coalition, the former with force and the latter with reluctance. As such, the invasion became a legacy for all four eventual states during post-communist times. For Poland and Hungary, commitment of troops abroad after 1989 would have constituted repetition of steps that they had taken earlier, although under strikingly different circumstances. Czechs and Slovaks would be more cautious about such engagements, for they had been on the receiving end in 1968. Coupled with their humiliation at Munich in 1938, an internal focus on rebuilding their two nations would have been the essence of common sense.

While a massive civil-non-violent resistance was the Czechoslovak people's reaction to the invasion, the quite formidable (200,000 strong vs. the initial invading force of around 250,000) Czechoslovak Armed Forces, as directed by Dubček, completely stood down (Bischof and Karner 2010). The experience of the country's Armed Forces being completely irrelevant to Czechoslovak self-defenses twice in the period of 30 years (1938–39 and 1968) must have had a profound influence on Czech and Slovak strategic cultures – reflecting their relative pragmatism but also, inevitably, contributing to relative devaluation of the military as relevant to the countries' security. Czechoslovakia's and its successor states' relative demilitarization after 1989 – less extreme than Hungary's, but clearly distinct from Poland's continuous existence on strong Armed Forces as a guarantee of the country's sovereignty – is clearly a reflection of this persistent historical pattern and the strategic culture it created.

### Themes between the 1968 invasion of Czechoslovakia and the 1980–81 Polish Crisis

The 1960s and 1970s were the "normal" or middle periods of communist military and defense policies in the countries under consideration. Factors of convergence and divergence between them continued to operate. On the one hand, the Soviet Union continued to insist on a relatively high level of military mobilization of its allies – which the Soviet leaders required to augment their own huge forces in Central Europe – that were expected to prepare to wage a strategically defensive but operationally aggressive mechanized war against NATO. As a result, the countries settled on fairly high levels of standing forces (if much lower than during high Stalinism), which for Poland numbered around 300,000, for Czechoslovakia 200,000, and for Hungary 100,000. These forces were also fairly well mechanized, modernized, and equipped, with high levels of professionalism, especially in more technical services (air forces, logistics, etc.). Their doctrines were all subordinated to and coordinated with the those of the Soviet Union, which in all cases envisioned a dual nature of the forces – highly mobile mechanized troops were to wage coalition warfare as a part of Soviet strike forces in Central Europe, whereas territorial defense forces were to defend the respective countries' land, air, and, in the case of Poland, also sea spaces. Coordination was maintained through multilateral and bilateral mechanisms of control. However, what we see as a persistent pattern entailed constant efforts by the communist-bloc allies to assert their autonomy against the Soviets, especially on the forum of Warsaw Pact institutions, with Romania clearly leading the way with theatrical displays of anti-Sovietism.[14]

However, factors of divergence were also in evidence, with Czechoslovakia (who, prior to 1968, was seen as "the most trusted ally") leading with the highest levels of military spending, which hovered between 5% and 6% of GDP in the 1960s, declined to 4% in the early 1970s, and climbed back again to over 5% in the early 1980s. Polish spending, in the meantime, was consistently above 4% in the 1960s and between 3% and 4% of GDP in the 1970s, climbing back up close to 4% in the 1980s. Hungary continued, in the meantime, with the already mentioned pattern of relative demilitarization which made it an outlier in the communist camp – the country was spending below 2% of its GDP in the 1960s, and never exceeded 3% of its GDP throughout the period until the fall of communism.[15]

## Late communism: the Polish Crisis of 1980–81 – dissolution of Soviet Empire and its legacies

"Late" communism was the period that shaped the Visegrád countries' military and defense policies and establishments in the way that most immediately affected their post-communist realities and policies. For one, the countries' post-communist militaries were initially, simply late communist militaries under a new leadership, which often featured (in the cases of Poland and Hungary) a high level of continuity with communist-era leadership. Late communism also started the trend of demilitarization of Europe, which continued into the post-communist period. From a long-term perspective, indeed, East-Central Europe had been demilitarizing since 1953, and the Gorbachev era's demilitarization simply reinforced this trend. Before this happened, however, the early 1980s brought about a volatile episode of neo-Stalinist re-militarization and war tensions of 1981–84. It was only after the failure of late communist/neo-Stalinist attempts to shore up the system's ideological and material basis that Mikhail Gorbachev's liberalization kicked in as a very different attempt to shore up the system's legitimacy and power – and ended up leading to a disintegration of the Soviet Empire.

Communist military and defense policies of the early 1980s largely continued those of the middle period. Polish, Czechoslovak, and DDR militaries (and, to a lesser extent, the Hungarian millitary) were still expected to participate in a potential Soviet confrontation with NATO. According to the existing war-plans, The Warsaw Pact allies' best/mobile "operational" forces were to be a part of massive Soviet armored thrusts through West Germany and Austria, while the territorial defense forces were to defend the respective homelands (Kajetanowicz 2013: 48).[16] The size of the countries' military forces did not change significantly, but they continued to be modernized, with substantial upgrading of equipment taking place throughout the 1970s and 1980s, as evidenced by the high and growing military procurement budgets of the countries in question (Crane 1987). Weapons systems such as Mig-23 and Mig-29 fighters, T-72 tanks, BTR-70 APCs, BMP-1 infantry fighting vehicles and Mi-24 "Hind" attack helicopters were either imported (BMP-1s, Mig-29s and Mi-24s) or domestically produced (T-72s, in Poland and Czechoslovakia). Nevertheless, all the countries in question resisted Soviet demands to further increase their military budgets and then, while formally agreeing to increased goals, never fully implemented them (Lewis 1982). Only East Germany completely fulfilled its promises to expand its military budget in the 1980s, marking the country's status as the favorite junior partner of the Soviets in the 1980s (Crane 1987).

In the meantime, Poland provided the Soviets with the most significant source of problems, the Polish Crisis of the 1980s being eventually unsolvable and leading to the demise of the entire communist bloc. The "Solidarity" Crisis was brought about by a non-violent uprising of the Polish population in the summer of 1980, which was the culmination of a tradition of social protest and resistance against communism that resulted in crises in 1968, 1970, and 1976. This time the wave of strikes and protests involved a newly found ability of the working class/farmers to create institutionalized forms of interest representation in alliance with dissenting intellectuals and the Catholic Church. Unwilling to use force,[17] the regime capitulated to the opposition demands, and, by fall 1980, authorized autonomous institutionalized forms of non-communist civil society, most importantly the Polish Solidarity, a massive social movement with some 10,000,000 members, masquerading as a "trade union" and led by charismatic Lech Wałęsa. While planning for the movement's disruption and eventual violent suppression, the Polish communist government and its military and police forces felt overwhelmed, while the Soviet leadership, beset by the ongoing crisis in Afghanistan, was extremely reluctant to intervene, pressuring the Polish communist leadership to suppress the revolution internally.[18] This marked the effective end of the "Brezhnev Doctrine," which was exercised in precisely one case, the 1968 Czechoslovakia (Quimet 2003).

One peculiar characteristic of the Polish Crisis was the ascendance of the Polish communist military, and its leader, General Wojciech Jaruzelski. He had been the Minister of Defense since 1968, became Prime Minister in February 1981, and moved on to be the First Secretary of the Polish United Workers' Party in September 1981. This unique merger of military and political powers was solidified in December 1981, when Jaruzelski introduced "martial law" in Poland. This crackdown was a massive,[19] country-wide, well-coordinated repressive operation, which not only violently suppressed the Solidarity movement and destroyed the Polish liberalization episode, but also formally suspended the supremacy of the Communist Party, by proclaiming the Military Council of National Salvation, with Jaruzelski at its head, to be the supreme state organ. This was followed up with a widespread militarization of all state institutions. No communist country of the Soviet bloc ever underwent this type of formal institutionalization of military rule, the phenomenon being specifically Polish, and perhaps harkening back to Piłsudski's coup of 1926.

The militarization of Poland, and Jaruzelski's propaganda, posing as a military-patriotic savior of the country from chaos or a potential Soviet invasion, appealed to a nationalistic-authoritarian streak in

Polish public opinion and political culture, which included trust in the military as a patriotic institution. Significantly, resistance to martial law, while widespread, was also relatively shallow and the regime had no problem asserting control. As late as 2011, two decades after the fall of communism, 51% of the Polish public saw the introduction of martial law in 1981 as a justified necessity,[20] thus implicitly accepting Jaruzelski's "patriotic" and nationalistic excuses, which recent historiography largely dismisses.[21] What matters for the purposes of this book is that the whole phenomenon testifies both to a persistent relative militarization and to a sort of authoritarian patriotism in Polish public opinion. In this case, even the communist military was mythologized by a section of the public opinion to be a "savior of the nation." Tellingly, of the countries examined in this book, only Poland avoided a direct Soviet military intervention during the communist period. Through a mix of nationalist concessions and repression, Polish communist rulers were able to assert control themselves.

Martial law was followed by a slew of American and Western sanctions against the Polish communist regime and the Soviet Union,[22] and this further escalated hostilities between the Soviet Union and the West, culminating in the (apparent) war scare of 1983 (Jones 2016). This period of volatility and high tension in East–West conflict was accompanied by Warsaw Pact efforts at military modernization, as reflected in increasing procurement budgets of the member countries (Crane 1987). However, this effort was clearly unsustainable in the context of the escalating economic crisis of communist countries, as they were reaching the top limit of their economic growth horizon possible under existing institutional arrangements. Caught among insolvable dilemmas of a desire for internal legitimacy, an economic crisis, militarism and the need for Western cooperation to foster the communist countries' economic growth, the Soviet leadership desperately looked for solutions.

Under Yuri Andropov (1982–83), a KGB head who became the first Secretary of the Soviet Communist Party after the death of the senile Brezhnev, a solution was to be found in a neo-Stalinist emphasis on law and order, militarism, and a crackdown on both dissent and corruption. These patterns were accompanied by relative pragmatism on select economic and political issues. Under the senile Konstantin Chernenko (1983–84), who was terminally ill when he ascended to the office, late Brezhnevian orthodoxy and corruption seemingly returned. After Chernenko's death, the ascent of Andropov's protégé Mikhail Gorbachev to the highest office finally marked the full and final attempt to restore dynamism to the decadent system.

Initially, Gorbachev's solutions seemed to follow his mentor's emphasis on law and order and militarism, but this soon led to liberalism, an opening to the West, and encouragement of liberalization among the bloc countries. A search of arms-control agreements/détente with the West and demilitarization was a part of the reform package that soon brought about cuts in military spending and demilitarization of the Warsaw Bloc countries. By 1988–89, Poland and Hungary were in full turn towards liberalization, encouraged by Moscow. By the end of 1989, through either peaceful negotiated transitions in Poland and Hungary or massive upheavals from below, accompanied by the collapse of the regimes in Czechoslovakia and the DDR, the communist regimes in East-Central Europe ended. This was encouraged by Moscow through the explicit repudiation of the Brezhnev Doctrine and its replacement by the jokingly formulated "Sinatra doctrine."[23] Importantly, though, the end of the Cold War in Europe was accompanied by Western guarantees that NATO/the US would not expand (with the exception of East Germany's absorption into a united Germany) into the strategic space left behind by the retreat of the Soviet Empire (Beschloss and Talbott 1993). Thus, the countries of East-Central Europe were left happily liberated from the Soviet imperial yoke, but they were also left in a strategic vacuum between the West and Russia, in which they needed to re/construct their post-communist defense policies and establishments.

The Polish Armed Forces were the largest, with around 347,000 troops and 15 mechanized or armored divisions (in 1988). Their capabilities also included specialized Air Forces, Naval Forces and Air and Air-defense and Territorial Defense Forces. The Czechoslovak military was the second largest, with 201,000 troops (in 1987) and 10 divisions, and was by far the best equipped among the Visegrád countries (for instance, it had 4,585 tanks as compared to Poland's 3,300, and the best aircraft, including Soviet Mig-23s and Su-25s). It was also similar in structure to the Polish military but lacked a Navy. Finally, the Hungarian military, with approximately 106,000 soldiers and 6 divisions, was by far the smallest and the least well-equipped among the Eastern European militaries on the eve of the transformation. Also, the Hungarian military had merged its Air and Air-defense Forces into one service.

Legacies of the communist period for East-Central European defense policies after 1989 are multiple and often hidden in plain sight, as the new regimes and post-communist societies embraced liberalism and deliberately distanced themselves from the communist legacies, including militarism. To some extent and by dialectical logic, it is precisely the process of distancing that constitutes one of the legacies – a phenomenon made clear to us by a recent wave of populist nationalism which swept the region and made us realize that the first two and a half decades of post-communism were a distinct and largely closed period of change.

As participants in the Soviet Empire, East-Central European countries had to abandon their pre-Second World War nationalistic realism and become a part of an institutionalized, hierarchical alliance system which defined both the countries' internal and external policies and their security interests. Significantly, after a very brief period of strategic ambiguity in the immediate post-communist period, East-Central European countries chose to join the Western security community, another institutionalized hierarchical system centered on the US. This new system was embraced enthusiastically and willingly, even though it defined the countries' defense policies and structures just as stringently, or even more so, as the Soviet imperial system did before. There is no doubt that what prepared the countries to participate in this new system was an earlier experience in the Soviet imperial system.

While the Soviet system was far from democratic, it dramatically transformed the countries in question away from pre-Second World War archaic social hierarchies into egalitarian, urban, and industrial societies through a process of "passive democratization." Post-communist social and political systems, while featuring a host of problems and social tensions, were thus uniquely suited to embrace liberalism. Embrace of liberal democracy, as well as the countries that embodied this ideology, was also conditioned by the rejection of communism as liberalism's ideological opposite. Ironically, as the memory of communism has faded in the countries in question, embrace of liberalism became weaker, and various forms of nationalistic populism rose to prominence.

One special way in which communist countries, especially Poland, were prepared to embrace a global multilateral security system centered on the West and the US, was their experience of participation in multilateral peacekeeping operations under the auspices of the UN. Poland, indeed, participated in ten such operations, starting with the Korean War, and including several peacekeeping and peace-monitoring missions in the Middle East, Asia, and Africa. This experience, to some extent, prepared the countries and their militaries for participation in much more intensive and violent operations under the auspices of NATO, the EU, and the UN in the post-Cold War era.

Neither former Warsaw Pact countries nor NATO defense policies and structures were prepared for post-Cold War turmoil or security challenges, for in the Cold War period, on both sides of the "iron curtain," defense policies, doctrines, and military establishments were geared toward countering each other for an epic high-tech conventional and nuclear clash that never took place. Some of the capacities acquired during the Cold War period were relevant to the new security environment of the 1990s, as conventional mechanized forces could be kept as a residual deterrent. They could also be adjusted to challenges to peace-keeping or peace-enforcement in places such as the former Yugoslavia. However, the imperatives of overseas expeditionary warfare that came with the "war on terror" in the early 2000s required new capacities and costly adjustments that came at the expense of conventional military modernization across Europe, including East-Central Europe. In turn, the new security environment that emerged after the August 2008 Russia-Georgia war, and, especially, after the Russian conflict with Ukraine in 2014, required re-investment into conventional military capacities.

So far, while all examined countries tried to meet challenges posed by these changing imperatives, only Poland, following its special cultural and unique structural position as the strongest country in the region, seems to have made a serious effort to meet these changing imperatives.

## Notes

1 General Stefan Mossor was the chief author of this defense policy concept and the corresponding military doctrine, clearly rooted in Dmowski's thought.

2 See, "Treaty of Peace with Hungary," part III, section I, article 12, The Library of Congress, "US Treaties" https://www.loc.gov/law/help/us-treaties/bevans/m-ust000004-0453.pdf, accessed March 18, 2017.

3 In an ironic twist, the bloody purges in the Polish military were carried out on the orders of Marshall Rokossovsky, who was himself a victim of earlier Soviet purges in the 1930s. In the Orwellian Soviet system, just like under Nazism, victims were taught to repress other victims.

4 The Polish communist military effectives in 1952 totalled 356,000 soldiers, while the country devoted at least 15% of its GDP towards military spending. The equivalent Hungarian figures were 230,000 soldiers, and up to 25% of GDP. In Czechoslovakia, the military effectives in 1953 totalled around 297,000 soldiers, and military spending reached 20% of GDP.

5 See "Treaty of Friendship, Co-operation and Mutual Assistance." Signed at Warsaw, on May 14, 1955 in the United Nations Treaty Collection, https://treaties.un.org/doc/Publication/UNTS/Volume%20219/volume-219-I-2962-Other.pdf, accessed March 26, 2017.

6 *Korpus Bezpieczeństwa Wewnętrznego*, KBW, was an internal security formation used mostly, paradoxically, to repress anti-communist resistance after 1945. Details of why and against whom the KBW units mobilized in 1956 remain obscure, but what mattered was the Polish public perception that the Soviets were somehow deterred by a prospect of Polish resistance involving elements of the Polish communist military.

7 The official name after 1952 was the Armed Forces of the Polish People's Republic (*Siły Zbrojne Polskiej Rzeczypospolitej Ludowej*).

8 Poland developed its own military doctrine starting in 1961. Pursuant to this doctrine, the country developed fairly substantial internal/territorial defense troops. Presumed to be used against NATO, these forces could also be used against a potential Soviet intervention. In terms of equipment since the early 1960s, Poland and Czechoslovakia co-produced a wheeled APC SKOT, superior to its Soviet BTR-60/-70 equivalent.

9 The formal and informal mechanisms of Soviet control over the Polish military were described by Col. Ryszard Kukliński, a high ranking Polish General Staff officer who was recruited by US intelligence and later defected to the US. See "Soviet Penetration of the Polish Military" declassified document, at http://bi.gazeta.pl/im/5/6056/m6056505.pdf, accessed March 26, 2017. The mechanisms included the existence of a Soviet liaison mission with high-level access to all the relevant documents, a constant Soviet supervision over and formal ability to evaluate the performance of Polish officers and units in terms of "military readiness," and access to information from social and friendship networks, wiretapping, and use of intelligence agents among the Polish military. Clearly, similar mechanisms were used in the Czechoslovak and Hungarian cases.

10 Hungarian casualties were about 2,500 dead and 20,000 wounded, mostly Budapest civilians. The Soviets lost around 700 soldiers, with 1,500 wounded, again mostly in Budapest. The victims of repression afterwards numbered around 30,000 arrested and 350 executed Hungarians, among whom were Imré Nagy and Pál Maléter, the Commander-in-Chief of the Hungarian military at the time of the Soviet invasion. In addition, some 200,000 Hungarians fled to the West and Yugoslavia (North Atlantic Council, 1957, p. 3).

11 A hybrid force of Hungarian military and insurgents formed the Hungarian National Guard led by General Béla Király.

12 This made Hungary, alongside Spain and Luxemburg, the lowest military spender in NATO and by far the lowest spender among newly admitted countries.

13 See Mr Griffith, "Policy Review of Voice for Free Hungary Programming, October 23–November 23, 1956," December 5, 1956, in National Security Archive, http://nsarchive.gwu.edu/NSAEBB/NSAEBB76/doc10.pdf, accessed March 18, 2017. See also Gati 2006.

14 Romania demanded and obtained the removal of Soviet forces from its territory, geared its military structures towards territorial defenses against a potential Soviet aggression, and refused to participate in but instead condemned the Soviet invasion of Czechoslovakia in 1968, etc. At all Warsaw Pact forums, Romania fulminated against Soviet control and demanded true multilateralism and respect for the national sovereignty of member states. The exposition effect of Romania's "bad" behavior on the East-Central European bloc countries must have been tremendous. The fact that the Soviet leadership tolerated it was astonishing, but perhaps it was explicable

due to Romania's marginal geographical position and to the fact that the country maintained the strictest Stalinist orthodoxy in its domestic political and economic order. The country also never formally quit the Warsaw Pact until the alliance's dissolution.

15 By Western standards stunningly high percentages of the respective countries' military budgets were devoted to equipment procurement, especially in the high-spending Czechoslovakia, in which, in 1983, an astonishing 59% of the military budget is presumed to have been devoted to procurement, most of it from domestic manufacturers. Poland was a middle-level spender, which systematically increased its military spending in the 1970s as compared to the 1960s; it continued to increase the military budget in the early 1980s, with procurement constituting 46% of the spending, most of it (53%) from domestic manufacture. While Hungary was a low-spender, it also devoted 46% of its budget to procurement, with the crushing majority of it (81%) devoted to imports of military equipment. See Crane 1987.

16 The so-called "Seven Days to the Rhine" 1979 war-plan/hypothetical scenario was typical of these plans. Czechoslovak troops were expected to co-participate in the Soviet strike against southern West Germany; the Poles were to attack northern West Germany, Denmark, and Holland in a strike supportive of the Soviet main offensive; and Hungary was to attack Austria alongside Soviet forces stationed in Hungary. This war-plan, presumably a counter against a NATO nuclear first-strike against Poland, also involved lavish use of Soviet nuclear weapons against targets in Germany, Belgium, Denmark, and Austria. See Mizokami 2016. This war plan was revealed by Polish Minister of Defense, Radoslaw Sikorski, in 2005, with the actual documents released in 2006.

17 One factor in this decision were byzantine intra-regime factional struggles, which resulted in three different Polish United Workers Party First Secretaries succeeding each other in the space of approximately one year (between September 1980 and October 1981). The last of them was General Wojciech Jaruzelski, who became the First Secretary in October 1981 and continued in this function until 1989. See Staniszkis 1984.

18 Several myths surround the Solidarity Crisis, including a widespread notion that the Soviet Union planned an outright military invasion of Poland in December 1980, only to be deterred by a threat of US political retaliation. More recent research shows that that there was no imminent Soviet/Warsaw Pact invasion threat, either in December 1980 or in December 1981. See, Paczkowski & Byrne 2008.

19 The operation involved at least 70,000 soldiers, 30,000 police personnel, and several thousand military vehicles. Around 10,000 people were detained, and 56 killed. This was by far the largest operation conducted by the Polish military between 1945 and 2017.

20 See MJ, PAP, "Sondaż: Większość Polaków za stanem wojennym," *Newsweek Poland*, www.newsweek.pl/polska/sondaz--wiekszosc-polakow-za-stanem-wojennym,85559,1,1.html, accessed July 29, 2017.

21 Most recent research indicates that Jaruzelski, far from trying to avoid the Soviet invasion, which was actually not on the cards, begged Moscow to intervene to prop up his crackdown, which succeeded way beyond expectations.

22 Sources are unanimous that both the Polish and Soviet communist leadership felt "betrayed" by the Western reaction to Polish martial law, as prior Western behavior was interpreted to have indicated that the West would not mind if Poland found "internal" solutions to the crisis and avoided a Soviet intervention. Evidence confirms that US/Western leaders were sending mixed signals to their communist counter-parts.

23 On October 25, 1989, referring to the Frank Sinatra song "I did it my way," the Soviet Foreign Ministry spokesman Gennadi Gerasimov retrospectively expressed Soviet approval of the then ongoing transition to liberal democracy in Poland and Hungary; that statement presaged Soviet approval for the upcoming revolutions in East Germany and Czechoslovakia.

# 4

# The Czech Republic: a reluctant ally

Assessing defense policy in the Czech Republic can center on a number of key pedestals that underpin the readiness of its forces to engage in critical deployments or to stand in readiness for coping with future challenges. First, what is the general orientation to defense policy, characteristic since the end of the communist era in 1989 and the 1993 separation from Slovakia? A second area of study includes a brief look at reforms enacted after 1993 that were designed to put post-communist defense policy on the path towards integration with Western partners. A key third topic consists of assessment of defense budgets over time. Although the end of the Cold War and the WTO called for reductions in defense budgets, an interest in integrating with Western institutions such as NATO and the EU pointed to the need to continue with a respectable budget in a comparative sense. Fourth, there is a need to study the related topic of the actual size of the military capability in terms of the number of troops over time. Fifth, and critically important, is participation in deployments outside the nation. Czech military forces possessed a number of unique capabilities that served both NATO and the EU well in missions such as Bosnia-Herzegovina, Kosovo, Afghanistan, and Iraq. The first two operations were relatively close to the geographic space of the Czech state, but the latter two were further afield and tied to America's perceived needs after the 9/11 attacks. The sixth and final focus will be the important questions that preoccupied the NATO alliance and its Czech partner after the Ukrainian Crisis of 2014 and the divisiveness of the American presidential election of 2016. A unifying thread is the question of what Czech priorities were as an individual Central European state as well as a partner in two significant regional alliances. It was impossible to separate the three entities in terms of overall defense policy, but it became an important challenge in light of political pressures connected with the Russian incursion into Ukraine, the pressure of Middle Eastern refugees into Western European nations, the rise of nationalistic political parties such as the Alternative for

Germany (AfD), and the emergence of nation-centered leaders such as Donald Trump.

## General orientation to defense policy

Collective security was important for the leaders and people of the new Czech Republic in the early 1990s, for their security had been so problematic earlier in the century. Following their loss at the Battle of White Mountain in 1620, the Czechs had succumbed to nearly three centuries of submission to the Austrian Empire and its leaders in Vienna. At the end of this period, the First World War tore Czechs apart in terms of the controls imposed by larger empires. Nearly 100,000 Czech Soldiers defected from the Austro-Hungarian Army and joined the Czech Legion, which became an ally of the pre-revolutionary Russian Empire. After the November revolution, the same Czech military units avoided solidarity with Lenin and the communists but then became trapped in Siberia during the Russian Civil War. Many other Czech military units stayed with the forces that Vienna led, and that subordination was paralleled by the alliance with Germany as well. Citizens of the Czech Lands dreamed of and planned for new options but were under imperial controls until independence in October 1918.

Jeopardized security continued to be the common theme during the existence of the Czechoslovak state from 1918 until its end in 1993. The Munich Agreement of 1938 was devastating, for the Nazis set up subordinate, puppet states in the Czech and Slovak geographic areas. The end of the the Scond World War brought a halt to Nazi controls, but within three-years the Soviet leaders imposed a new controlling system under the leadership of the Czechoslovak Communist Party. Admittedly, there was considerable local sentiment that supported the overture from the East but, in general, Czech security was in the hands of Moscow and its associates in Prague and Bratislava. The one effort of Czechs to gain some control over their own security matters ended in failure, for the Prague Spring of 1968 threatened to create too important a fissure between the northern and southern sectors of the Warsaw Pact. As result, the challenge of designing their own security framework was greatly important in 1993 and after.

In effect, Czech leaders sought to establish a new "strategic culture" that would link citizens and leaders together in a common purpose during the upcoming period of democratization (Lefebvre 2010, 329). Emergence of the Partnership for Peace (PfP) program of NATO provided one concrete direction for Czech strategic planners. While the end of the Cold War may have provided a strong hint that lower defense spending was possible, the possibility of admission to NATO pointed in the opposite direction. In the early years of the new republic, President Havel and Foreign Minister Dienstbier emphasized increasing Czech participation in the common values of Europe, and the Organization for Security and Cooperation in Europe (OSCE) was for them the top priority. Since the Warsaw Pact had immediately collapsed after the end of the Cold War, there was an expectation in some quarters that a similar fate awaited the Atlantic alliance. However, emerging crises in the Balkans put the spotlight back on NATO as the main guarantor of security. Just as this nod towards NATO pointed the Czechs west and towards Europe and its Atlantic partners, so too did the new orientation downplay the Visegrád security basis for the Czech Republic, Slovakia, Hungary, and Poland (Lefebvre 2010, 339–45). Connections with the EU and hoped for membership in it also loomed as important strategic factors. Czech aspirations for a future of assured security would flourish through balancing NATO and EU priorities, and their work on developing "capable Armed Forces" would serve the needs of both regional organizations (Lefebvre 2010, 368–9). Thereby, they laid the foundation for the development of a vibrant and meaningful "strategic culture."

With respect to the EU as a centerpiece of a Western-based strategic culture, there was initial participation in its Common Foreign and Security Policy (CFSP), but after 9/11 this gave way within the alliance to a more hardheaded European Security and Defense Policy (ESDP). Five years after Czech accession to the EU, the Lisbon Treaty in 2009 replaced the ESDP with the Common Security and Defense Policy (CSDP) (Kříž and Chovančík 2013, 50–2). With Czech participation in the EU at the ten-year mark at the time of the Lisbon Treaty, these security themes and accompanying programs had also become a full part of the emerging Czech strategic culture. However, the far greater capacity of NATO made it into a firmer source of protection than the EU.

An important testament to the renewed focus on Czech security assurances and protections was the November 2002 NATO Summit. Brussels-based alliance planners possessed sufficient confidence in the Czech Republic as a security partner to hold this critical meeting in Prague. There, the NATO leadership invited Estonia, Latvia, Lithuania, Slovenia, Slovakia, Romania, and Bulgaria to become full members, which they all did two years later in 2004. Inclusion of Slovakia was of particular importance in light of both the break-up of Czechoslovakia in 1993 and the earlier full membership granted to the Czechs in 1999. In addition, the Prague Summit resulted in enunciation of a Prague Capabilities Commitment as well as a Statement on Iraq in light of the upcoming probability of an American-led war there in the near future. Importantly, the alliance also approved for the first time the creation of a NATO Response Force. In light of the previous decade of post-Cold War challenges, this force would consist of 21,000 troops and be capable of deployment within a 5–30 day window (Simon 2004, 251). Clearly, the Cold War tensions seldom required any sort of actual mobilization of troops in a crisis. However, deployment by NATO forces to a variety of war-torn settings made deterrence of dangers yield to actual combat in its operations.

## Czech defense policy reforms after 1993

In 2001, leaders of the Czech Republic added a new constitutional amendment that addressed issues of foreign policy and its new commitments. Essentially, that amendment provided the policy-makers with the "flexibility" to deploy troops under existing NATO and EU missions. Prior to that reform, Czech Army capabilities had centered on territorial defense mainly, but membership in NATO in 1999 required expanded horizons on the potential locations of military commitments. Based on an Army Reform of 2001, Czechs would also prepare themselves to follow NATO guidelines that might entail deployment of 3,000 troops for six months in a single peacekeeping operation with no rotations. Further, Czechs would be prepared to deploy 1,000 troops for six months in a single operation with no rotations. The reason for the lower number of troops in this option centered on the fact that there was a parallel requirement to keep 250 troops in readiness for a second six-month operation with no rotations (Kříž and Chovančík 2013, 58). One year later, at the end of 2002, there was another Army Reform that took Czech responsibilities to a somewhat higher level. Czech plans would center on the ability to provide 5,000 troops to a six-month peacekeeping operation and to maintain 250 troops in a specialized unit for another operation. In light of the increased threat of terrorism and the capture of hostages, they would also develop an elite police unit of 200 personnel to work with NATO in teams of 50.

Between 2005 and 2011, there were other significant reforms for military preparedness and operations. In 2005, the Czechs abolished compulsory military service in order to professionalize the Armed Forces in tune with NATO expectations. In 2008, a further reform made it explicit that deployment of Czech troops outside the geographical space of NATO and the EU was permissible. Of course, such deployment had already taken place in the Balkans, Afghanistan, and Iraq. In a sense, this reform simply brought guidelines up to date and compatible with existing reality. Finally, a reform at the beginning of 2011 called for deepened interactions with other alliance partners (Kříž and Chovančík 2013, 54–7). It was an achievement to be able to dispatch Czech troops to foreign locations to partner with the allies, but it was another step needed to make Czech military capabilities compatible with those of NATO. This reform pertained to language, army equipment, and air force planes. The time needed for this reform would be lengthy but would harness the nation's capabilities more tightly to those of the alliance and benefit future missions.

## Changing Czech defense budgets

Examination of Table 4.1 reveals the trends in Czech defense spending since the split of Czechoslovakia into two nations. From beginning to end, there has been a sharp drop in the proportion of GDP devoted to defense from 2.61% in 1993 to 1.03% in 2016. No doubt the higher figures in the 1993–94 period were holdovers from the Cold War, when defense preparedness was a high priority. Underlying factors behind those relatively higher figures were pressure from the Soviet Union for a strong Czech contribution to the WTO and perceptions of the American-led Western threat. It was also the case that the Czech military engaged in frequent exercises after 1968 with Soviet troops and other WTO allies such as East Germany, Poland, and Bulgaria. Those exercises required a full military capacity and development of multi-faceted defense capabilities. By the mid-1990s, there was no fear of a revival of the Cold War and no apparent overwhelming enemy on the horizon. Hence, the proportion of GDP devoted to defense noticeably dropped between 1995 and 1997.

**Table 4.1** Czech defense expenditure as a percentage of GDP, 1993–2016

| Year | % GDP | Year | % GDP | Year | % GDP |
|------|-------|------|-------|------|-------|
| 1993 | 2.61 | 2001 | 2.10 | 2009 | 1.43 |
| 1994 | 2.60 | 2002 | 2.23 | 2010 | 1.29 |
| 1995 | 2.26 | 2003 | 2.21 | 2011 | 1.17 |
| 1996 | 2.16 | 2004 | 1.90 | 2012 | 1.10 |
| 1997 | 1.90 | 2005 | 2.00 | 2013 | 1.06 |
| 1998 | 2.07 | 2006 | 1.72 | 2014 | 0.91 |
| 1999 | 2.25 | 2007 | 1.55 | 2015 | 0.96 |
| 2000 | 2.35 | 2008 | 1.35 | 2016 | 1.03 |

*Source*: Ministry of Defense of the Czech Republic, 2016b.

By 1998, it was clear that Poland, Hungary, and the Czech Republic would become full NATO partners the next year, which added a new external variable to domestic considerations of what the appropriate defense budget should be. Alliance standards had included a 2% threshold for all members, whether old or new. As a result, the percentage went up to the NATO standard in 1998 and then increased in each of the next two years. With the exception of the 1993 figures, those in 2000 represented the highest percentage in the entire twenty-four-year period. A dip in 2001 was followed by a small increase in 2002, which may reflect a somewhat higher emphasis on defense preparedness after the 9/11 attacks.

However, the entire period from 2003 through 2016 demonstrates a relentless decline in percentages, and the only year in which the Czechs met NATO standards was 2005. By that time, Czech troops were taking part in NATO-led operations in both Kosovo and Afghanistan. They had also participated in the NATO deployment in Bosnia-Herzegovina and continued under the European Union Force (EUFOR) after the NATO hand-over of responsibilities occurred in December 2004. Czech troops were also part of the mission in Iraq: some of those forces were under NATO command, while many were under exclusive leadership of the US. Certainly, the low point in security preparedness from the vantage point of the NATO standard was the most recent 2014–16 period, for the proportion that Czechs devoted to defense was almost exactly one half of what NATO expected.

It is fair to ask why all of these defense figures and trends mattered for a relatively unthreatened small state in the center of Europe. After meeting NATO standards in the years surrounding Czech accession to the alliance, there were many years before and after when it did not seem to matter what the contributions of the Czechs and other new alliance members were. However, American challenges in fighting wars in both Afghanistan and Iraq peaked in the 2007–9 period. Reluctance of the new members to contribute fully in keeping with NATO standards did prompt Secretary of Defense Robert Gates to reprimand them at that time and remind them of the need to increase defense spending. Similarly, during the 2016 American presidential campaign, Republican candidate Donald Trump at times asked why the US should defend, through NATO, countries that were not contributing themselves very much to defense. He did not specifically refer to the 2% alliance benchmark but no doubt sought to convey the impression that some NATO members were not doing enough in light of the strong threat from ISIS and other enemies.

## Size of the military over time

Examination of the data on the size of the Armed Forces reveals that the total personnel employed by the Ministry of Defense in 2015 was less than 50% of what is was in 1992 (Table 4.2). Even more notable is that the proportion of Generals in 2015 was about 40% of what it was in 1992. No doubt, the highest figures in the early 1990s relate to the holdover in military strength from the Cold War. Those higher figures parallel the situation regarding the proportion of GDP devoted to defense spending, for Czechs never approached the higher figures of the 1993–95 period in any later year. It is clear that the Czech leadership expected that the end of the Cold War meant that a lessened priority on defense was a clear policy expectation.

Attention to the 1992–97 data in Table 4.2 reveals interesting patterns.

**Table 4.2** Changes in the composition of the Czech Armed Forces, 1992–2015

| Year | Generals | Career soldiers | Civilian employees | Ministry of Defense total |
| --- | --- | --- | --- | --- |
| 1992 | 49 | 38,049 | 25,286 | 63,335 |
| 1993 | 39 | 33,282 | 23,634 | 56,916 |
| 1994 | 30 | 30,413 | 27,726 | 58,139 |
| 1995 | 25 | 27,654 | 26,456 | 54,110 |
| 1996 | 21 | 26,340 | 27,060 | 53,400 |
| 1997 | 19 | 23,759 | 21,797 | 45,556 |
| 1998 | 23 | 22,966 | 21,481 | 44,447 |
| 1999 | 29 | 23,721 | 21,301 | 45,022 |
| 2000 | 28 | 23,184 | 21,157 | 44,341 |
| 2001 | 29 | 20,627 | 20,888 | 41,515 |
| 2002 | 25 | 21,249 | 22,675 | 43,924 |
| 2003 | 25 | 21,055 | 20,808 | 41,863 |
| 2004 | 32 | 22,145 | 17,288 | 39,433 |
| 2005 | 32 | 23,110 | 14,971 | 38,081 |
| 2006 | 32 | 24,229 | 13,358 | 37,587 |
| 2007 | 26 | 24,334 | 11,946 | 36,280 |
| 2008 | 25 | 24,103 | 10,575 | 34,678 |
| 2009 | 20 | 23,136 | 9,017 | 32,153 |
| 2010 | 22 | 22,261 | 8,303 | 30,564 |
| 2011 | 22 | 21,751 | 8,248 | 29,999 |
| 2012 | 18 | 21,733 | 8,288 | 30,021 |
| 2013 | 20 | 21,011 | 7,530 | 28,541 |
| 2014 | 21 | 20,864 | 7,487 | 28,351 |
| 2015 | 19 | 21,970 | 6,411 | 29,512 |

*Source*: Ministry of Defense of the Czech Republic, 2016b.

The sharp drop in the number of Generals stands out, with a decrease from 49 to 19 soldiers with that rank in just five years. No doubt the highly ranked personnel from the late Cold War years were retiring at a high rate or being dismissed, with no replacements in sight. The drop in the number of personnel overall was also striking but not quite as drastic. The balance between career soldiers and civilian employees is interesting: the data demonstrate that the number of civilian employees was not much lower than the number of career soldiers in 1997, whereas the civilian number had been far lower in relation to military personnel in 1992. In 1997, there was not such a heavy focus on entry as a full member into NATO, and the explosion of terrorist activity was still several years away.

The 1998–2003 period outlined in Table 4.2 also encapsulates in the data the impact of policy priorities and global events on numbers of personnel in the Armed Forces. The overall number of Ministry of Defense employees continued to drop in this period but not as sharply as in the previous five years. The difference between the numbers of career soldiers and civilian employees continued to shrink, with the result that they were nearly the same by 2003. In that way, defense planners could reduce the size of the army but maintain a credible level of defense preparedness. There was a notable increase in the number of Generals in the period, and their high water mark was the year of NATO admission and the two years after that. The 9/11 attack had a marginal impact, as the number of career soldiers as well as civilian employees was higher in 2002 than during the previous year. Events such as admission to full NATO membership and the al Qaeda attacks made a clear difference in the personnel decisions of the Ministry of Defense.

With regard to the 2004–9 period, as revealed in Table 4.2, the most striking change is the balance between the number of military and civilian employees. There were modest increases in the number of career soldiers but a sharp drop in the number of civilians, and that was quite a contrast to the previous period. Perhaps the changed international environment with increased threat perceptions led to a heavier reliance on career soldiers who would be serving or who may have served in theaters of combat such as Afghanistan or Iraq. Numbers of Generals remained constant in 2004–6 but dropped sharply after that, and the same was true at a slower rate for the total personnel numbers. It may be that it was vital to keep the same military personnel levels in the 2001–06 period, for it was the one in which pressures on the Czech Armed Services were greatest. They contributed entire units to Bosnia, Kosovo, Afghanistan, and Iraq. For many NATO members, the period from 2007 on was a time of rethinking priorities, after such a commitment to American-led operations.

There is a constant theme in the personnel patterns revealed in Table 4.2 for the 2010–15 period. For Ministry of Defense personnel and for the category of Generals, strength levels remained about the same during the five-year period. Minor dips in the number of Generals and total Ministry of Defense personnel were signs of stability in this period. There were sharply lowered expectations for Czech participation in the foreign operations of NATO and the EU, and yet defense preparedness for future challenges was still a priority. The imbalance between the number of career soldiers and number of civilian employees continued to increase, and this could have been a symbol of and increased priority on professionalization within the military. There would be normal participation in NATO operations but at a reduced rate due to the lessened global threat that pulled in alliance military units.

In general, it is clear that the data on composition of the Czech Armed Forces are revealing in terms of the impact of outside events that accompanied the advent to full alliance membership in 1999. Czech planners were surprised that alliance expectations for their assistance in Kosovo accelerated sharply, for the NATO operation in that region of Serbia occurred just after the Czechs joined the alliance in the spring. Further, the 9/11 attacks put pressure on the Czech military to take part in related missions, and they did so with conviction. Continued professionalization of the military continued apace, as the balance of career soldiers to civilian employees increased at a steady rate. By the end of the period under review, the Czech military had emerged from the shadow of the Cold War into the status of a reliable NATO ally with a military that was prepared for self-defense and also contributions to regional missions that Western alliance partners had designed.

## Deployments outside the Czech Republic

The Czech Ministry of Defense was very active in and committed to the responsibility of dispatching important military units in deployments to crisis centers in the region and beyond. After the break-up of Yugoslavia, there were major civil wars in both Croatia and Bosnia-Herzegovina, and Czechs contributed to missions in both countries. Further, there was a concern that Macedonia would succumb to a similar internal conflict, and the Czechs made a contribution there as well. After the 1995 Dayton Accord that resolved the Bosnian Civil War, a NATO peacekeeping force that later became the responsibility of the EU moved in with Czech participation. Following the NATO bombing campaign in Kosovo in 1999, Czechs were also involved in the military force that took part in local rebuilding efforts as well as protection of citizens. The

War in Afghanistan required the efforts of many military forces from Europe, and Czech units participated fully in the US and NATO-led operations from the beginning in 2001 until the end in 2014. In spite of the controversy surrounding the origins of the Iraq War in 2003, Czech units were quite active there as well. Despite the concerns of Czech citizens about costs and potential casualties in these operations, defense planners had no hesitation in committing forces into nations on the southeastern edge of Europe as well into southwest Asia and the Middle East.

### Former Yugoslavia

During the Balkan Civil Wars of the 1992–95 period, Czechs played a full part in the peacekeeping mission called the United Nations Protection Force through provision of 2,250 troops. Interestingly, the units were part of the Czechoslovak Army until the rupture into two states, at which time they represented the Army of the Czech Republic. Serbian incursions into Croatia were not as engulfing as their moves into Bosnia, but the battles raged in both geographic arms of Croatia. After the end of the fighting, the UN set up its UN Confidence Restoration Operation, and Czechs sent 874 military personnel to help restore stability to Croatia (Simon 2004, 41–2). Their location was Krajina, the southern arm of the country that was largely Serb in ethnicity. From January 1996 until January 1998, they provided a field hospital of 100 troops to take part in UN Transitional Administration for Eastern Slavonia, Baranja, and Western Sirmium. This unit was an early reminder that Czechs could provide niche units that had specialties of benefit to the allies, and the pattern would be repeated (Ministry of Defense of the Czech Republic 2016a).

### Macedonia

After the Balkan conflicts in Croatia, Bosnia, and Kosovo; there was considerable concern about unrest in Macedonia, with its sizeable 40% Muslim minority. The concerns prompted a UN peacekeeping operation entitled Essential Harvest. In keeping with their growing reputation as a country with an ability to contribute specialized forces in a niche capacity, the Czechs contributed 120 parachutists, whose job was to collect weapons from Albanian rebels (Simon 2004, 109). They remained for two months near the end of 2001, a time that overlapped with the 9/11 attacks on the US. During 2003, two Czech soldiers took part for eight months in an EU operation known as Concordia: this was important, for the crisis had died down, but observers worried about another outbreak of tension (Ministry of Defense of the Czech Republic 2016a).

*Bosnia-Herzegovina*
After the signing of the Dayton Accord in 1995, the presence of Czech troops in Bosnia was a substantial one. Overall, 6,300 Czech personnel took part in the peacekeeping operation there, and this accorded with the NATO expectation that its PfP members most likely to join in the near future would provide considerable assistance in this region that was in their neighborhood. One example of their involvement was the dispatch of a Czech Stabilization Force (SFOR) unit that constituted a 650-man battalion. However, this large presence by the Czechs in SFOR ended in December 2001 (Simon 2004, 58, 108). In spite of that, the 9/11 attacks a few months earlier led Prime Minister Zeman to provide one TU-154 with 15 crew members to the efforts in Bosnia (Simon 2004, 114).

Between 2002 and the end of 2004, there were continued connections with SFOR through provision of 42 soldiers who provided assistance to projects connected with civilians as well as service at command posts. After December 2, 2004, the EU had responsibility for these forces in their EUFOR mission called ALTHEA, for NATO had turned peacekeeping over to them. Therefore, Czechs sent 421 soldiers back under that mission between December 2004 and June 2008 (Ministry of Defense of the Czech Republic 2016a). Protection of base security was a high priority for these military personnel. For example, in 2005, Czechs took over security responsibilities from the Austrians at Eagle Base, the EU headquarters. Another 80 soldiers worked with the Austrians to protect Tuzla Base. Further, airmen from the Czech base at Přerov flew helicopters that both took part in investigative flights over Bosnia and transported military material (Peterson 2011, 66).

Even after 2008, the Czech military sent specialized soldiers to carry out missions of importance. For example, In June 2010, two Czech officers became members of the EUFOR headquarters in Sarajevo. As late as 2016, the two Czech officers worked on training and development of the Bosnian Armed Forces. One of the Czechs was Chief of the Management Storage Group, while the other possessed a specialty in weapons of mass destruction (Ministry of Defense of the Czech Republic 2016a). Importantly, there had been a Czech presence in Bosnia for over two decades and this ongoing commitment reflected a continuing effort to help build stability in a nation that war had nearly devoured.

*Kosovo*
As early as 1998, there was considerable Western concern about the prospects for a repeat of the Croatian and Bosnian tragedies in the Yugoslav Republic of Kosovo. Within the state, Kosovo was unique

with its overwhelmingly Muslim population. Czechs announce their willingness to send a military field hospital of 84 troops if violence broke out and an allied intervention took place. In the case of a NATO bombing intervention, Czechs granted the alliance over flight rights. In addition, the Czech Republic promised to contribute 20–30 observers to be part of the OSCE verification operation in the afflicted Yugoslav Republic (Simon 2004, 80).

Czech troops played a continuing role right after the 1999 NATO bombing campaign that pushed Serbian forces back out of the Muslim inhabited areas. Czech troops were still there as part of this NATO mission after Kosovo declared its independence as a nation in 2008. In sum, the Kosovo Force (KFOR)'s peacekeeping force included 980 Czechs between 1999 and February 2002 (Ministry of Defense of the Czech Republic 2016a).

However, their role increased in the next three years, as a full 2,400 were in Kosovo at one time or another as part of a joint Czech-Slovak battalion (Ministry of Defense of the Czech Republic 2016a). That battalion took up its positions in March 2002, and consisted of 400 Czechs and 100 Slovaks (Simon 2004, 109). The group worked under a unit that troops from the UK headed and was based in the Kosovo capital of Priština. Czechs renewed their commitment for a number of years after 2005 (Peterson 2011, 72).

After 2005, more than 8,000 Czech troops made contributions during the ensuing six years (Ministry of Defense of the Czech Republic 2016a). Many of those activities centered on the Multinational Brigade (C) in Priština, as the Czechs headed that unit in 2005–6. There were 500 Czech troops in charge of a unit of 1,600. NATO had actually divided up Kosovo into a number of similar regional units, and each one had a mission that related to key problems in the area. Czechs worked to deactivate land mines, to stop illegal cutting in forests, and to halt drug trafficking. By mid-2009, there were 550 Czech soldiers who took part in Mission Pardubice, including the 131st Combined Artillery Battalion as well as the 14th Logistical Support Brigade. Furthermore, there were 60 Czech troops in mid-2008 who were based at Šajkovac and whose mission included restoration of energy sources and drinkable water (Peterson 2011, 72–3). Such work had a positive impact on many citizens of Kosovo and contributed to restoring the province to normal life. In 2010, the Czechs assumed command of Šajkovac with 422 soldiers from the 31st Chemical, Biological Radiological, and Nuclear (Weapons) Brigade, the 152nd Engineering Battalion Rakovník, and the 153rd Engineering Command Olomouc. The last unit stayed back in readiness in the Czech Republic (Peterson, forthcoming).

In sum, the Czechs took part in KFOR operations from 1999 through 2016. In 2016, there were still 13 Czechs located at Priština as part of the 11th Army of the Czech Republic KFOR Task Force. Three of them were specialists from the Deployable Communications Module from Lipik nad Barvou in the Czech Republic. Their Task Force Commander was Kamil Chadim, and the deployment dates of the unit were from August 2016 until February 2017 (Ministry of Defense of the Czech Republic 2016a). Clearly, the Czech commitment to KFOR was a deep and continuing one.

### Afghanistan

Service in Afghanistan by Czech soldiers was extensive and relatively diversified. Units included field hospitals, helicopter units, Special Forces, training personnel, airport protection, and assistance with Provincial Reconstruction Teams (PRTs). Czech military involvement began a little more than six months after the 9/11 attacks and continued at least through 2017. In 2014, five Czechs were killed in a "green on blue" shooting; one had earlier died in a landslide. Such sacrifices were emblematic of the reliability of the nation as a Western ally in the most difficult of conditions.

Initial support by Czechs came in the provision of medical assistance on the battlefield and in dangerous areas. The first Czech operation included dispatch of 269 military personnel who were part of the 6th and 11th field hospitals. Their stay lasted from 2002 to 2003; an 11-person field surgical team replaced them in the first part of 2003.

From 2004–7 the Czech involvement took several different directions. In that three-year period, there were 350 Czech soldiers stationed at Kabul Airport with responsibility for ordnance disposal and meteorological work (Ministry of Defense of the Czech Republic 2016a). A field hospital unit at the airport helped to transport those who had been injured in combat. In addition, their 5th contingent helped to inoculate Afghan children against a variety of diseases. At Pardubice in the Czech Republic, the 601st Special Forces Group was located, consisting of 120 persons; in the middle of 2004, they spent several months on patrol in the mountains of Fajzabad (Peterson 2011, 92–4). From early 2005 until the end of 2007, 600 Czech troops contributed to the German PRT in Fayzabad (Ministry of Defense of the Czech Republic 2016a), and also worked with Danes to protect the base and its transport vehicles. Another group of 35 served in Helmand Province in 2007, joining a British group that had responsibility for equipment (Peterson 2011, 90). Finally, after March 2004, there was a group of 200 Czech soldiers who worked to rebuild the Logar PRT (Peterson 2011, 94).

After 2007, the Czechs continued to provide valuable military resources that were usually of a specialized nature. In 2007–8, they provided 658 soldiers as part of a field hospital as well as a chemical detachment at the Kabul International airport. From 2008–9, Czech protection contingents consisted of two rotations of 63 soldiers each in Uruzgan. From 2009–11, their helicopter units were quite active with 700 personnel involved overall. Their Special Forces returned to Afghanistan with two rotations of 100 each from mid-2011 to mid-2012. Moderately sized contingents then worked in Wardak Province in the 2012–13 period with the goal of training and mentoring the Afghan military police and other forces. A Military Advisory Team of 59 soldiers was active at the same time in Wardak, while another of 64 was active then in Logar Province. In sum, Czech contributions in Logar over the 2008–13 period were quite impressive, with more than 2,500 serving there. A number of the soldiers had performed several tours of duty as part of that group (Ministry of Defense of the Czech Republic 2016a).

During the transitional time after January 1, 2015, Czechs continued to take part in the NATO renamed operation Resolute Support Mission. Their 14th Task Force came in with 264 personnel at the very end of 2016, and their mission centered on protection of Hamid Karzai International Airport. A variety of units played a role in that operation, including a Military Police Protection Unit, the twentieth Air Advisory Team, the 18th Field Surgical Team, and a Deployable Communications Module. There were also Czechs stationed at the Headquarters in Kabul and Bagram (Ministry of Defense of the Czech Republic 2016a). Given that the post-2014 NATO mission in Afghanistan was overwhelmingly American in composition, the Czech roles were striking.

*Iraq*

Preoccupation of the West with Iraq clearly preceded the invasion of March 2003, and Czech involvement in the United Nations Guards Contingent in Iraq was a continuing project from the end of the Persian Gulf War in 1991 to the American-led invasion in 2003. The numbers of Czechs involved was 320: it was the Czechoslovak Army that dispatched them in 1991, and the Army of the Czech Republic that took over the responsibility in 1993. Involvement after the beginning of the second Iraq War in 2003 centered again on their niche capability of a field hospital. From the beginning of the war until the end of 2003, 526 soldiers from the 7th Field Hospital were available to offer medical assistance in Basra to those who were wounded. From December 2003 until the end of 2006, a large number of Czech Military Police took part in six rotations in the area of Shaibah. In the 2003–8 period, there were

423 Czech soldiers who took part in the National Training Mission in Baghdad (Ministry of Defense of the Czech Republic 2016a).

The results of this involvement were impressive, for their units assisted in the training of 12,000 Iraqi police officers in 2003–6. They provided much needed skills on the critical issues for Iraq of self-defense and border patrol. On this project nearly 100 Czech soldiers worked at Al Shaiba base near Basra with British and Danish military units (Peterson 2011, 117). Czechs also worked with the Iraqi National Army and National Police at Basra Airport. They built a new military academy in Baghdad, and sold Czech airplanes to the Iraqis. In addition, they assisted with T-72 tanks and the NP-1 Aircraft.

After the withdrawal of forces in 2011, there was limited outside involvement in Iraq until the rise of the ISIS threat in 2014. After that, specialized assistance by outside powers took place. They promised the provision of 35 Czech airmen from the end of 2016 until late December 2018. The group would include pilots, ground technicians, and instructors, and would train Iraqis on the L-159ALCA aircraft that the Czechs had supplied to Iraq. A Field Surgical Team also went to Iraq, which included surgeons, anesthetists, middle-level medical personnel, and other specialists. This group would work with an American field hospital of ROLE 2 level (Ministry of Defense of the Czech Republic 2016a).

## Concluding matters of concern

In terms of the themes of convergence and divergence, the former were more powerful in the post-communist period than the latter. Pressures to participate in NATO operations emerged right away in the 1990s and culminated in formal membership in 1999. Heavy involvement by Czech forces was characteristic of their participation in KFOR in Kosovo as well as in Operation Enduring Freedom in Afghanistan. At the same time, EU membership became a reality in 2004, and increasingly there were foreign policy pressures from them as well. The Czech role in Bosnia after December 2004 was exclusively in the management hands of the EU. However, there was also a contrasting pressure from the Visegrád Group that came into being in 1991, although its historical roots penetrated more deeply into the past. In 2016, that organization became a fulcrum of opposition to the EU quotas for distribution and re-location of refuges from Syria, Iraq, and Afghanistan (Interview with Michael Žantovský, August 4, 2016). In a sense, convergence tugs emanated from several directions at once and at times were in conflict with one another.

A certain divergence theme thus became apparent in those situations of conflict. For example, Czech leaders were reluctant to go along with the full Western sanctions on Russia after their take-over of Crimea in spring 2014. Czech President Miloš Zeman was one of the few European leaders to attend the end of the Scond World War celebration events in Moscow in 2015. At the same time, Czechs were wary of Russian intentions toward Central Europe after the Crimean take-over, and the population may have been more worried than the leaders seemed to be (Interview with Michael Žantovský, August 4, 2016). Some of this concern about Russia had appeared at the time of discussion of the Missile Shield Proposal in 2008 and 2009. At that time, Czechs were anxious not to alienate Russia by locating the radar system of the Missile Shield Proposal on their own territory.

It is fair to ask how much Czech concern existed about the fact that they lived in "the shadow of the bear." That shadow was quite visible during the afore-mentioned Ukrainian and Missile Shield events, and Czechs did what they could to stay on the sidelines of the shadow. Perhaps their long-standing connections with the Soviet Union and its successor state in the previous century prepared them to live in the shadow without concluding that the consequences of it were too ominous. Czech leaders and populations worried less than did Poland and the Baltic states about the bear becoming aggressive and actually using its sharp claws against them.

# 5

## Hungary: imperial legacies and post-imperial realities[1]

The Hungarian case confronts us with multiple paradoxes. Like Poland, and unlike the Czech Republic and Slovakia, Hungary is a carrier of distinctly imperial and post-imperial legacies (described in chapter 2). Indeed, the essential similarity between Polish and Hungarian political history and culture is a well-known fact in the region, creating a sense of affinity between the two nations. However, unlike Poland, post-communist Hungary emerged with a material reminder of its imperial/pre-Trianon boundaries: some 2.3 million Hungarians living in neighboring countries, specifically Romania (Transylvania 1.3 million), Slovakia (0.5 million), Serbia-Yugoslavia (0.25 million in Vojvodina), and Ukraine (in Transcarpathia 0.156 million). Given these legacies, and Hungary's dangerous proximity to the Western Balkans/former Yugoslavia, one would expect the country, regardless of its small size, to pursue a uniquely vigorous and well-funded defense policy. After all, a small size did not prevent Hungary from pursuing a policy of aggressive revisionism during the interwar period.

The reality is in fact contrary to the above presumption – post-communist Hungary has emerged in many ways the precise opposite of Poland, which, as we will shortly learn, is an outlier among the Visegrád Four in terms of robust defense policies and anti-Russian character. Hungary, on the other hand, is an outlier in the other direction, a "chronic under-spender" (Kufčak 2014), the country with perhaps the most neglected defense policies and a marginalized military establishment. Indeed, when referring to the post-communist Hungarian military, Lt. Gen. Ferenc Végh (Chief of General Staff, 1996–99) and Minister of Defense Ferenc Juhász (2002–6) used terms like "operetta military" and "army of a banana republic" (Simon 2002, 38, 92; Kufčak 2014).[2] Only recently has the inadequacy of Hungarian military spending been acknowledged by Minister of Defense Csaba Hende. In 2012, both he and his successor István Simicskó promised to increase military spending, and some modest increases have indeed occurred since 2015

(Hungarian Republic Ministry of Defense 2012; MTI 2014; Than and Szakacs 2017).

Hungary's outlier status and what it means in practice for its post-communist defense policies will be analyzed below. A historical-cultural explanation of the phenomenon is partially given in chapter 2. Defeat in the Second World War, the paroxysm of Stalinist militarization, the revolution of 1956, and the subsequent destruction and demoralization of the Hungarian military all contributed to a Hungarian state and public opinion that are uniquely de-militarized. Indeed, the country had already become a "chronic underspender" under the Warsaw Pact. Hungarian society and polity transitioned into post-communist reality with these already profoundly anti-military values and priorities, which actually caused Hungarians to be all the more ready to embrace Western liberalism precisely because of its anti-militarism. However, with admission to NATO, Hungary bumped into the paradox of the same West requiring a new form of limited militarization, which Hungarian public and politicians have largely embraced in rhetoric and sabotaged in practice.

The paradox of Western liberalism being a mix of anti- and pro-military values explains the paradox of Hungary's success in being admitted to NATO in the first tranche of countries in 1999. Inasmuch as liberalism meant the rejection of both communist and nationalist militarism, Hungary's public and elite found no problem adjusting to liberal institutional and policy requirements such as subordination of the military to civilian leadership and demilitarization. Indeed, Hungary's political and institutional success in adjusting itself to Western democratic liberalism was so conspicuous that the country appeared as a leader in terms of post-communist transformation. The country's admission into NATO (1999) and EU (2004), coupled to a general transformation of Hungary's neighborhood into a zone of liberal peace and stability solved the country's strategic dilemmas and allowed it to focus on internal economic development. One way to conceptualize the absence of Hungary's robust defense policies is to understand its security policy as a victim of its own success.

Liberal internationalism, indeed, promised a way to solve the challenging strategic predicament of displaced Hungarian minorities in neighboring countries. This security dilemma, coupled with neighboring countries' fear that Hungary would seek to revise their borders, or otherwise undermine the countries from within, had the potential to generate a mutual cycle of national oppression and state-to-state hostilities insolvable in a realist-nationalist world. In a liberal internationalist world, though, Hungarian minorities could enjoy the constitutional rights and autonomy guaranteed to all citizens because integration into a Western security (NATO) and socio-economic (EU) community meant a diminishing importance of national borders and accompanying security dilemmas on all sides. Post-communist Hungary, indeed, rejected militaristic realism and nationalism,[3] and explicitly chose liberal internationalism as a logical way to solve its strategic dilemmas. This strategy, from a 2017 vantage point, has succeeded wildly, with five out of seven of Hungary's neighbors also becoming members of either NATO or the EU. Only Ukraine and Serbia have formally remained on the outside of Western institutionalized national communities, though both have embraced liberalism and have been seeking membership in NATO (Ukraine) and the EU (Ukraine and Serbia). Peace has been achieved – regardless of the persistence of tensions with Romania and Slovakia – in bilateral relationships between Hungary and all its neighbors, highlighted by friendly treaties with Ukraine (1991), Slovakia (1995),[4] and Romania (1996) (Nagy 1997). Indeed, liberal internationalism has remained the doctrinal basis of Hungarian foreign, security, and defense policies throughout the post-communist period, and was forcefully reasserted in the country's 2012 National Security Strategy and 2012 National Military Strategy, regardless of the nationalist populist turn the country took during the 2010 elections (Republic of Hungary 2012, 20; Hungarian Republic Ministry of Defense 2012, 1–2). A logical question to be asked in this context is: Why should Hungary need to implement defense policies that go beyond token spending and loyal engagement with NATO, if the liberal anti-militaristic policies pursued so far have succeeded so much in terms of satisfying the country's security needs?

## Formation of a new strategic culture

Initially, the continuous presence of Soviet troops, who did not leave until June 1991, made for fairly cautious rhetoric concerning Hungarian defense policies. While the country achieved a democratic breakthrough during its May 1990 elections, ushering in a non-communist parliamentary majority, Hungary's new leaders, minding the lessons of 1956, asserted their military sovereignty with caution, leaving the Warsaw Pact only with its multilateral dissolution in Budapest on February 25, 1991. The wars of Yugoslavian succession, which raged between 1991 and 2001 on Hungary's southwestern border, validated the country's discretionary stance on defense, vividly displaying the tragedy and insecurity that could result from renewed realist, nationalist, and ethnic irredentist sentiment. When UN-, OSCE- and European-initiated solutions to the Yugoslavian crises failed to stop the misery, and only

NATO- and US-backed solutions provided (semi-)lasting solutions, the lesson to all European and Visegrád countries, but especially to Hungary, was that NATO and Atlanticism represented reliable national security.

In spring of 1993, Hungary passed two parliamentary resolutions to embody its commitment to Euro-Atlantic security integration "Basic Principles of Security Policy of the Republic Hungary" and "Principles of National Defense of the Republic of Hungary," which stated: "The acquisition of full-fledged membership in the European Communities will provide a fundamental guarantee of the security of the Republic of Hungary (paragraph 4 of the 'Basic Principles of Security Policy')." Achieving membership in NATO was a goal embraced by all six of Hungary's otherwise bitterly competitive political parties (paragraph 16 of "Principles of National Defense") (see table 5.5) (Gazdag 1994; Calopareanu 2011). Their unwavering commitment was met with success (Törö 2001). Hungary was officially invited to the NATO Summit of July 8, 1997, and, in 1998, passed "Resolution on Basic Principles of Hungary's Security and Defense Policy," which reasserted Hungary's commitment to multilateral Euro-Atlantic defense principles .

Hungary's journey to Euro-Atlantic integration required dismantling the second-rate conscript-based Cold War military it inherited in 1989 and replacing it with NATO-compatible forces. It also necessitated an institutionalization of liberal norms through military subordination to civilian leadership. Though the country's leadership unanimously embraced both tasks, they were accomplished only after a messy and drawn-out process, which began in 1990 and was not completely resolved until 2007. Between 1990 and 1993 a series of political battles began when the Hungarian Supreme Court upheld a new (1993) Defense Law decisively asserting the supremacy of the civilian Prime Minister and Ministry of Defense over the military. However, the military insisted on its independence by exploiting the division of power ambiguities between Presidential (formally, the Commander-in-Chief) and Prime Ministerial powers in the Hungarian semi-presidential constitutional system (Simon 2002 13–22).[5] Due to the intensely competitive[6] nature of Hungarian political life, which made institutional reforms difficult, as well as a lack of military expertise among civilian leadership, it wasn't until 2007 that the Hungarian General Staff was firmly integrated into the Ministry of Defense and made fully subordinate to civilian leadership.[7]

The dismantling of Hungary's late communist military and abolition of conscription, likewise, wasn't accomplished until 2004 through a continuous decline in personnel. Hungarian military forces shrank by close to three quarters by 2002 (from 122,400 to 36,170 soldiers) and

**Table 5.1** Hungarian military and defense personnel, 1989–2002

| Year | Total personnel | Conscripts | Career soldiers | Contract soldiers | Total military | Civilians | % change in total personnel from year to year |
|------|-----------------|------------|-----------------|-------------------|----------------|-----------|-----------------------------------------------|
| 1989 | 155,700 | 91,900 | 30,500 |  | 122,400 | 33,300 |  |
| 1990 | 143,200 | 81,000 | 29,700 |  | 110,700 | 32,500 | -8 |
| 1991 | 121,500 | 65,300 | 28,700 |  | 94,000 | 27,500 | -15 |
| 1992 | 100,000 | 51,100 | 22,900 |  | 74,000 | 26,000 | -18 |
| 1993 | 100,000 | 52,340 | 22,000 |  | 74,340 | 25,660 | 0 |
| 1994 | 97,720 | 51,560 | 22,100 |  | 73,660 | 24,060 | -2 |
| 1995 | 92,321 | 46,350 | 21,911 |  | 68,261 | 24,060 | -6 |
| 1996 | 80,902 | 37,595 | 24,099 |  | 61,694 | 19,208 | -12 |
| 1997 | 72,012 | 34,385 | 21,346 | 2,200 | 57,931 | 14,081 | -11 |
| 1998 | 68,800 | 33,000 | 20,700 | 4,000 | 57,700 | 11,100 | -4 |
| 1999 | 64,300 | 32,400 | 19,800 | 4,300 | 56,500 | 7,800 | -7 |
| 2000 | 45,500 | 13,000 | 19,900 | 5,100 | 38,000 | 7,500 | -29 |
| 2001 | 43,900 | 13,000 | 19,900 | 3,500 | 36,400 | 7,500 | -4 |
| 2002 | 42,270 | 13,260 | 18,910 | 4,000 | 36,170 | 6,100 | -4 |

*Source:* Simon 2002, 33.

total Ministry of Defense personnel diminished by a factor of 3.5 (from 155,700 to 42,700) over the same period. Real and relative budget cuts coincided. In 2016, as a percentage of GDP, defense spending was about a third of what it was in 1989 and half of what it was in real terms.

A deeper analysis of Hungarian defense personnel, spending, and policies in the pre-NATO and post-NATO accession period shows a pattern of almost constantly shrinking defense budgets, which defeated most efforts at a meaningful military modernization beyond simply dismantling the communist-era military. Despite a slight increase in spending during the years immediately following NATO induction. Hungary's simultaneous cuts in personnel and in real spending meant that no viable budget for military modernization could be created. The personnel cuts themselves were costly, as pensions for retired soldiers took an increasing share of the budget. Still, current operations and personnel costs (see table 5.4) took the lion's share, leaving only token amounts for procurement of new equipment. By 1995, the Magyar Honvédség/ Hungarian Defense Forces (MH/HDF) had exhausted their material reserves, finding themselves in crisis, with conscripts and career soldiers untrained due to lack of funds. With exercises, equipment and physical infrastructure deteriorating, the increasingly demoralized forces were hemorrhaging career soldiers (Simon 2002, 30–3).

The only deviation from this pattern of dissolving resources and reserves in the 1990s occurred under Minister of Defense György Keleti (1994–98), who represented the ("successor") Hungarian Socialist Party. He took advantage of an in-kind settlement of Russia's debt to Hungary to acquire a huge fleet of 450 BTR-80 APCs. He also bought 100 T-72 tanks at bargain prices from Belarus and acquired (as a gift) 20 ex-DDR Mi-24 helicopters from Germany. These, added to 28 Mig-29s acquired from Russia in 1993, also as a part of debt settlement, were the last major equipment acquisition programs in post-communist Hungary. The sole exception was the 2001–17 lease of 14 Saab Gripen fighter-bombers, rammed through by Prime Minister Orbán in a controversial 2001 decision (Simon 2002, 80–4; Kufĉak 2014).[8] Despite the commitment of this handful of Hungarian politicians, these equipment acquisitions hardly served to viably modernize or mobilize the Hungarian military; Most of the acquired equipment, except for the Gripens and the BTR-80s, are today retired or obsolete (Csiki 2015).[9]

Hungary's declining defense infrastructure was public knowledge, and country politicians and public figures, especially Chief of General Staff Lt. Gen. Ferenc Vegh (in his position between 1996–99), openly criticized the catastrophic underfunding of the country's military. According to Lt. Gen. Vegh, the HDF operated on half of the necessary

**Table 5.2** Hungarian military spending, 1989–2016

| Year | Real spending in constant in US 2015 $m | % change from year to year | Forints (bn) (current, non-adjusted) | % of GDP |
|---|---|---|---|---|
| 1989 | 2,648 | | 45.5 | 2.8 |
| 1990 | 2,291 | –13 | 52.9 | 2.5 |
| 1991 | 1,721 | –25 | 55.4 | 2.4 |
| 1992 | 1,662 | –3 | 61.7 | 2.2 |
| 1993 | 1,432 | –14 | 64 | 1.9 |
| 1994 | 1,418 | –1 | 66.5 | 1.7 |
| 1995 | 1,068 | –25 | 77 | 1.48 |
| 1996 | 1,004 | –6 | 87 | 1.32 |
| 1997 | 1,235 | 23 | 96.8 | 1.4 |
| 1998 | 1,104 | –11 | 122 | 1.5 |
| 1999 | 1,261 | 14 | 164.5 | 1.6 |
| 2000 | 1,392 | 10 | 192.3 | 1.51 |
| 2001 | 1,528 | 10 | 223.6 | 1.6 |
| 2002 | 1,669 | 9 | 261.4 | 1.6 |
| 2003 | 1,801 | 8 | 302.2 | 1.7 |
| 2004 | 1,668 | –7 | 346.9 | 1.5 |
| 2005 | 1,651 | –1 | 288.1 | 1.4 |
| 2006 | 1,480 | –10 | 283.1 | 1.3 |
| 2007 | 1,508 | 2 | 278.2 | 1.3 |
| 2008 | 1,401 | –7 | 319.7 | 1.2 |
| 2009 | 1,249 | –11 | 298.6 | 1.14 |
| 2010 | 1,120 | –10 | 280.9 | 1.04 |
| 2011 | 1,135 | 1 | 296 | 1.05 |
| 2012 | 1,080 | –5 | 297.5 | 1.00 |
| 2013 | 1,021 | –5 | 286.3 | 0.95 |
| 2014 | 1,006 | –1 | 281.4 | 0.87 |
| 2015 | 1,131 | 12 | 315.9 | 0.94 |
| 2016 | 1,254 | 11 | 353.1 | 1.01 |

Sources: Simon 2002; SIPRI https://www.sipri.org/sites/default/files/Milex-constant-2015-USD.pdf. Accessed July 5, 2017.

budget, which, in the long term could only sustain an "operetta army" (Simon 2002, 38). Despite this, Hungary sailed to NATO membership in 1999 rather smoothly because of its ability to present itself as thoroughly reformed in terms of its institutions and values through smart applications of limited resources during missions that showcased its utility to NATO and the US aided by Hungary's strategic geographic position.

## Hungary in NATO: the alliance game

The Yugoslavian Crisis presented both a risk and a strategic opportunity for Hungary. The risk of military spill-over into Hungary was real, and, if the government acted too brashly in an effort to protect its borders, ethnic Hungarians living in Serbia faced insecurity. In this respect, it helped that, in the early 1990s, Hungary still possessed substantial conventional military assets, which were strengthened by Keleti's acquisition programs. Hungary's proximity to the conflict, more importantly, provided the country with an opportunity to demonstrate its utility as a new liberal internationalist democracy. Hungary became a staging area for NATO military operations, deployed peacekeeping troops to former Yugosolavia without costly overseas logistics, and firmly upheld sanctions and embargoes in the region

Hungary utilized the mix of danger and opportunity resulting from conflict in the Balkans masterfully to gain NATO recognition and membership (Szenesz 2007). Indeed, the very fact that Hungary faced real dangers when cooperating with NATO, both in Bosnia and, later, in Kosovo, evidenced not simply its usefulness but, more importantly, its loyalty (Hendrickson 2000; Simon 2002). With the waning of the Balkan conflict, in turn, engagement in multilateral deployments became Hungary's solution for national security in the face of its rapidly disintegrating military infrastructure.

The consequence of Hungary's shrinking defense budget was a loss of territorial defense capabilities. NATO, along with the promise of continued liberalization in the region, offered a solution through investment in multilateral deployments for peacekeeping and peace-enforcement. These missions required less costly capacities, such as light-infantry and Special Forces trained in civilian affairs and logistical/civil reconstruction. The practical ways Hungary contributed to NATO and EU alliance missions, and to the US-led "war on terror," offered the country a role in an international network of "niche capabilities." As a result, under-spending on indigenous self-defense became much less relevant to national security.

After Hungary was admitted to NATO in March 1999, the country's new defense policies were formally enumerated in key documents. A new National Security Strategy was issued in 2002 and again in 2004 (see table 5.5). These developments culminated in the 2009 National Military Strategy of the Republic of Hungary (Republic of Hungary 2002, 2004; Hungarian Republic Ministry of Defense 2009). The doctrinal thrust of these documents was the assumption that Hungary, as a result of membership in NATO and the peaceful liberalization of

**Table 5.3** Hungarian participation in key multilateral missions

| Name of mission | Place | Organization | Duration | Hungarian units | Maximum troops |
|---|---|---|---|---|---|
| UNFICYP | Cyprus | UN | 1993–2017 | A company | 155 |
| MFO | Sinai | UN | 1995–2015 | An observer unit | 55 |
| IFOR | Bosnia | UN | 1995–96 | An engineering unit | 300 |
| SFOR | Bosnia | NATO | 1996–2004 | A company | 200 |
| EUROFOR-Althea | Bosnia | EU | 2004–17 | A company | 100 |
| KFOR | Kosovo | NATO | 1999–2017 | A company | 223 |
| Multinational division Iraq | Iraq | US-allied | 2003–4 | An engineering company | 300 |
| ISAF | Afghanistan | NATO | 2003–14 | Multiple units, including special forces | 540 |
| Resolute Support | Afghanistan | NATO | 2014–17 | A training unit | 100 |
| Inherent Resolve | Iraq | US-allied | 2015–17 | A company | 125 |

*Source*: Simon 2002, Szenesz 2007. Last updated September 2015, www.providingforpeacekeeping.org/2015/09/11/peacekeeping-contributor-profile-hungary/. Accessed July 17, 2017.

Hungary's neighbors, was free from conventional military threats. The HDF was urged to adjust to a new era of utility through the establishment of quick reaction forces, easily mobilized for the type of missions Hungary executed in Yugoslavia, Iraq, and Afganistan. In the words of the 2004 National Security Strategy:

> The Hungarian Defense Forces need to possess rapidly deployable and sustainable forces suited for flexible use and available also for expeditionary operations that are able to cooperate with allied forces and can be used in crisis spots without any geographical limitations. The necessary capabilities need to be developed in a way coordinated with NATO, coordinating force contributions committed in the NATO and EU framework and by making use of the opportunities lying in bi- and multilateral international cooperation and development programs. The goal is to develop an armed force that is new in the sense of operational philosophy, able to fulfill the commitments made to NATO, that is financially affordable, capability-based and specialized in the framework of the North Atlantic Treaty Organization, that constitutes an integral part of the society and enjoys the latter's support, that is placed under democratic and civilian control, and that is composed of members committed to their countries and profession, properly trained and motivated, commanding the respect of the society. Respective goals and tasks need to be set down in the National Military Strategy." (Republic of Hungary 2004, 22–3)

These transformative defense policies culminated in Hungary's first National Military Strategy in 2009 (Hungarian Republic Ministry of Defense 2009). This were accompanied by HDF structural reform throughout the 2000s. After an extensive Defense Review process conducted between 2001 and 2002, conscription was suspended in 2004 and an all-volunteer force created by 2006, which stabilized at around 20,000 troops and 10,000 civilian employees by 2009. The troops centered initially around three, and then two, infantry brigades (comprised, altogether, of seven battalions), one intended mostly for collective defenses and one for international deployments, plus an Air Wing and support services for specialized tasks. Command structures were unified, comprising of a General Staff and a Joint Forces Command integrated in the Ministry of Defense.

Modernization and capacity-building influence during the first decade of Hungarian membership in NATO is undeniable, albeit narrowly focused on "niche capabilities" (Biró 2005; Pecsvarady 2010; Racz 2012; Racz and Erzsebet 2012; Magyarics 2013; Matei 2013; Kufčak 2014; Wagner and Marton 2014; Csiki 2015). Capacities such as Special Forces[10] and strategic lift capabilities were acquired, mostly in the course of multilateral or bilateral cooperation. Cooperation with the US on issues such as doctrine and training was close, and it was the US who provided Hungary with modern equipment necessary for foreign missions, such as MRAP mine-resistant and HMMW vehicles, communication equipment, and assault small arms used by Hungarian Special Forces in Afghanistan.

Without pressure from external allies, it is unlikely the Hungarian military would have taken on even the small-scale modernization efforts it did during its first two decades as a liberal internationalist democracy. Hungarian public opinion is historically inclined to see all military spending as a luxury, and membership in NATO hardly changed the pervasive political culture of anti-militarism. In fact, widespread opposition to deployments in Afghanistan, Iraq, and the former Yugoslavia was likely aided by the fact that Hungary's small professional military operates in a somewhat detached way from a wary public. Taking on missions unapproved by the public – like the one in Afghanistan – hardly contributed to building a culture of popular consensus and approval for defense policies as a part of Hungary's self-identity (Sherr 2000; Talas and Csiki 2013; Csiki 2015).

## Hungary's defense policies today

2010 was a watershed in Hungarian politics, as the right-wing nationalist populist FIDESZ-Hungarian Civic Alliance won the country's parliamentary elections by a landslide, defeating disintegrating left and liberal parties. FIDESZ won again in 2014, and remains popular today, in contrast to Hungary's left and liberal opposition parties, whose continued weakness was dramatically illustrated by FIDESZ' overwhelming victory in the 2018 parliamentary elections. Significantly, as of 2018, the second largest party in Hungary is "Jobbik," an even more nationalistic and populist organization than FIDESZ.

With its supermajority, FIDESZ created a new Constitution of April 2011, passing over 200 laws and modifying every aspect of Hungarian domestic politics. The Constitution and the laws have been criticized as nationalistic and anti-democratic. Viktor Orbán, in particular, became famous with statements that proclaimed exhaustion of liberalism as an ideology and liberal democracy as a political system. Orbán also praised authoritarian rulers like Putin, and engaged in an "opening to the East" policy, which will be discussed in the Conclusion of this chapter. As a nationalist, Orbán asserts Hungary's sovereignty against the global capitalist system and depicts the EU as an oppressive institution that represents the interests of global elite as opposed to the national interests of Hungary (Orbán 2014).

One would expect Orbán's self-proclaimed "national revolution" to immediately impact Hungary's security and defense policies, channeling them in a unilateral direction towards a strategy of territorial self-defense. However, the essential structure, spending, and doctrine of the Hungarian Armed Forces have stayed fairly conservative in every essential national security document since the Constitution of 2011. In fact, the only concrete change that has resulted from Orbán and FIDESZ' rhetorical shift has been a modest increase in military spending, which is on track to match the average spending of European NATO Member States as a percentage of GDP by 2022.[11] Without a substantial increase in funds allocated, Hungary will likely not be able to develop a military infrastructure capable of the unilateral territorial defense that the new ruling party is advocating. Therefore, it is only logical that Hungary continues to enjoy the historically unprecedented security of Euro-Atlantic defense alliances through policy that reaffirms its commitment to multilateral peacekeeping missions. It is too early to say whether a true long-term change is on the cards, but there are signs that Hungary's defense strategy has shifted and that the country's underfunded military is transforming.

Indication of a shift in defense planning can be found in the "Foreword" to the 2012 National Military Strategy:

> We have to abandon the previously denizened, comfortable, but altogether dangerous attitude that national defense is feasible without substantive military strength, relying on a bare minimum of our own capabilities, and trusting solely in the solidarity of NATO and EU nations. This approach, which is a far cry from that of the Alliance, can only lead down the bitter path of further deterioration of our defense force. Only a strong, confident and proud defense force can be of service to Hungary, Europe, and Hungary's National Military Strategy" (Hungarian Republic Ministry of Defense 2012, 1–2).

This frank admission of weakness, written by then Minister of Defense Dr. Csaba Hende, is followed by an equally frank elaboration – within the body of the strategy itself – that new capacities of the Hungarian military are to be initially found through "flexibility and efficiency" as a temporary "scarcity" of "available budgetary resources" is a given.

While renunciation of war is conspicuously absent, other liberal and liberal internationalist principles of foreign policy, such as Hungary's membership in the EU (Article E), cooperation with "all peoples and countries in the world" (Article Q (1)),[12] and commitment to all principles and specific provisions of international law (Article Q (2) and (3)), are significantly reasserted in the Constitution of 2011. Further down, the Constitution outlines the principles of Hungary's universal military service (Article XXXI), acknowledging the existence of HDF (Article 45) whose chief duties "shall be the military defense of the independence, territorial integrity and borders of Hungary, the performance of collective defense and peacekeeping tasks arising from international treaties, as well as the carrying out of humanitarian activities in accordance with the rules of international law." These military forces are to be subordinated to civilian leadership (Article 45, paragraph (2)), and their professional members are banned from membership in political parties and political activities (Article 45, paragraph (4)).

The Constitution also reaffirms a 2003 amendment whereby the government is authorized to deploy troops within the framework of NATO or EU decision-making upon mere notification of the parliament. Prior to Constitutional Amendment 40/C, in response to Hungary's notoriously anti-militaristic citizenry, a two-thirds parliamentary approval was necessary for any national military action, but, article 43 paragraph 7 of the Constitution of 2011 reinstated the 2003 removal of bureaucratic barriers to military action. This can be understood as another sign of Hungary's continued commitment to multilateral defense organizations. However, it also highlights the dichotomy that exists when an anti-militaristic culture is governed by populist-nationalists. On the one hand, FIDESZ and Orbán embody the essence of the people's political aspirations; on the other hand, they must coax militancy from the people in order to live up to the rhetoric that got them elected.

This can be observed most recently by Hungary's response to the 2015 Ukrainian and refugee/migration crises at the Hungarian border, during which the government made statements about "doubling the size" of the military. However, the chief way in which Orbán dealt with the personnel problem[13] of policing a large numbers of immigrants at the Hungarian border was recruiting a special 3,000-strong auxiliary force of Határvadász/Grenzenjäger, also called the "Border Chasseurs" or "hunters" formation[14] To address the cultural problem of Hungarian anti-militarism, Orbán promised to increase military pay and pursue "patriotic education of children"[15] focused on instilling military and patriotic values in school. This last program is certain to be described as nationalistic indoctrination by the political opposition, and is likely to backfire, creating even greater public cynicism about the nation's military. On the other hand, increasing military pay might address the issue to some extent.[16]

In accordance with Dr. Csaba Hende's admission in the "Foreword," an increase in resources was set into motion by the 2012 Security Strategy. Specifically, by freezing the nominal value of the Hungarian defense budget until 2015, then, starting in 2016, increasing the budget with "annual increases no less than 0.1% of GDP." In reality, in 2014, Hungary's defense budget decreased to 281.4 bn forints, marking the lowest real budget in the history of post-communist Hungary. However, in response to the Ukrainian Crisis, Hungary lived up to its promise and increased nominal and real spending to fulfill and even slightly exceed the level of spending promised in the "2012 Military Strategy" (see table 5.2). This trend continued in 2016 and in 2017, thus restoring Hungarian defense spending to roughly 1% of GDP and $1.2 bn real level (in 2015 constant dollars); in other words, back to what it was in 2010.

In spring of 2017, new Hungarian Defense Minister Istvan Simicsko (who replaced Csaba Hedbe in 2015) set an even higher military spending goal, promising to continue the increases with the goal of spending 2% of GDP on defense by 2026 – or roughly doubling the current spending. In 2018, the Hungarian military budget is set to increase by 21% (Staff 2017).[17] These budgetary increases will finance a newly unveiled (but unavailable in detail) "Zryini 2026" defense development plan, which emphasizes reserve and territorial defense forces, military pay increases, personal equipment, and helicopter procurement.[18] Until the Hungarian military is able to restore a healthy 40/30/30 budget (in terms of personnel, operations, and procurement), it will not be able to modernize its technology. However, with the budget increases that occurred between 2016 and 2018, there are timid signs that it is on its way.

Within the existing framework, however, there is no indication of a change of course and no trace of Orbán's "national revolution" – to the contrary, the formulation of Hungary's grand defense strategy is as liberal and liberal internationalist as can be. The HDF defined as

**Table 5.4** Structure of Hungarian military budget, 2009–16

| Year | Equipment (%) | Personnel (%) | Infrastructure (%) | Other (operations and maintenance, etc.) (%) |
|------|------|------|------|------|
| 2009 | 12.67 | 50.43 | 3.88 | 33.02 |
| 2010 | 12.1 | 56.35 | 2.07 | 29.48 |
| 2011 | 12.29 | 50.64 | 1.31 | 35.76 |
| 2012 | 5.84 | 47.69 | 2.11 | 44.36 |
| 2013 | 11.08 | 48.96 | 2.32 | 37.64 |
| 2014 | 7.76 | 49.77 | 1.07 | 41.4 |
| 2015 | 8.17 | 48.27 | 0.64 | 42.92 |
| 2016 | 13 | 50.21 | 2.27 | 34.52 |

*Source*: Based on Kufčak 2014.

"the primary institution" which "need well-equipped and trained forces as well as flexible, usable, deployable and sustainable capabilities to defend the sovereignty and territory of the country, to contribute to collective defense within the NATO-framework and to UN, NATO, EU or OSCE-led international peacekeeping, stabilization or humanitarian operations." The 2012 National Security Strategy goes on to emphasize civil-military cooperation in multilateral deployment missions such as disaster relief. Sound familiar? The 2012 National Security Strategy pushes for the Hungarian military's continual refinement as a liberal internationalist ally.

Though the 2012 "National Military Strategy"[19] holds some indications of Hungary's intentions to restore its high-intensity, conventional warfare capability, its assertions are ambiguous at best.[20] It restates the notion that Hungary's immediate neighborhood is "stable" and a risk of conventional attack against Hungary and its allies is "marginal," but one can also find concerns about stability of (implicitly) the Western Balkans: "the security of those regions previously struck by crises remains fragile." It sets forth the necessity for personnel who "have received high-level education and training, have adequate physical and psychological endurance, are capable of high-level performance in an international environment, and are motivated and committed to executing its tasks." However, it provides little operational guidance on how to achieve these goals. Therefore, in this interim period, when it is hard to gauge what will happen next, Hungary's goal for, "armed forces that can be employed in the full spectrum of possible operations from low to high intensity" is, in its ambiguity, the best prediction available for the future of HDF.

### Concluding matters: Russia, refugees, and the future

The Ukrainian Crisis exploded in February 2014 with Putin's takeover of Crimea. Orbán's response to the issue has been unsurprisingly two-fold – on the one hand, his government, alongside other V4 countries, condemned the violation of Ukraine's sovereignty,[21] and diplomatically supported and sustained EU sanctions against Russia (Kucharczy & Meseznikov 2016). On the other hand, in a display of political schizophrenia, Orbán publicly criticized the sanctions his government helped to draft (Kucharczy & Meseznikov 2016) and raised the issue of Hungarian minority rights in Transcarpathia; a display of inferred support for Russian claims of Ukraine's minority rights violations. Though Orbán's rhetoric painted the EU as an enemy and Russia as a friend, his political actions, in many ways, could not have been further from his words.

**Table 5.5** Evolution of Hungarian defense policy doctrine

| Year | Documents | Premises | Goals | Main/new threats | Main means |
|---|---|---|---|---|---|
| 1993 | Basic Principles of Security Policy of the Republic of Hungary | Hungarian strategic autonomy as a temporary reality | Integration into NATO and EU | External instability and local conflicts | Peaceful economic, social, and political development |
| 1993 | Principles of National Defense of the Republic of Hungary | Hungarian strategic autonomy as a temporary reality | Integration into NATO and EU as full members | External instability and local conflicts | Adjustment of Hungary to multilateral institutions. Sufficient mix of forces to preserve sovereignty |
| 1998 | Hungary's Security and Defense Policy – Resolution on Basic Principles | Hungary's membership in NATO as a given | Integration into NATO and EU | External instability and local conflicts | Adjustment of Hungary to multilateral institutions. Continuous liberal development with emphasis on non-military aspects of security |
| 2002 | National Security Strategy of the Republic of Hungary | Euro-Atlantic and European integration. Safety from conventional threats | Liberal development of Hungary and in the broader world, especially immediate neighborhood | External instability and local conflicts. "New" global threats | Liberal development and international cooperation |
| 2004 | National Security Strategy of the Republic of Hungary | Euro-Atlantic and European integration. Safety from conventional threats | Liberal development of Hungary and in the broader world, especially immediate neighborhood | External instability and local conflicts. "New" global threats | Liberal development and international cooperation |

| | | | | |
|---|---|---|---|---|
| 2009 | National Military Strategy of the Republic of Hungary | Euro-Atlantic and European integration. Safety from conventional threats | Development of alliance-compatible and integrated military capabilities | External instability and local conflicts. "New" global threats. Defense capacities to counter the "new" threats | Liberal development and international cooperation |
| 2012 | National Security Strategy of the Republic of Hungary | Hungarian membership in the Western Security community. Safety from conventional threats | Liberal development of Hungary and in the broader world, especially immediate neighborhood | External instability and local conflicts. "New" global threats | Liberal development and international cooperation |
| 2012 | Hungarian National Military Strategy | Inadequacy of Hungarian Defense Forces. "Dealing with challenges of the future" | Stronger and more flexible Hungarian Defense Forces, to be capable of both expeditionary warfare and territorial defense functions | External instability and local conflicts. "New" global threats. Threats can materialize suddenly, globalization brings about "new" threats | The need to strengthen military capacity across a spectrum of capacities. Emphasis on counter-insurgency and network-centric warfare |
| 2017 | National Security Strategy (still under discussion) | Increases in threat environment? | "National development?" | "Muslim invasion?" | Emphasis on territorial defenses? |

Hungary also played a prominent role in the drama of mass migration from Africa and the Middle East which has shaken Europe since 2015. On this issue, Hungary took a much more defiant stance against the EU, engaging in a drawn-out conflict with mostly Western EU members over refugee admission quotas. In the fall of 2015, Hungary sealed its borders with Serbia, and then with Croatia, constructed border fences, and declared a state of emergency in March 2016, rushing 1500 soldiers to the borders.[22] The militarization of the crisis led to personnel problems in the underfunded military and the resignation of Minister of Defense Csaba Hende, who was held responsible for the slow construction of a border fence with Serbia in September 2015.[23] Significantly, and in contrast to policy on Russia, in which Poland took a strong anti-Russian position, all V4 countries shared Hungary's reaction to the immigration issue, showing that factors stronger than the particular ideological predilection of Hungary's current leaders were at work.[24]

As of right now, it is unclear where Hungary's true allegiance lies. In many ways, Hungary's "opening to the East" policy pre-dated the Ukrainian crisis and even Orbán's coming to power in 2010. Indeed, Hungary's post-1991 policy towards Russia has been generally friendly, especially under Orbán's chief enemies, the Hungarian socialists (MSZP). In 2008, the MSZP formulated a foreign policy strategy of "global opening," which called for Hungary's increasing economic and political intercourse with non-EU countries, including Russia. Thus, Orbán's friendliness towards Russia is not necessarily new, but its loudness and ideological undertones are. Still, the core of Orbán's "Eastern opening" seems to be pragmatic and economic – it puts economic advantage over liberal "ideological criteria" such as concerns about human rights. The chief practical expression of this policy, so far, has been the January 2014 signing of a contract with Russian company Rosatom to expand Hungary's nuclear power station at Paks (the so-called Paks-2 project).[25] This project puts Hungary squarely in the Russian camp of European energy security battles. However, the economic motivation for Paks-2 is less a confirmation of Russian allegiance and more an expression of economic pragmatism (Vegh 2015).[26]

With all of the above ambiguities, Hungary's routine, institutionalized defense policies continued unabated. In July 2017, the country co-hosted a large-scale NATO "Saber Guardian 17" military exercise (with some 25,0000 soldiers), clearly aimed at deterring Russia.[27] Moreover, with the election of Donald Trump to US presidency, Hungary's commitment to Atlanticism has been reinforced, since Orbán sees a fellow nationalist populist, instead of mistrusted Obama, as the leader of a key NATO country (Kalan 2012). Trump's call to "defend the Western civilization" in his Warsaw speech of July 6, 2017 was enthusiastically welcomed by Orbán, who sees a vindication of his own ideology in Trump and his policies (Orbán 2017).

What is real and what is rhetoric remains questionable when dealing with nationalist populist politicians like Orbán or Trump. Hungary hardly needs increased high-intensity warfare capacities to deal with terrorism or immigration – the threats emphasized by Orbán. (Orbán, at least rhetorically, considers a Russian threat non-existent.) Nevertheless, Hungary has continued to play the NATO "alliance game" through recent (unenthusiastic) participation in hollow displays of defense against Russia, which, in actuality, would require a tremendous (re) building of Hungary's conventional capabilities after some 60 years of neglect.

The ultimate irony of Hungarian defense policy could be that the current government, dedicated to the cause of restoring Hungary's sovereignty, is actually illustrating the impossibility of full-on small country nationalism in a world enmeshed in international institutions. However, with the rise of Trump, Brexit, and wave after wave of populist nationalism across the globe, one wonders about the endurance of international institutions. If EU and NATO core states like the US start destroying international institutions from within, the liberal internationalist model on which Hungarian defense doctrine is based might revert to a realist world of self-help and shifting alliances, as happened in the interwar period. Even Orbán would presumably not like a return of to that world.

## Notes

1 Jacek Lubecki would like to extend special thanks to Professor András Rácz of Péter Pázmány Catholic University in Budapest for helping with research for this chapter. The author is fully responsible for any errors that remain.

2 In the words of an anonymous Lt Commander at the US European Command "working with Hungary is like watching a bad comedy set on auto repeat." See www.greekchat.com/gcforums/archive/index.php/t-54509.html, accessed July 10, 2017.

3 The hallmark of this rejection was Hungary's constitutional renunciation of war in its post-communist (amended 1949) Constitution, where article 6, paragraph (1) stated: "The Republic of Hungary renounces war as a means of solving disputes between nations and shall refrain from the use of force and the threat thereof against the independence or territorial integrity of other states." The subsequent paragraph (2) stated: "The Republic of Hungary shall endeavor to co-operate with all peoples and countries of the world." Signficantly, similar provisions have long existed in post-Second World War German, Japanese, and Italian constitutions. Among

post-communist countries, we find a similar provision in the Slovenian 1991 Constitution. Significantly, paragraph (1) and its renounciation of war did not make it to the Hungarian Constitution of 2011.

4 See "Treaty on Good-Neighbourly Relations and Friendly Co-operation between the Republic of Hungary and the Slovak Republic" www.kbdesign. sk/cla/projects/slovak_hungarian_treaty/related/treaty_sk_hu.htm, accessed July 12, 2017.

5 Hungarian constitutional evolution progressively diminished presidential powers. This was solidified with the adoption of the 2011 Constitution. The Hungarian system of government can be described as a weak semi-presidential one. See "The Fundamental Law of Hungary" at www. kormany.hu/download/e/02/00000/The%20New%20Fundamental%20 Law%20of%20Hungary.pdf, accessed July 17, 2017.

6 Just like in Poland, most of Hungary's post-communist political life revolved around fierce competition between post-communist, successor "left," derived from the former ruling Communist Party, and the former anti-communist opposition "right," divided into conservative and liberal wings. This competition was accompanied by a constant alternation in power until 2010 (the right ruled during 1991–94, the left 1994–98, then right again 1998–2002, and left 2002–10), with electoral outcomes, like in the 2002 elections, being decided by razor-sharp margins of vote, and power distribution being decided by parliamentary coalitions where minor parties held the deciding edge. The most important development in this story is a collapse and disintegration of the left, which, racked by scandals, crumbled between 2006 and 2010, leaving the right and its chief party, FIDESZ with Viktor Orbán as its head, as hegemons in Hungarian political life. Significantly, Poland followed a very similar pattern in its political development.

7 This also meant that professional voices which lamented the catastrophic state of Hungarian military and rightly blamed civilian leadership for this state of affairs were silenced, at least when in office.

8 By consensus, the Gripen program turned into a "bottomless pit of money," halting modernization of other weapons systems.

9 77 Hungarian reserve T-72 tanks were donated to the government of post-2003 Iraq and 58 remaining Hungarian reserve tanks were recently sold to either Czech Republic or Ukraine. Apparently, a token force of 11 T-72 tanks are in active service as of 2017. The Mi-24s are not in active service, but are to be overhauled in the course of the newly announced "Zrinyi 2026" program.

10 In particular, the 34th Bercsényi László Special Operations Battalion was designated as a Special Forces unit in September 2005 and gained new capabilities with heavy US training assistance and military hardware support. However, Maj. Szabolcz Péscsvarady, in a monograph on the subject, noted conceptual confusion, overlapping of responsibilities, and waste of resources involved in the creating Hungarian special forces (Pécsvarady 2010).

11 The paltry 1.39% of GDP sum, one has to say, falls far short of the NATO

recommended 2% of GDP. The whole notion that a country's defense spending is to be decided by an average of the proportion of what one's immediate allies spend certainly only makes sense under liberal internationalist premises – namely, based on a notion that "doing one's fair share" in a multilateral alliance framework should define a country's strategic needs.

12  An identical formulation was in the pre-existing Constitution, article 6 (2). See "Act XX of 1949 The Constitution of the Republic of Hungary," amended in 1989–90, at http://lapa.princeton.edu/hosteddocs/hungary/1989–90%20 constitution_english.pdf, accessed July 24, 2017.

13  Apparently, because of appalling service conditions (lack of winter gear and proper living accommodation) during the emergency border deployment, many soldiers and officers/non-commissioned officers quit the regular military, hence, the well-paid but poorly trained "Border Chasseurs" formation became a stop-gap measure to deal with the crisis. This information was given to the authors by Professor András Racz.

14  See "Orbán has Launched the Training of His Border Chasseurs" on "Visegrad Post – English," https://visegradpost.com/en/2016/09/18/orban-has-launched-the-training-of-his-border-chasseurs/, September 18, 2016, accessed July 26, 2017.

15  See "Orbán plans to DOUBLE the Hungarian army and Rise Patriotism Among Children" on "Visegrad Post – English," https://visegradpost.com/en/2016/10/19/orban-plans-to-double-the-hungarian-army-and-rise-patriotism-among-children/, October 19, 2016, accessed July 25, 2017.

16  Increases in military budget since 2015 have indeed been accompanied by increased (up to 50%) in military salaries. See "The Hungarian Defence Forces must be made a Major Military Force in the Region by 2026" at Hungarian Ministry of Defense website, www.kormany.hu/en/ministry-of-defence/news/the-hungarian-defence-forces-must-be-made-a-major-military-force-in-the-region-by-2026, accessed July 28, 2017. How these can be reconciled with the goal of rebalancing military spending towards procurement is not clear, but overall budget increases could address the problem.

17  Orbán himself re-emphasized the theme of a strong Hungarian military "able to defend Hungary from all external attacks" in his July 24, 2017 speech entitled "Will Europe Belong to Europeans?" See Orbán (2017). In this same speech he announced the creation "of the first factory for the Hungarian arms industry." From Minister of Foreign Defense February 2017 statements we know that the industry in question is to manufacture communication and information equipment.

18  See "The Hungarian Defence Forces must be made a Major Military Force in the Region by 2026" at Hungarian Ministry of Defense website, www.kormany.hu/en/ministry-of-defence/news/the-hungarian-defence-forces-must-be-made-a-major-military-force-in-the-region-by-2026, accessed July 28, 2017.

19  A new national security strategy is apparently in the pipeline, but its content has not been made public. See, "Hungary's Government Drafting New

Security, Military Strategy" at Hungary Daily News https://dailynewshun-gary.com/hungarys-government-drafting-new-security-military-strategy/, accessed July 28, 2017.

20 Given the current size of Hungarian operational forces (some 4,000–5,000 out of the total of some 23,000 soldiers), Hungary alone is clearly incapable of the country's self-defense in an event of external conventional aggression.

21 See Johannes Wachs and Lisa Herman, "Hungary's Reaction to the Ukraine Crisis Illustrates the Tensions within Fidesz's Foreign Policy Discourse Ahead of April's Elections" on London School of Economic "EUROPP" website    http://blogs.lse.ac.uk/europpblog/2014/03/20/hungarys-reaction-to-the-ukraine-crisis-illustrates-the-tensions-within-fideszs-foreign-policy-discourse-ahead-of-aprils-elections/, accessed July 28, 2017.

22 See "Breaking News: Hungary Declares State of Emergency as Migrant Crisis Turns Unpredictable" at "Hungary Today," March 9, 2016, http://hungarytoday.hu/news/breaking-news-hungary-declares-state-emergency-migrant-crisis-turns-unpredictable-96001, accessed July 28, 2017.

23 See, Reuters, "Hungarian Defense Minister Resigns as Migrant Inflow Continues" at World News, September 7, 2015, www.reuters.com/article/us-europe-migrants-hungary-minister-idUSKCN0R71VN20150907, accessed July 28, 2017.

24 See "Visegrad Leaders Oppose Migration Quotas" at *The Economist* http://country.eiu.com/article.aspx?articleid=1823495766&Country=Poland&topic=Politics_1, accessed July 28, 2017.

25 The station provides some 50% of Hungary's electricity supply, and the project is worth some 10 bn Euros, with the credit to be financed by Russia.

26 He famously said that ideological economic policy is what "smart countries impose on dumb countries."

27 See Rick Docksai, "Eucom, European Partners Work to Deter New Threats," at US Department of Defense Website, https://www.defense.gov/News/Article/Article/1261004/eucom-european-partners-work-to-deter-new-threats/, accessed July 28, 2017.

# 6

# Poland: return to the West?

## Emergence of new defense policy and structures

The new Polish government's initial foreign and security policy actions were cautious. The crumbling of the Soviet Union was a surprise to Polish anti-communist opposition, who, in the fall of 1989, found themselves in power unintentionally through their negotiated transition with the Communist Party.[1] While the Warsaw Pact was formally dissolved between February and July 1991 (through the Budapest and Prague declarations respectively), the last Soviet troops did not leave Poland until September 1993. The period in-between was fraught with external strategic and internal ambiguity. Overall, Poland was unsure what course to follow and appeared to be the least likely candidate for liberal democratic reforms in the defense establishment.

With few exceptions, Poland's new non-communist government expected that, at best, Poland could gain limited semi-independence from the Soviets based on the Finish model or "Finlandization." There was a faction of domestic opposition ("independists" in Roman Kuźniar's formulation) who envisioned full-blown Polish independence and total rejection of any Russian influence. However, their strategic thought did not go much beyond that. The dominant theme among Polish and East-Central European dissident thought, as illustrated by the writings of Václav Havel, Györgi Konrád, and Adam Michnik, was that both NATO and the Warsaw Pact represented a nasty logic of "imbecilic militarism" (Konrád) and imperialism. For these dissidents, both NATO and the Warsaw Pact would hopefully disappear in a better world (Konrád1984; Havel & Keane 1985; Michnik 1987).

Akin to the partitions, Poland's time subjugated by the Soviet Union was not a period of stagnation in Poland's independent strategic thought. Independent thinkers and institutions existed in the country among illegal and semi-legal oppositional milieus and among exiles in the West. Amidst the latter, an outstanding think-tank was created around the Paris-based magazine *Kultura*, edited by Jerzy Giedroyć.

It was in this milieu, and especially in the writings of political thinker Juliusz Mieroszewski, that Poland's specific interpretation of liberal democratic thought was born. Mieroszewski, who was active between 1949 and 1975, embraced Piłsudski's notion that Poland's independence necessitated the independence of all countries west of Russia: "without free Ukraine, Belarus and Lithuanian (UBL) there is no free Poland." Mieroszewski's understanding was not based in neo-imperial designs that these countries could somehow represent a "Polish sphere of influence." He fully recognized the borders resulting from the Second World War, as well as the fact that Poland had to divest itself of any post-imperial sensibilities about its former territories in the East. Most importantly, in an act of departure from Piłsudski's thought, Mieroszewski decisively rejected the notion of "eternal" or geopolitically pre-determined Polish-Russian hostility. For him, departure from the vicious cycle of Polish–Russian confrontation could be fueled by an understanding of Poland as "a bridge" between Russia and Europe: a Europeanized Russia living in harmony with Poland based on mutual respect of each other's sovereignty (Kuźniar 2008: 32). This vision, rooted in modern liberalism, was accepted almost unanimously by Polish domestic anti-communist opposition.[2]

Contrary to oft-repeated hopes, Poland's prospects for liberal democracy were initially not that rosy. Internally, it mattered that interwar Poland, unlike pre-Second World War Czechoslovakia, did not sustain a liberal democracy and the reasons for its collapse in 1926 had everything to do with Poland's inability to effectively establish civilian control over the military. Likewise, in 1989, unlike both Czechoslovakia and Hungary, Poland confronted the unique legacy of a militarized communist regime in the 1980s.

Externally, Poland in 1989 had to take into account the potential for an insecure western boundary with Germany, not settled until December 1991 when the Bundestag ratified a treaty confirming the Oder-Neisse frontier. Until then, Poland could not be sure if continued alliance with Russia was preferrable to opening strategically to the West. Likewise, the US was bewildered by Eastern Europe, though they promised not to exploit the security vacuum left behind by the Soviet Empire.

Polish post-communist political life was uniquely fragmented and polarized between the "left" (represented by the Social-Democracy of the Polish Republic, or SDRP party, later renamed Union of Democratic Left, SLD) and the democratic opposition parties (multiple, with ever-changing names), divided, in turn, between their liberal and conservative-nationalist wings.[3] Within that latter camp loomed large the charismatic, mercurial and impetuous figure of Lech Wałęsa who deliberately self-styled himself as Piłsudski's avatar, a "liberator and savior" of the nation, standing above party divisions and willing to violate liberal-democratic norms in the name of his power and what he deemed the national interest.

In 1991, Poland's first truly free parliamentary elections placed the anti-Russian, anti-communist "right" of the Polish political spectrum in power, with a platform advocating Poland's membership in NATO. However, this view was by no means domestically dominant, welcome in the West, or representative of an elite consensus among the recently legitimized parties.

By 1991 Poland was strategically independent, possessed substantial military assets, and was suspended between the West and Russia like a percipient pendulum. Polish national interests and the ruling liberal consensus – embodied in Mieroszewski's "Eastern" policy – demanded good relationships and settled borders with all neighbors. However, all vestiges of Poland's dependent status had necessarily to be removed first and foremost through the exit of Russian troops, accomplished by fall 1993. The significant, if brief, period of strategic ambiguity which followed the fall of communism in Poland comes as no surprise given this state of Polish political thought.

Poland's defense policy during the 1990s had to address complex and contradictory security risks and opportunities. While threats of conventional military invasion were largely gone, the "forced" self-sufficiency created by the fall of the Soviet Union made it imperative to maintain a relatively large conventional military force. In addition, new and non-conventional threats appeared on the horizon: social instability and civil ethno-nationalist conflicts precipitated by communist collapse often ended in chaotic authoritarian and nationalist regimes, not liberal democracies.[4] The risk of dangerous external spill-over and internal instability was real and looming. The gravitational pull of the West, combined with a ruling liberal-democratic ideology informed by Polish history and the weight of Poland's cultural and geostrategic position soon created – in convergence with other countries of the region – a consensus that Poland must be fully integrated into Western security structures.

Liberal internationalist sections of the Polish foreign policy elite embraced the notion that Poland should put its trust in all-European security structures embodied in a reinforced and reformed Conference on Security and Cooperation in Europe (Kuźniar 2008: 88–92). Indulging the inter-war *Intermarium* idea, President Lech Wałęsa briefly toyed with the idea of NATO-bis: a separate collective security alliance of all former Warsaw Pact members minus Russia (Onyszkiewicz, 1999:

135). Another expression of a separate East-Central European defense structure was the Visegrád Three (later the Visegrád Four with the 1993 addition of Slovakia), a ratified organization with members Poland, Czechoslovakia, and Hungary. The V4 emerged from two summits in Visegrád and Budapest in Februrary 1991.[5] This organization was imbued with much hope but featured internal tensions and was not very active in the 1990s (Kuźniar 2008: 68–70). Still, its continuous existence was indicative of dramatic progress in the region compared to the interwar and communist period, marked by hostilities and mutual acts of military aggression (Czechoslovak–Hungarian, Polish–Czechoslovakian, Polish–Slovak, and Hungarian–Slovak border wars, invasion of Czechoslovakia in 1968, etc.).

Still, Poland was formally self-sufficient between 1991–98, and its national security doctrine of 1992 reflected this reality. In *Principles of Defense Policy*, we find Poland "does not see any existing country as a threat" and is able to counter conventional aggression from "any direction" if Polish sovereignty, territorial integrity, and democratic order are threatened. Regarding internal risks, dismantling the communist-era military-industrial complex had to be done gradually, so as not to create an organized pool of unemployed and impoverished former military and security personnel, able and willing to destabilize, corrupt, or destroy the new liberal-democratic order in a country where, just recently, the military was in charge.[6] This consideration dictated either maintaining a relatively large force of career soldiers in place or retiring them in large numbers with generous pension packages. As a result, a quantitatively large and costly military force was kept in place but not really modernized due to budgetary constraints. The 1990s thus marked a slow decay and decapitalization of Polish military assets: equipment, bases, training standards, etc. (Simon 2004). Backed by a Ministry of Defense (MON) budget that nominally represented a shrinking percentage of the country's GDP but a considerable and actually growing sum of money in real terms (see table 6.2) (Simon 2004: 89), the size of the Polish Armed Forces steadily diminished (see table 6.1).[7]

By late 1992, Wałęsa had fully converted to the idea of future Polish membership in NATO and the EU; by 1994, the post-communist left embraced this strategy and it became the consensus of all major Polish political parties and elites (Lis 1999: 351). However, it wasn't until the defeat of Wałęsa in the presidential elections of 1995,[8] and the hegemony of the post-communist left (represented by Aleksander Kwaśniewski, President between 1995 and 2005) and the liberal wing of post-Solidarity "right" (which controlled the parliament and Prime-Ministership between 1997 and 2001), that the full scope of institutional

**Table 6.1** Polish Armed Forces, 1991–2003

| Year | Total forces | Conscripts | Career soldiers | Civilians | Total personnel |
|------|-------------|-----------|-----------------|-----------|-----------------|
| 1991 | 305,000 | 191,100 | 113,900 | NA | NA |
| 1992 | 296,500 | 167,400 | 129,100 | 88,800 | 385,300 |
| 1993 | 287,500 | 162,400 | 125,100 | 89,000 | 376,500 |
| 1994 | 283,600 | 160,000 | 123,600 | NA | NA |
| 1995 | 278,600 | 158,100 | 120,000 | 84,000 | 362,100 |
| 1996 | 248,500 | 147,100 | 101,400 | 83,500 | 332,000 |
| 1997 | 241,750 | 141,600 | 100,150 | 82,400 | 324,150 |
| 1998 | 213,500 | 114,500 | 99,000 | 81,600 | 295,100 |
| 1999 | 205,000 | 104,500 | 94,900 | 80,000 | 279,400 |
| 2000 | 197,000 | NA | NA | 64,000 | NA |
| 2001 | 180,000 | 91,800 | 88,200 | NA | NA |
| 2002 | 165,000 | 83,400 | 81,600 | NA | NA |
| 2003 | 150,000 | 73,000 | 76,392 | 57,000 | 206,392 |

*Source*: Adapted from: Simon 2004, 89.

military reforms could be enacted, and indeed was. This happened, in particular, with the adoption of key legal acts: the 1997 Constitution, the Law on Universal Military Service (1996), and the Law on the Use of Armed Forces Abroad (1998) (Wolpiuk 1998; Simon 2004). By 2001, principles of civilian control over the military, including over military intelligence services, were firmly established.[9]

Radical personnel cuts followed Polish membership in NATO in 1999 (see table 6.1), which meant the proportion of military budget (item 29 of National Budget, MON) devoted to "national security" dramatically diminished (section 752) compared to the portion for "social security" (largely, pensions for retired military). Indeed, table 6.2 vividly illustrates how the Polish military budget absorbed ever growing spending on items other than "national security," (see the gap between "national security" and "non-national security" items in the MON budget, in column 5 of table 6.2), making it more difficult to modernize despite the numerically shrinking force. This insight also illustrates how relying on a mere "percentage of GDP" metric of defense spending can be deceptive.

NATO and the imperatives of post-Cold War security required institutional overhaul: the modernization of Armed Forces and the professionalization of personnel geared for quick, expeditionary deployment. As early as 1995, plans[10] to rationalize and rebuild the Polish military-industrial complex were created, followed by the much more elaborate "Outlines of the Government Program for the Armed

**Table 6.2** Polish MON budget, 1991–2003

| Year | MON budget (Part 29 of state budget) as % of GDP | Section 752 of the budget ("national defense") as % of GDP | Total MON budget (in 2006 $m) | Gap between total MON budget and section 752 (in 2006 $m) | 752 section of MON budget (in 2006 $m) |
|---|---|---|---|---|---|
| 1991 | 2.25 | 2.23 | 520.3 | 4.03 | 516.27 |
| 1992 | 2.23 | 2.21 | 732.7 | 8.11 | 724.59 |
| 1993 | 2.47 | 2.12 | 1,099.0 | 153.51 | 945.49 |
| 1994 | 2.43 | 1.96 | 1,462.0 | 282.71 | 1,179.29 |
| 1995 | 2.15 | 1.71 | 1,884.1 | 384.29 | 1,499.81 |
| 1996 | 2.16 | 1.56 | 2,375.2 | 659.97 | 1,715.23 |
| 1997 | 2.15 | 1.55 | 2,878.9 | 800.29 | 2,078.61 |
| 1998 | 2.12 | 1.52 | 3,339.1 | 950.91 | 2,388.19 |
| 1999 | 2.00 | 1.51 | 3,497.8 | 866.54 | 2,631.26 |
| 2000 | 1.92 | 1.44 | 3,757.0 | 947.69 | 2,809.31 |
| 2001 | 1.89 | 1.22 | 4,009.2 | 1,494.03 | 2,515.17 |
| 2002 | 1.88 | 1.26 | 4,168.7 | 1,501.97 | 2,666.73 |
| 2003 | 1.90 | 1.30 | 4,378.0 | 1,455.94 | 2,922.06 |

*Source*: Adapted from: Lepianka 2004, 38.

*Note*: It is deceptive to look at the overall MON budget (part 29 of the Polish state budget) as indicative of effective Polish spending on national defense – especially equipment procurement. In fact, the "national defense" (section 752) portion of the MON budget shrank systematically as a % of GDP and state budget (even though section 752 increased dramatically overall in real terms). What accounts for the growing gap between MON budget and effective defense expenditure is a systematic increase in spending on social security (section 753 of MON budget), mostly for the retired military. For instance, as of 2003, social security represented nearly a quarter (25.65%) of the MON budget – see Lepianka 2004, 45). Other not-directly-military sections of the defense budget are small, but add up to another 13% of MON budget (as of 2004, education 7.33 %, health care 0.52 %, military lodging 2.12 %). Overall, nearly one third of the Polish defense budget in 2004 went towards budgetary items other than "national defense."

Forces Modernization 1998–2012" ("Program 2012") in September 1997. Prepared with a view of impending Polish membership in NATO, "Program 2012" envisioned a smaller, more efficient, NATO-interoperable military force of around 150,000 officers and soldiers (down from 241,000 in 1997)[11] predicated on radically increased equipment, infrastructure, and research and development spending: from $0.32 billion in 1997 to 1.23 billion in 2012.[12]

"Program 2012" was never fully funded; the 1997–2001 right-wing government of Poland chose to focus on other fundamental reforms (health care, social security, territorial government, education) and spending priorities. However, international pressures from NATO and the country's strategic reformulation in the 1999 (2000) National Security Strategy of the Polish Republic[13] resulted in another more serious effort to modernize Polish Armed Forces. On May 25, 2001 "The Program of Restructuring and Technical Modernization of the Armed Forces of Poland for 2001–2006" was passed by the Polish parliament together with proper budgetary provisions. Following NATO guidelines, the Program guaranteed a minimum 1.95% of GDP spending and provided a minimum monetary level of expenditure in case of recession.[14] However, no sooner was the law passed, when Poland indeed found itself in the most severe recession since 1991, which forced the Council of Ministers to postpone modernization of the Polish Armed Forces. Accordingly, in October 2002, an amendment to the May 2000 law was passed by the Polish parliament cancelling the minimum spending floor and cutting down the sums intended for equipment procurement in the defense budget.[15] Substantial efforts to modernize Poland's military matériel had to wait until Poland's economic recovery.

The last column of table 6.2 vividly illustrates that real spending on Polish military nearly tripled between 1991 and 2003, befitting a country with a uniquely strong emphasis on its military defenses. The growing burden of pensions and a slowly shrinking military budget as a percentage of GDP fail to exemplify the dramatically expanding scope of Poland's military deployments abroad on UN- (prior to 1999), NATO- (2001–15) and EU- (2005–18) led operations, as well as bilateral deployment in Iraq in US-led "Operation Iraqi Freedom" (Polish deployment in Iraq between 2003 and 2008).

## Poland in NATO and the "war on terror:" assertion of defense identity

The Polish National Security Strategy of 1992 rightly pointed out that instability in former Soviet territories posed a more pertinent security risk than direct military aggression from any country of the region. Though emphatically opposed to Poland's membership in NATO (Calka 1998), Russia could do little to prevent the membership of its erstwhile "ally" in the Western security organization. Russia of the 1990s was famously weak and chaotic, with a disintegrating military humiliated in Chechnya. Poland recognized that Russia understood the "language of power" which related Polish membership in NATO with a thaw in Polish–Russian relations based on mutual respect (Magdziak-Miszewska 1998). This is precisely what happened. Punctuated by President Kwaśniewski's visit to Moscow in July 2000 and President Putin's to Warsaw in January 2002, an era of good feeling and economic cooperation between Poland and Russia seemed to be dawning, though few potential conflicts were specifically addressed.[16] This positive trend was not to last. By 2005 Polish–Russian hostility arose once more, this time over the direction of Ukraine's democratic development. Poland pursued the neo-Piłsudskite "eastern policy" of supporting Ukrainian democracy and independence from Russia. Russia interpreted these actions as an infringement upon its legitimate sphere of influence.

NATO membership created the guise of near-absolute freedom from conventional military threats, and trans-Atlantic allegiance became the cornerstone of Poland's 2000 National Security Strategy, which acknowledged, "In the foreseeable future Poland's independent existence is not threatened; Our country is not threatened by a direct military aggression."[17] Instead of focusing on traditional military defenses, therefore, the new comprehensive formula for Poland's security took into account a whole range of "fashionable" non-conventional threats, including terrorism and international organized crime. Poland was looking forward to upcoming membership in the EU to further reinforce the new aspects of its military and non-military defense. A reformulation of Polish defense documents in 2003 put even more emphasis on a US-oriented coalitional strategy geared towards global, non-conventional threats. Poland was increasing its reliance on NATO, and specifically the US within NATO (Atlanticism), as the ultimate guarantor of Poland's security.[18] This framework emphasized Polish compatibility with globalized defense strategies and actions over Poland's indigenous and autonomous defensive capabilities in local and regional contexts. Given fissures in the Western security community, beginning in 2003 over Iraq, coupled with the growth of Russian power from high energy prices and authoritarian stability, this was a potentially dangerous course of action for Poland to follow.

The events of 9/11 shook the world of global security. US and NATO operations in Afghanistan and the US-led invasion and occupation of Iraq shattered the premise of Poland's new found sense of security. The

Western alliance was fractured in the run-up to the war in Iraq. The overall European political pattern was a balancing within the Western alliance against the Franco-German tandem opposing the US. Given the firmly Atlanticist foundation of Poland's defense strategy and policy, Poland, like all East-Central European, and indeed most peripheral European countries (the UK, Spain, Portugal, Italy, Denmark, the Netherlands), took a firmly pro-US course. Thus, both in Western and Eastern Europe, the weaker or peripheral countries chose to preserve their freedom of action by supporting the US in the "war on terror."[19]

For East-Central European or former Soviet countries, fear of a Russian neo-imperial revival emphasized reliance on the US as the only reliable ally against Russia. This was clearly behind respective countries' support of the US "war on terror" (see table 6.4). Poland was in a group of high-contributing countries, sending by far the largest number of troops among all former Soviet countries in absolute terms, the second largest in relative terms, after Georgia. Estonia, Croatia, and Romania were also high contributors. Among Visegrád countries, Slovakia, Hungary, and the Czech Republic were moderate contributors, with Hungary leading the way. Polish exceptionalism is thus clearly visible in this regional East-Central European context, making the country more akin to Baltic countries, or Georgia and Romania – countries with high security concerns about Russia.

Realist considerations aside, Poland's exceptional willingness to deploy troops on multilateral missions in support of its allies has been conceptualized in terms of "alliance loyalty," the embodiment of a strategic culture steeped in fear of abandonment by allies. Indeed, Polish President Kwaśniewski, in his farewell speech to units deployed as a part of Stabilization Force Iraq, invoked lessons of September 1939, when "Poland was abandoned by its allies," saying, "We will not be allies who abandon our friends in need, as this will guarantee that we, when in need, will not be abandoned in turn and can count on US support."[20] However, in Kwaśniewski's speech at National Defense University on January 13, 2003, he reasserted an Atlanticist interpretation of Poland's partnership with the US:

> Today's leadership of the US in the world is not questioned and it should be exercised. But it should be clearly said that in order to be effective it has to be cooperative and based upon the rules acceptable by all the parties. If these rules are not applied, then leadership can be perceived as hegemony or domination.[21]

Further evidence of Poland's Atlanticism can be found in documents and statements from the Polish Ministry of Foreign Affairs. In the official

**Table 6.3** Polish participation in multilateral missions and operations, 1989–2017

| Name of mission | Place of deployment | Organization/ agency | Duration | Polish armed units | Max. number of Polish troops | Casualties |
|---|---|---|---|---|---|---|
| UNDOF 1 | Golan Heights | UN | 1974–93 | A logistics company | 150 | 0 |
| UNDOF 2 | Golan Heights | UN | 1993–2009 | An operations battalion | 360 | 9 dead |
| UNTAC | Cambodia | UN | 1992–93 | A logistics battalion | 700 | 5 dead |
| UNIFIL | Lebanon | UN | 1992–2009 | A logistics battalion, a field hospital, a maneuver company | 500 | 7 dead |
| UNPROFOR | Croatia | UN | 1992–95 | An operations battalion (mechanized) | 1,240 | 7 dead |
| UNCRO | Croatia | UN | 1995 | An operations battalion (mechanized) | 1,060 | 0 |
| IFOR | Bosnia | NATO | 1995–96 | An operations battalion (mechanized) | 660 | 1 dead |
| SFOR | Bosnia | NATO | 1996–2006 | An operations battalion (mechanized) | 500 | 1 dead |
| AFOR | Albania | NATO | 1999 | An operations company | 140 | 0 |
| KFOR | Kosovo | NATO | 1999–2017 | An operations battalion (mechanized) | 800 | 4 dead |
| Enduring Freedom | Afghanistan | USA | 2002–6 | A sapper company | 120 | 0 |
| ISAF | Afghanistan | US/NATO | 2007–15 | Two operations battalions, a special forces unit, a reconnaissance group, an air support group | 2,600 | 43 dead 361 wounded |
| Resolute Support | Afghanistan | US/NATO | 2015–17 | A training/advising company | 200 | 1 dead |
| Iraqi Freedom | Iraq | US | 2003 | A company of special forces, chemical platoon | 200 | 0 |

| Mission | Location | Org | Years | Description | Number | Casualties |
|---|---|---|---|---|---|---|
| Multinational Division | Iraq | US | 2003–8 | A motorized brigade, a command battalion, a logistics battalion, air cavalry battalion, a company of special forces | 2,200 | 23 dead, 150 wounded |
| EUFOR BH | Bosnia | EU | 2004–17 | A maneuver company | 200 | 2 dead |
| Allied Harmony | Macedonia | EU | 2002–3 | A maneuver company | 200 | 2 dead |
| EUFOR CONGO | DRC | NATO | 2006 | A maneuver company | 130 | 0 |
| EUFOR TCHAD | Chad | EU | 2007–9 | Two maneuver companies, an engineering company, a logistics company, an air support group | 400 | 0 |
| | | | | Totals | 12,623 | 615 (104 dead) |

*Sources*: Kajetanowicz 2013, 242; Polish MON website, http://en.mon.gov.pl/missions. Accessed May 31, 2017.

**Table 6.4** Contribution of the former Soviet Bloc/East-Central European and Balkan countries to the "war on terror"

| Country | ISAF peak deployment | Operation Iraqi Freedom – peak deployment | Total personnel in Afghanistan and Iraq | Populations (c. 2008) | Total troop commitment as % of population (from highest to lowest) |
|---|---|---|---|---|---|
| Georgia | 1,600 | 2,000 | 3,600 | 3,720,000 | 0.0968 |
| Poland | 2,600 | 2,500 | 5,100 | 38,116,000 | 0.0134 |
| Estonia | 120 | 40 | 160 | 1,340,602 | 0.0119 |
| Croatia | 450 | 60 | 510 | 4,453,500 | 0.0115 |
| Romania | 1,600 | 730 | 2,330 | 21,680,974 | 0.0107 |
| Macedonia | 135 | 80 | 215 | 2,061,315 | 0.0104 |
| Lithuania | 200 | 120 | 320 | 3,369,600 | 0.0095 |
| Latvia | 70 | 136 | 206 | 2,270,700 | 0.0091 |
| Hungary | 540 | 300 | 840 | 10,041,000 | 0.0084 |
| Bulgaria | 767 | 485 | 1,252 | 15,217,711 | 0.0082 |
| Slovakia | 293 | 110 | 403 | 5,379,455 | 0.0075 |
| Albania | 140 | 120 | 260 | 3,619,778 | 0.0072 |
| Czech Republic | 415 | 300 | 715 | 10,424,926 | 0.0069 |
| Azerbaijan | 100 | 250 | 350 | 8,676,000 | 0.0040 |
| Slovenia | 70 | 0 | 70 | 2,039,399 | 0.0034 |
| Ukraine | 3 | 1,650 | 1,653 | 48,457,102 | 0.0034 |
| Armenia | 40 | 46 | 86 | 3,231,900 | 0.0027 |
| Bosnia | 0 | 36 | 36 | 3,981,239 | 0.0009 |
| Moldova | 0 | 24 | 24 | 3,383,332 | 0.0007 |
| Kazakhstan | 0 | 29 | 29 | 15,217,711 | 0.0002 |

*Source*: Compiled from various sources, including former ISAF and Multinational Assistance Force-Iraq website, various ministries of defense, etc. ISAF: https://www.nato.int/isaf/ (no longer available). Accessed October 2, 2010. Multinational Assistance Force Iraq: www.mnf-iraq.com (no longer available). Accessed October 2, 2010.

2003 *Yearbook of Polish International Affairs*, Minister of Foreign Affairs Włodzimierz Cimoszewicz stated that: "European security policy can only be developed on a solid foundation of transatlantic cooperation, whose tested framework is offered by NATO."[22] However, in a newspaper editorial exchange in the pre-eminent Polish daily *Gazeta Wyborcza*, Cimoszewicz defended Polish participation in stabilization forces in Iraq, invoking the logic of balancing power within Europe: "this is not just about the pro-American option, but also about our place in Europe: that we want to determine ourselves, not be determined by others."

Poland committed itself to missions in Iraq and Afghanistan and to EU missions in Europe and Africa, and maintained this active alliance through three different governments represented by the three opposing factions of Polish politics – the post-communist "left" (the SLD party in power 2001–4), the conservative "right" (the PiS, Law and Justice party, in power 2005–7), and the liberal "right" (Citizens' Platform Party, PO in power 2007–15). When political commitment to the criticized mission in Iraq crumbled in 2006–8, an even greater commitment to the Polish mission in Afghanistan replaced it. This happened despite the fact that these deployments were clearly opposed by the Polish public,[23] received fairly negative media coverage,[24] and were criticized by a substantial portion, if not the majority, of the country's intellectual elite.

Indeed, the deployments and their fallout generated a vehement debate about the future direction of Poland's security and defense policy. The elite opinion split roughly into three factions, reflective of Poland's ideological divisions: "realists" (the conservative right) saw Poland's bilateral alliance with the US as the centerpiece of Polish security; "Atlanticists" (present in all the mainstream parties) saw Polish support for the US as the best course for maintaining a Western alliance while also serving Poland's national interests; and "Europeanists" (present among liberal right and the non-post-communist left) prioritized European security and defense policy.[25]

Defense Minister Janusz Onyszkiewicz, who served in Hanna Suchocka (1992–93), and Jerzy Buzek's (1997–2001) "right-wing" governments, represented most prominently the pro-American "realists." In his 1999 book, Onyszkiewicz states the US is Poland's source of security and that Poland should continue to cultivate the "special status in the relationship " it initially garnered during the 1991 Persian Gulf War (Onyszkiewicz 1999, 233). However, he also admitted that, "Only NATO is the security structure able to meet the challenges of the twenty-first century" (Onyszkiewicz, 246–7) Onyszkiewicz switched to an even more firmly "realist" position following 9/11. According to him, 9/11 blew the "myth of NATO," exposing a Western European incapacity to act, stating, "Solidarity does not come from formal guarantees but from action."[26] This statement idenitifies the US, with its capabilities and will to act, as Poland's true source of security, as opposed NATO and its "paper guarantees." Through this lens, Polish military participation in Iraq reads as a "test of solidarity" essential for US reciprocal action in the future. This and similar views were expressed in many editorials, including one by Jerzy Jastrzębowski, who rhetorically asked, "Who will help us when in need?"[27] Today, this point of view is especially prominent among the PiS (Law and Justice) right wing party elite and will be explored further below.

The mainstream "Atlanticist" perspective, expressed by Ryszard Wojna's statement that "maintaining the transatlantic link" is the "key task" of Polish foreign policy, as, "militarily, NATO would not survive without the US," takes only a small step back from Onyszkiewicz's realism.[28] Institutionalized in the Polish Security Strategy of 2000 and repeated in its updated 2003 version, "Atlanticism" is the official doctrine of Polish foreign security. Changes to the policy that occurred between 2000 and 2003 are telling. Section 3.2.1 of Poland's Security Strategy 1999 states: "The Atlantic Alliance is the main factor of political and military stability of our continent. For Poland it constitutes a real base for security and defense."[29] The 2003 Security Strategy has a different formulation: "Poland is a part of an allied defense system. NATO and bilateral political and military cooperation with the USA and other main states-members of the alliance constitute the most important guarantee of external security and peaceful development of our country. Our bilateral relationship with the USA is a crucial link in the transatlantic chain." The 2003 Security Strategy goes on to mention the "military and stabilization operation in Iraq" as a part of an accumulated "capital of Polish security policy."[30] Furthermore, section 3.2.3 of the 1999 Security Strategy states: "Poland fully supports the development of European Security and Defense Identity [sic] within the Alliance as a way of strengthening NATO's European pillar." The 2003 Security Strategy contains a somewhat lengthy elaboration of the same idea. Thus, Poland's Atlanticism is inextricably connected to support for the CFSP as a potentially complementary strategy. All subsequent Polish security and defense strategies have subscribed to this view (see table 6.8); it is hegemonic among all dominant Polish political parties and forces. The post-communist left and liberal right (PO) have most consistently embraced this view.

Zdzisław Najder, a former anti-communist dissident and one of Poland's foreign policy pundits, rejects the subordination of ESDP to the goal of trans-Atlantic unity, representing the "European" faction. In a policy paper published by the prestigious Institute of Public Affairs, Najder stated that Poland should support the formation of a coherent ESDP as its foremost goal. He also dismissed the Polish government's 2003 policy on Iraq as contrary to the national interest.[31] His position was most consistently supported by Janusz Reiter, former Polish Ambassador to Germany, who declared that government policies were weakening both trans-Atlantic and European unity in favor of a bilateral alliance with the US.[32] Similar views have been expressed by Roman Kuźniar, former Director of Strategic Planning at the Ministry of Foreign Affairs, who resigned in 2002 to protest Polish participation in the Iraqi War.[33] These views are present especially among the liberal right and (non-post communist) left and gained ground during the liberal right (PO) rule of 2007–15.

Polish opinion-makers and politicians opposed to multilateral overseas mission used the argument that these missions of questionable strategic utility consumed scarce monetary resources that could otherwise be used to modernize the Polish military (Koziej & Brzozowski 2015). In fact, the monetary cost of Polish deployment in Iraq was low: The US covered transportation and logistical burdens; Poland only payed for personnel and equipment. In contrast, the cost of Afghan operations within the framework of International Security Assistance Force/NATO had to be fully born by the Polish side, resulting in dramatically higher costs for Poland. At its annual peak in 2010, operations in Afghanistan amounted to 7.5% of Polish MON spending, while the highest annual cost in Iraq (2004) was around 2.5% of the budget, averaging only 1% for the period 2002–8 (see table 6.5). The notion that, in purely monetary terms, the cost of Polish deployments caused a significant delay in Poland's military modernization, while evoked by many, is disputable (Kajetanowicz 2013: 241–3). More credible is the notion that deployments actually helped reform, modernize, and restructure the Polish Armed Forces, but towards global deployability and coalitional expeditionary counter-insurgency warfare, which may not necessarily have been the most useful direction of Polish military development (Koziej & Brzozowski 2015). After 2011, when Poland started refocusing its defense policy on territorial defenses, this notion was embraced with consensus.

The peak decade of Polish foreign missions between 2001 and 2011 was marked by substantial efforts at military modernization. The steady and accelerating shrinkage of Poland's large Warsaw Pact, conscript-based force, accompanied by an increasing military budget (in real terms), made resources available for this effort. Regardless of the high

**Table 6.5** Polish annual MON budgets, 2001–11 and cost of Polish participation in multilateral missions

| Year | Polish defense budget 2001–11 | | Cost of key Polish missions abroad ($m) | | | |
| | MON budget (part 29) in $m | % of GDP | Mission in Iraq | Mission in Afghanistan | Total on missions | Missions as % of MON budget |
| --- | --- | --- | --- | --- | --- | --- |
| 2001 | 4,673 | 1.89 | 0 | 0 | 0 | 0 |
| 2002 | 4,883 | 1.88 | 0 | 10.6 | 10.67 | 0.02 |
| 2003 | 5,123 | 1.90 | 57 | 4.90 | 61.9 | 1.49 |
| 2004 | 5,437 | 1.93 | 102 | 3.43 | 105.4 | 2.51 |
| 2005 | 5,870 | 1.90 | 54 | 3.50 | 57.5 | 1.23 |
| 2006 | 6,390 | 1.95 | 39.7 | 13.37 | 53.0 | 0.85 |
| 2007 | 7,033 | 1.99 | 39.3 | 113.00 | 152.3 | 2.35 |
| 2008 | 6,587 | 1.68 | 63 | 133.27 | 196.2 | 3.30 |
| 2009 | 7,673 | 1.80 | Na | 261.67 | 261.6 | 3.41 |
| 2010 | 8,423 | 1.88 | Na | 633.67 | 633.6 | 7.52 |
| 2011 | 8,907 | 1.89 | Na | 366.67 | 366.6 | 4.12 |

*Source*: Compiled from various sources, including Polish Mission in Iraq website: http://pkwirak.wp.mil.pl/pl/28.html, www.money.pl/gospodarka/raporty/artykul/afganska;misja;kosztuje;miliardy;wyjscie;nie;takie;proste,244,1,632308.html, SIRI. Accessed May 10, 2017.

and persistent cost of military pensions, – which in the 2001–17 period held steady at around 20% of total military budget – the May 25, 2001 "Program of Restructuring and Technical Modernization of the Armed Forces of Poland for 2001–2006" renewed and adjusted in 2004[34] after the country's economic crisis passed, funded procurement programs, which, for the first time since the fall of communism, modernized the equipment of the Polish military (Bursztyński 2009). One element of the Polish procurement effort, a new generation of fighter-bombers for the Polish Airforce, was so costly (estimated at a total of $7.5 bn – compare to Polish military budget in table 6.5) that it had to be financed separately. In June 2001, the Polish parliament declared the purchase of 60 multipurpose fighter-bombers in a statute that simultaneously established a separate financing mechanism for the purchase. The decision to buy 36 F-16Cs and 12 F-16Ds, over the competing Mirage 2000 and Saab Gripen offers, was made in June 2002,[35] and the airplanes were purchased and fully paid for by 2015. The decision to procure 690 Rosomak (Wolverine) APCs, a licensed variant of Finnish Patria's Armored Modular Vehicle, in turn, was made in December 2002, and the vehicles were delivered by 2013. Many other programs followed, involving mostly land and air equipment most useful for the expeditionary warfare Poland waged in the 2000s. For the moment, the Polish Navy remained largely neglected.

With material modernization, a decisive structural reform was also underway. By 2010, Polish forces consisted of an all-volunteer, small, professional force suitable for NATO- or EU-led expeditionary warfare. The thrust of doctrinal and structural changes was predicated on Poland's safety from conventional or nuclear attack (see table 6.8). During the time expeditionary warfare waged by relatively small professional forces, and not territorial defenses, was to be the future of the Polish Armed Forces (see table 6.6). These premises were becoming increasingly unsustainable as Poland's neighborhood heated up in the East.

It was 2004: Ukrainian elections finally gave Poland its first opportunity to play an unabashed role as champion for Ukrainian independence consistent with Mieroszewski's doctrine. When, on November 22, 2004, Victor Yanukovych proclaimed victory over Yushchenko in a clearly rigged second round of presidential elections, Yushchenko deemed the result fraudulent and called for his already mobilized and organized supporters to take to the streets. The dramatic standoff that developed divided Ukrainian society and threatened a civil war with unimaginable consequences. President Kwaśniewski's efforts to mediate and internationalize the conflict prevented bloodshed and brought the EU and US squarely behind Yushchenko's idea that a repetition of the second round of elections, this time without fraud, would be the only democratic solution to the crisis. Poland, now securely integrated into NATO and the EU, could enjoy a freedom of action to pursue its strategic priorities.[36]

Already, prior to the elections, Poland had shown its ability to stand up to Russia on energy issues – hence, the Russian decision to build an underwater gas pipeline across the Baltic instead of Poland.[37] Coupled with the US unambiguous rejection of Yankovych's claim to victory, threatened with unspecified sanctions against both Russia and Ukraine if fraudulent elections were to prevail, Kwaśniewski's actions created an environment in which Ukrainian pro-Russian President Kuchma agreed to a second round of elections and secured a peaceful transition of power to Yushchenko. Significantly, Kwaśniewski's actions in support of Ukrainians' revolt garnered enthusiastic support from the entire spectrum of Polish political forces and public opinion. His actions were a slap in the face for Putin, who supported Yanukovych and his claim to power to the last moment. For the first time since 1999, Poland defied Russia and won a major strategic battle in their own backyard.[38] This

**Table 6.6** Polish military effectives and structure of forces, 1990–2015

| Year | Total forces | Conscripts | Career soldiers | Civilians | Total personnel | Units (land) | Tanks | APCs and IFVs | Combat airplanes | Combat Ships |
|------|------|------|------|------|------|------|------|------|------|------|
| 1990 | 314,000 | 206,000 | 108,000 | 113,000 | 427,000 | 2 armies, 1 corps | 2,488 | 2,572 | 668 | 40 |
| 1995 | 218,000 | 158,000 | 120,000 | 84,000 | 362,000 | 4 corps | 1,772 | 2,420 | 396 | 19 |
| 1999 | 199,400 | 104,500 | 94,900 | 80,000 | 279,400 | 2 corps | 1,676 | 1,400 | 286 | 17 |
| 2005 | 151,000 | 73,000 | 78,000 | Na | Na | 4 divisions | 957 | 1,384 | 93 | 17 |
| 2010 | 98,000 | Na | 98,000 | Na | Na | 4 divisions | 906 | 1,536 | 132 | 17 |
| 2015 | 120,000 | 20,000 (reserves) | 100,000 | 44,000 | 164,000 | 3 division and 3 brigades | 914 | 1,938 | 98 | 19 |

*Source:* Simon 2004, 88–89; Kajetanowicz 2013, 212 and 218; Polish MON www.mon.gov.pl/. Accessed May 11, 2017.

left Russia resentful and decisively ended the 2001–4 Polish-Russian thaw.

Russian–Polish political clashes over energy issues between 2005 and 2008 strained their relationship further. In August 2008, Russian Armed Forces crushed Georgia in a conventional conflict over South Ossetia, revealing Russian army and air forces, though still largely un-modernized, were capable of flexing their muscles against a determined opposition – gone was the humiliation of 2004–5. In the meantime, Yuschenko's reforms in Ukraine failed to prevent a fair-and-square electoral victory to Yanukovich in the elections of 2010. A new standoff between Poland and Russia over Ukraine was looming, with potential negative security implications for Poland. The writing was on the wall, but Polish policy-makers trusted their special strategic relationship with the US, NATO, and the EU, which had received lavish displays of Polish allegiance between 2003 and 2011 (see tables 6.3, 6.4 and 6.5).

Political turbulence surrounding the American missile shield exemplifies the growing tension between Poland and Russia, as well as the complexities of the Polish–US alliance. Since 2002, US President G.W. Bush's administration had been in talks with European nations to deploy a system ostensibly aimed against Iranian long-range missiles. Interceptor elements of the system were to be deployed in Poland while the radar was installed in the Czech Republic (see chapter 4) (Peterson 2011). For East-Central Europeans, the real threat was Russia, not Iran. Therefore, US negotiations with Poland, which formally started in 2007, were subject to Polish attempts to tie them to a quid pro quo that would involve direct US commitment to Polish security vis-à-vis Russia, or otherwise: a commitment of US aid to strengthen Polish defenses.

Polish domestic politics surrounding the issue are notably embodied in the division between "realist" pro-American conservative right and Atlanticist or "Europeanist" liberal right opinions. Thus, the right-conservative government of PiS, the Law and Justice party (2005–7), represented by President Lech Kaczyński and his twin brother Prime Minister Jarosław Kaczyński, was willing to allow the US to deploy the system unconditionally as a sign of alliance solidarity. In contrast, the subsequent government of 2008–15, led by the PO Civic Platform party and representative of the liberal right and Atlanticist and Europeanist sentiments, made deployment conditional on specific US concessions to Polish security, most importantly, deployment of US Patriot missiles to Poland. The US agreed to the concession, and the US–Polish agreement was signed on August 20, 2008, against strenuous Russian opposition and warnings shortly after the South Ossetian war of 2008.[39] However, the agreement was cancelled by the Obama administration in

2009 (coincidentally, on September 17, the 70th anniversary of Soviet aggression against Poland in 1939), who cited the diminishing threat of long-range missiles from Iran, cost, and technological feasibility as impetus (Peterson 2011).

Polish (and Czech) reaction to the cancellation was mixed. The conservative right was disappointed and felt betrayed. The PO government and public opinion were more relaxed, especially after Vice-President Joe Biden, during a fence-mending trip to Poland in October 2009, promised to deploy SM-3 medium-range missile interceptors (instead of the original system aimed against long-range missile) as part of a European Phased Adaptive Approach. This project, after some turbulence, has continued to the present day. The construction of a $1 billion American base for the missiles, located at Rędzikowo near Słupsk, began in 2016 and is to be finished and operating in 2020. Formally, the project is still aimed against Iran, though a Polish–American understanding of the actual goal of the project – which will be accompanied by a permanent presence of US troops on Polish soil – make it clear that the political, strategic, and potential tactical use of these interceptors involves defenses against Russian missiles. Significantly, the second land base for SM-3 interceptors is in Romania – another frontline state with security concerns about Russia.[40]

By the time the construction of Rędzikowo Base began in 2016, another Ukrainian Crisis had hit Poland's immediate neighborhood, this time ushering in Russian-supported armed revolts in Eastern Ukraine and the Russian takeover of Crimea. A new era in Polish defense policies, which continues to this day, had begun.

## Poland's defense policy today

By 2010, Polish defense policies, military doctrine, force organization, and even equipment were largely adjusted to NATO and EU alliance politics and policies. Poland had a fairly small and decently equipped professional military force (see table 6.6) which participated at unusually high rates in NATO-, EU-, and US-led expeditionary operations across the globe (see tables 6.3 and 6.4). Poland had developed a "special" alliance with the US through unflinching loyalty in the "war on terror." The residual domestic security concern of Russian neo-imperialism seemed inconsequential to a member of the most powerful political and military alliances in the world. Poland was operating under the assumption that they no longer faced conventional regional military threats (see table 6.8).

This assumption was decisively shattered when a new Ukrainian

Crisis hit the region in fall 2013. As President Yanukovich cancelled further talks with the EU over a Ukraine–EU Association Treaty, street revolts erupted across western and central Ukrainian, threatening a another round of instability and repression. Keeping with Poland's "eastern policy," following the pattern established during the 2004/5 crisis, President Bronisław Komorowski and foreign Minister Radosław Sikorski, backed by the West, intervened in the crisis and engineered a political compromise: New elections were to take place. The compromise unraveled, Yanukovich fled to Russia, pro-Western Ukrainian forces took over, and, in response, Russia annexed Crimea, a border state with an ethnic Russian majority, and sponsored armed pro-Russian insurgencies across Eastern Ukraine. The brutal, though limited, warfare that followed featured mixed paramilitary and conventional forces on both sides. It was waged under the threshold of open inter-state warfare, leading experts to coin a fashionable and vague new term: "hybrid war." In this conflict, Russia showcased a modernized military machine suited for this particular form of warfare.

The revival of Russian neo-imperialism dawned in 2013–14 with Poland and other Visegrád countries facing stark realities: a debilitating weakness in their capacity for conventional territorial defense, a similar weakness in their NATO allies, and a waning US commitment to European-NATO defense in material terms (Kalan 2012).The Obama administration's "pivot to Asia" had refocused Euro-Atlantic military efforts on the global South. Compounded by the 2008 global economic crisis, across the Euro-Atlantic world, defense budgets were slashed, conventional militaries dismantled, and remaining military forces further adjusted to global expeditionary asymmetrical warfare, away from conventional threats (Peterson 2011). Poland's response to this crisis stood out once more from its Visegrád neighbors (indeed from most of Europe) in its strength and depth, showcasing a Polish "exceptionalism" further pronounced in the wake of unexpected tragedy.

On April 10, 2010, the 70th anniversary of the Katyn crime, an eerie premonition of looming Polish–Russian hostilities took the form of sudden and tremendous loss. On this day, a Polish delegation composed of President Lech Kaczyński, the military Chiefs of Staff for the Army, Navy and Airforce, the Head of the National Security Office and other vital members of Polish leadership were traveling to commemorate the mass killing of 1940 that had exterminated Poland's intellectual elite when, in a forest near the military airport in Smolensk, the Russian-produced TU-154 airplane carrying 96 of Poland's most influential people crashed, killing everyone aboard. Poland's grief and national unity was met with sympathy from all over world.

The subsequent investigation into the cause of the crash led to dramatic domestic disputes when it became politicized. The apparent cause of the catastrophe was accidental – the airplane crashed in a nasty fog, while attempting to land at a primitive and badly maintained air base, with apparent air safety violations abounding both on Polish and Russian sides. However, because the deceased President had represented the nationalist conservative PiS (Law and Justice) party, led by his twin brother Jarosław Kaczyński, while the Prime Minister at the time, Donald Tusk, represented the Civic Platform party (PO), a vicious partisan struggle over accountability began. Tusk and PO were accused of colluding with Moscow, borderline covering up a Russian plot to murder the Polish President. Rumors that PO was sheltering "deep state" structures, secretly maintaining the former communist establishment, were brought into the spotlight. This vicious feud shoved Polish domestic politics in an anti-Russia direction. In 2015, PiS won both the presidential and parliamentary elections in Poland and "toughness against Russia" became fundamental for establishing credibility in Polish domestic politics.

So, mutual distrust between Poland and Russia was growing before the 2013–14 Ukrainian Crisis. An additional factor was PO–PiS disputes over foreign and defense policies. PO has long advocated for Atlanticism with a pro-European/pro-CSDP tilt, warning against dependence upon Poland's bilateral alliance with the US. PiS takes the opposite, "realist" position, seeing the US–Polish alliance as the centerpiece of Poland's defense policies. Significantly, PO criticized Polish deployment to Iraq, pulling out from "Operation Iraqi Freedom" in 2008, while doubling up on the country's commitment to Afghan deployment, a NATO operation beginning in 2010. This relatively costly mission led to an inevitable restructuring of the Polish Armed Forces towards a relatively small professional/expeditionary warfare-oriented structure corresponding to the actions undertaken by Poland in Afghanistan given objective budgetary constraints. These forces were admittedly ill-suited and insufficient for the traditional task of territorial defense. Thus, contradictory and perhaps unavoidable imperatives of Polish political development and its alliance politics led Poland under PO to follow its allies in creating an essentially Western-style military. The insufficiency of these forces for the task of traditional territorial defenses was criticized before the Ukrainian Crisis, especially by PiS (Sanecka-Tyczyńska 2011; Kajetanowicz 2013).

The Ukrainian Crisis forced PO's government to acknowledge the limitations of their defense policies. Adjustments included a comprehensive Strategic National Security Review (2010–12) with the resulting *White Book of National Security* (2013) divided into classified and unclassified sections (Koziej & Brzozowski 2015). On September 17, 2013, a Council of Ministers resolution established and consolidated a list of 14 priority military modernization programs, confirmed and expanded in June 2014. Finally, in 2014, a new *National Security Strategy of the Polish Republic* was created.[41] Taken together, these programs represent a major adjustment to Poland's defense policy, strategy, doctrine and direction. Still, they were criticized by the PiS party, who have since conducted their own Strategic Defense Review and created a *National Defense Concept for the Republic of Poland* after election to office in 2015.[42] The consensus, clash and debate between these two visions has defined Polish defense policies since 2010 and will continue to for the foreseeable future.

The 2014 *National Security Strategy* put forth by PO repeated the key premises of all previous strategies since 1992, the central goals being peaceful internal and external liberal development and reliance on NATO and EU/CSDP. Professional, fully modernized Armed Forces were understood to be a key element of the defense sub-system of Polish national security. However, for the first time in Polish post-communist defense policy, Russia was mentioned several times implicitly and explicitly as a threat, as a country that does not respect international principles of sovereignty and as possessing a potentially offensive military whose revival comes at "the expense of its neighbors," therefore having a "negative influence on regional security" (Rzeczpospolita Polska 2014: 10, 19–21). The strategy identified hybrid warfare ("armed operations below the threshold of classical war") as a possible threat, with all-out conventional war being less likely (Rzeczpospolita Polska 2014: 20).

The heightened new perception of Russian threat prescribed a strengthening of both NATO and EU policies and response mechanisms. Most importantly, both NATO and CSDP were to be reconsolidated around territorial defense as their primary function, with expeditionary global capacities, though important, as secondary (Rzeczpospolita Polska 2014: 29). Polish Armed Forces, especially, were to possess "full spectrum capacity" focused on territorial defense and deterrence capacities – the ability to impose genuine pain on any potential enemy contemplating aggression (Rzeczpospolita Polska 2014: 30–1). In concrete terms, the 2014 *Strategy* called for the stepped-up modernization of Polish Armed Forces. For defensive technologies, the priority was air and anti-missile defense systems, as well as information and cyberwarfare capacity. In June 2014, Prime Minister Tusk announced deterrent capabilities were to be centered around programs unveiled under the moniker "Polish fangs"; These included up to 400 US-produced medium range (to 370 km) Lockheed AMG-158 JSSM air-launched self-guiding

**Table 6.7** Polish MON budget and procurement, 2013–17

| Year | MON budget (part 29) in $bn | % of GDP | Procurement in $bn | Procurement as % of MON budget |
|------|------|------|------|------|
| 2013 | 9.373 | 1.76 | 2.033 | 22 |
| 2014 | 10.679 | 1.96 | 2.700 | 25 |
| 2015 | 10.840 | 1.82 | 4.500 | 42[a] |
| 2016 | 11.817 | 1.91 | 3.267 | 28 |
| 2017 | 12.285 | 1.98 | 3.333 | 27 |

*Source*: Polish MON website, www.mon.pol.gov. Accessed May 14, 2017.

*Note*: [a] The sudden jump in 2015 was mostly due to paying the last tranche of F-16s acquisition, which was financed separately, hence the unusually high number.

cruise missiles to be installed on Polish F-16s, new submarines equipped with under-water guided ballistic missiles, and a medium-range (to 300 km) HOMAR multiple-launch rocket system. The *Strategy* also called for the rebuilding of a territorial defense force and a military reserve system – both neglected with the professionalization of Armed Forces in 2010 (Rzeczpospolita Polska 2014: 45–6). Otherwise, Polish troops were to be trained for increased mobility and C3 (command, control, and communication) capacity to respond to strategic and tactical surprise. Financial capacity for these new programs was immediately created; the programs implemented forthwith visible adjustments to Poland's defense budget (see table 6.7).

PO's program of reform did not hinder PiS' predictable criticism that they weren't going far enough to protect Poland from contemporary Russian threat. With the 2015 PiS victory in both presidential and parliamentary elections, the conservative right-wing government could create its own defense strategy based on a radical break from the past 25 years of Polish policy. Minister of Defense Antoni Macierewicz, a highly controversial anti-Russian, anti-communist figure, began a wholesale purge of military personnel, accompanied by mass resignations by officers and Ministry of Defense cadres. These and other controversial and damaging moves created the image of a Ministry in disarray, presumably damaging dearly bought Polish prestige in NATO (Ćwieluch & Rzeczkowski 2017). On May 14, 2017, many former Polish Defense Ministers signed a letter which decried Macierewicz's tenure as "sowing mistrust in the military and defense potential of Poland" and calling for his resignation.[43]

On May 23, 2017, Macierewicz presented a new *Defense Concept of the Polish Republic* authored by a team led by Undersecretary of State at the MON, Tomasz Szatkowski. As expected, the document differed radically in term of tone and even format[44] from all the previous Polish strategic documents (Ministerstwo Obrony Narodowej 2017). Russian aggression is mentioned in the first sentence and Poland's dependence upon its military forces is emphasized. The document states:

> Over recent years, our forces developed based on erroneous assumptions. There was a lack of both an accurate assessment of Poland's geopolitical situation and of a sound strategic diagnosis supported by the careful observation of trends in our neighbourhood. This resulted in a wrong conviction that the risk of an armed conflict in our part of Europe was marginal, and that any potential threats would be attributed mainly to non-state actors.

The document went on to say, "The scale of threats resulting from the Russian aggressive policy had not been adequately assessed in the past." This diagnosis, according to the document, calls for radical change in Polish defense policies in order to create defenses commensurate to the existing level of threat, which could supercede "actions below the threshold of war" to include open, interstate armed conflicts (Ministerstwo Obrony Narodowej 2017: 19–20). Polish autonomous defensive capacity is considered crucial, operating in concert with NATO and EU missions, which remain pillars of Polish security, though also threatend by Russian institutional aggression. The *Concept* then engages in a speculative, opaque, and abstract discussion of the EU and NATO as subject to future and unspecified "changes" – perhaps a code word for weakening or disintegration. In this threatening environment "real capacities and actions" matter first and foremost.

The *Concept* goes on to state that Poland aims at spending 2.5% of its GDP on defense, making the country (based on 2016 figures) the third largest spender in NATO after the US and Greece.[45] Substantial new sums are to be put into force enlargement and armaments programs. A new division is to be added to the existing land force structure, while Territorial Defense Forces, modelled on the British system of reserves (or US Army-National Guard), are to be implemented for the first time since the fall of communism. These 53,000-strong Territorial Forces are designed to be attached to particular provinces, where they will train for guerrilla operations in the case of an area overran by an enemy's regular troops (Likowski 2017).[46] Overall, by 2025, the Polish Armed Forces are to be 200,000-strong and superbly equipped, with substantial deterrent capacities. They are also to be led by a new command structure with a Commander in Chief in times of war being also the Head of General Staff.

If we look beyond the *Concept*'s aggressive rhetoric, it is remarkable to acknowledge that PO's 2014 *National Security Strategy* included most of the specific ideas the PiS *Defense Concept* touts as completely new: the emphasis on territorial defenses, the increased spending and modernization programs, and the idea of creating a new territorial defense force with deterrent capacities were all already in PO's 2014 program. This might be a good sign – beyond the heated rhetoric, the evolution of Polish defense policies is perhaps more cohesive and constructive than meets the eye. It is remarkable, too, what did not make it to the official document. Though PiS rhetoric puts a special emphasis on Russian nuclear weapons and Poland's inadequate deterrence capabilities against these weapons, Vice-Minister Szatkowski denied a desire to develop Poland's own nuclear weapons, instead proposing nuclear "sharing," borrowing nuclear weapons of the allies[47] – a statement denied by the MON as mere "opinion".

## Conclusions and comparisons

Poland's geographical position and size, geopolitics in other words, explain a lot about the country's exceptionalism in terms of military defense policies. However, cultural factors and legacies of the past also explain Poland's preoccupation with its military security and fear of Russia. Both structurally and culturally Poland is actually not exceptional but very similar to countries like Georgia, the Baltics, Finland, and Romania. However, as we would expect from Poland, its concern over its military security and therefore the strength of its response to the development of the 2010s was uniquely robust as compared to other Visegrád countries and, really, most of Europe. Indeed, the ambiguity or even pro-Russian character of Czech (President Miloš Zeman's in particular), Hungarian (Prime Minister's Viktor Orbán's) and Slovak (Prime Minister's Robert Fico's) responses to the new security situation indicated an opening divergence between Poland and its Visegrád partners, which, between 1989 and 2012, travelled on more or less the same trajectory.

Briefly, political, military, and defense reactions and policies of the three countries in question did not follow the Polish adjustment – to the contrary, the countries largely followed the course taken in the early 2000s, reducing its military spending and forces to numbers to sufficiently fulfill minimum alliance commitments, generally following the all-European pattern of demilitarization, and, borderline, freeriding on America's waning security guarantees. Conversely, Polish policies converged with those of Baltic countries and Romania – these same

**Table 6.8** Evolution of Polish post-communist defense strategy and military doctrine

| Year | Documents | Premises | Goals | Main/new threats | Main means |
|------|-----------|----------|-------|------------------|-----------|
| 1992 | Principles of Polish Security Policy | Polish strategic autonomy and self-sufficiency as temporary reality | Liberal development | Internal instability | Peaceful economic, social and political development |
|      | Security Policy and Defense Strategy of the Polish Republic | | Integration into NATO and EU | External instability and local conflicts | Sufficient mix of conscript and professional of military forces to defeat external aggression |
| 2000 | Security Strategy of the Polish Republic | Poland is safe from conventional threats. Polish membership in NATO and future membership in EU | Continuous liberal development | Local crises and instability | Sufficient mix of conscript and professional of military forces to defeat external aggression |
|      | Defense Strategy of the Polish Republic | | Loyal participation in NATO and shaping of stable regional and global environment | Non-conventional threats | Alliance solidary, and shaping of global and regional environment. Forces sufficient to fulfil alliance missions |
| 2003 | National Security Strategy of the Polish Republic | Poland is safe from conventional threats. Polish membership in NATO and alliance with the US | A comprehensive approach to security. Continuous liberal development | Non-conventional threats: terrorism, WMD proliferation, international organized crime | Alliance solidary, and shaping of global and regional environment. Buildup of forces to meet NATO obligations. Participation in shaping of global and regional environment |

**Table 6.8** (continued)

| Year | Documents | Premises | Goals | Main/new threats | Main means |
|------|-----------|----------|-------|------------------|------------|
| 2007–9 | National Security Strategy of the Polish Republic and Defense Strategy of the Polish Republic (2009) | Poland is safe from conventional threats. Polish membership in NATO and alliance with the US | A comprehensive approach to security. Continuous liberal development | Non-conventional threats, Russian energy imperialism, Polish demographic challenges, breakdown of NATO and EU, local and regional conflicts | Strengthening and expansion of NATO and EU/CSDP. International institutional development. |
| 2010–13 | Strategic Review of National Security | Crisis of EU and NATO reality of Russian aggression. De-prioritization of international missions and expeditionary warfare. Refocusing aon territorial and conventional/ hybrid threats | A comprehensive approach to security. Continuous liberal development | Non-conventional threats, Russian energy imperialism, Polish demographic challenges, breakdown of NATO and EU, local and regional conflicts | Strengthening of NATO and EU/CSDP. International institutional development. |
| 2013 | The "White Book" of National Security | | Crisis of CFE Treaty | Russian "stealth" neo-imperialism and a threat of hybrid warfare | Buildup of Polish conventional military and civilian defense capacities. NATO troops in Poland. Buildup of territorial defenses |
| 2014–15 | National Security Strategy of the Polish Republic | | Re-prioritization of territorial defenses | | |
| 2017 | Defense Concept of the Polish Republic | | Re-prioritization of territorial defenses | Russian open imperialism and a threat of open warfare | |

countries with which Poland enjoyed anti-Soviet alliances during the inter-war years (Polish-Romanian and Polish-Latvian) – or otherwise shared concerns about potential Soviet aggression. Significantly, the Baltics and Romania, and not Visegrád countries, are recently cited as Poland's chief defense partners in the region of East-Central/Eastern Europe.

However, rhetorical policy differences between Poland and the remaining Visegrád countries perhaps should not be exaggerated – Hungarian, Czech, and Slovak ambiguity or pro-Russianness were often rhetorical, theoretical, tactical, or token, and the countries generally maintained NATO and EU solidarity on the issue of military responses (as expressed at NATO Wales and Warsaw summits) and EU sanctions against Russia.

As befitting a country with a uniquely strong – as compared to its Visegrád neighbors – emphasis on a "hard" military component of defense policies, Poland took a robust and well-funded approach to rearming. However, turbulence in Polish domestic politics – struggles between liberal (PO) and conservative (PiS) right wing parties – unhinged some of these efforts, and ushered in new debates over the direction of Polish defense policies. These struggles happened against the background of a rise of nationalist populism across the world, epitomized by the election of Donald J. Trump as US president in fall 2016, and questions being raised about US commitment to NATO. Still, regardless of the sometimes heated rhetoric that accompanied the rise of nationalist populism across the world, it appears that the newly found Polish commitment to robust territorial defenses and rededication of US efforts towards territorial defenses of NATO allies that began under President Obama will actually continue under President Trump. Just like in the Polish case, it seems that the rise of nationalist populism across the world brings to the fore a lot of heated rhetoric which makes no difference in terms of actual policies.

Reflecting broadly on Poland's post-communist "return to the West" which is in the title of this chapter, one cannot help but point to the tragedy and irony of the whole process. The dream of Polish dissidents and Mieroszewski, after all, was a peaceful liberal Poland that would serve as a bridge between the West and Russia – a liberal Russia, reconciled with independence of its "Western" neighbors, including the Baltics, Belarus, and Ukraine. For Mieroszewski, the idea of Poland as a bridge was the only escape from Poland's vicious cycle of history, characterized by reciprocated hostility towards Russia and a constant fear of "betrayal" by the West. What Poland became after 25 years of liberal development is a reverse of Mieroszewski's dream – a country defined by its relative militarization and hostility to Russia, and with no illusions about prospects for any immediate Russian liberalization. Moreover, in Poland, Hungary, and even in the US and Western Europe, forces sympathetic to the Russian model of non-liberal development are on the rise, even when they are defined, like the PiS party in Poland, by hostility to Russia. Without trying to essentialize geography, if the "West" stands for liberalism and the "East" for authoritarianism, after 25 years of post-communist development has Poland returned to the West, or to the East? Has the West become the East?

## Notes

1 Briefly, as a result of the Spring 1989 "round-table" talks, the communist and opposition parties agreed to share power, utilizing a formula for semi-free elections, a government arrangement which almost guaranteed that key controls over government power – particularly in the realm of security and military issues – would remain in communist hands. However, the bargain crumbled when the opposition defeated the communists in the "free" component of the semi-free elections. With the Soviet-communist empire collapsing all around, the anti-communist opposition found constitutional authority to a significant chunk of executive power (Prime Ministership under a semi-presidential system) while still keeping their part of the "round-table" bargain. As a result, General Jaruzelski became the first elected President of post-communist Poland, replaced by Lech Wałęsa by January 1991.

2 On closer inspection, there were many prequels to this idea in the Polish liberal tradition of the nineteenth century. Polish romantic liberals of the first half of the nineteenth century, and Polish-Russian liberals of late nineteenth and early twentieth centuries (Aleksander Lednicki and Alexander Kierensky come to mind) embraced a similar vision. See Janowski 2002.

3 This structuring of party cleavages was very similar to Hungary's, and very different from the Czech Republic's, where the post-communist left was legally and politically marginalized.

4 As duly noted by the authors of the 1992 *Security Policy and Defense Strategy of the Polish Republic,* no doubt under the influence of Yugoslavian wars and armed conflicts in Russia (1993, 1995), Transdniestria, Georgia, and Azerbaijan.

5 The organization is still very much in existence. See www.visegradgroup.eu/, accessed May 15, 2017.

6 The tragedy of post-2003 Iraq, where the entire military and state apparatus were let go overnight, vividly illustrates this imperative. Also, see Michta 1997.

7 According to Palak and Telep (2002, 16), the Polish defense budget was reduced by 60% between 1989 and 1993. However, according to the Congressional Budget Office ("Integrating New Allies into NATO. Chapter

II. Military Budgets." 2000. www.cob.gov/ftpdoc.cmf?index=2665&type=0&sequence=3, accessed October 21, 2007), Polish defense spending actually did not fall so dramatically as a percentage of GDP, mostly staying at above 2% of GDP throughout the 1990s as compared to 2.5 percent in 1988. What explains Poland's seemingly inconsistent figures is the country's macroeconomic situation: first, a transition depression shrank the country's GDP by about 18% between 1988 and 1991, and then the country entered a period of rapid economic growth between 1993 and 2000. During the depression period defense spending declined in real terms, even though it remained steady as a percentage of GDP, while, vice-versa, during the growth period, defense spending increased in real terms, even though it shrank as a percentage of GDP.

8  In fairness to Wałęsa, he was also instrumental in accelerating Polish admission to NATO. See Lis 1999; Onyszkiewicz 1999.

9  When, in August 2002, Colonel Ryszard Chwastek publically criticized his superiors and the civilian leadership, he was summarily dismissed from the military and subjected to Court Martial proceedings; this accompanied by Prime Minister Leszek Miller's statement promising "no more Drawskos."

10  See Palak and Telep (2002); Michta (1997).

11  This numerical goal was indeed achieved by 2004.

12  "Program 2012" was met with approval by SACEUR and was a crucial piece of Polish effort to gain membership in NATO, which indeed followed in 1999. Whether the Program was a serious plan or a PR ploy to gain membership remains open to speculation.

13  Government of Poland, "Strategia Bezpieczeństwa Narodowego Rzeczypospolitej Polskiej" (National Security Strategy of the Republic of Poland or SBRP 2000), *Zbiór dokumentów – Dokumenty z zakresu polityki zagranicznej Polski i stosunków międzynarodowych* No. 1 (2000), www.zbiordokumentow.pl/2000/18.html, accessed January 24, 2003. This was the first reformulation of the country's national security strategy since 1992. The military reform priority of SBRP 2000 was the same as in Program 2012 – to achieve NATO-like force interoperability and standards. The SBRP 2000 was replaced by a 2003 document with slight modifications – see Rzeczpospolita Polska, "Strategia Bezpieczeństwa Rzeczypospolitej Polskiej" (National Security Strategy of the Polish Republic), *Biuro Bezpieczeństwa Narodowego* (Office of National Security) 2003www.bbn.ogv.pl/pl/document/strategia_bezpieczenstwa.html, accessed March 15, 2004

14  See, see Rafał Domisiewicz, "Modernization of the Armed Forces in Polish Foreign Policy" 2002 www.sprawymiedzynarodowe.pl/yearbook/2002/druk/domisiewicz.htm.

15  The ratio of equipment procurement expenditure in the overall defense budget was reduced from 19% to 13.3% in 2003. Even more importantly, the minimum 1.95% of GDP defense spending goal was reformulated to include all spending on national defense, not just Ministry of Defense (part 29) budget. See Lepianka 2004.

16 Autorzy Rzeczpospolitej. "Polska-Rosja. Po pierwsze pragmatyzm" (Poland-Russia. First of All, Pragmatism). *Rzeczypospolita* (Warszawa), January 15, 2002; Autorzy Rzeczpospolitej. "Dobra atmosfera, malo konkretó" (Good Atmosphere, Few Specifics). *Rzeczypospolita* (Warszawa), January 18, 2002.

17 "W dającej się przewidzieć przyszłości niepodległy byt Polski nie jest zagrożony, kraj nasz nie jest narażony na bezpośrednią agresję militarną" Government of Poland, in "Strategia Bezpieczeństwa Narodowego Rzeczypospolitej Polskiej" (National Security Strategy of the Republic of Poland or SBRP 2000) and "Strategia Obronna Rzeczypospolitej Polskiej" (Defense Strategy of the Polish Republic)in *Zbiór dokumentów – Dokumenty z zakresu polityki zagranicznej Polski i stosunków międzynarodowych* No. 1 (2000). In the conclusion of this latter document we find the following statement: "The safety of the Republic is not under threat for the first time in a few centuries. Poland is safer than in any time of its modern and early modern history [...]. However, indivisibility of security means that efforts to improve Poland's security must start far away from the borders of the Republic. We firmly strive to assure that in the twenty-first century Poland will be not only a consumer, but also a creator of security." These last two sentences were to prove prophetic.

18 Changes that the doctrine underwent between 2000 and 2003 are telling. Thus, Section 3.2.1 of Poland's 2000 Defense Strategy stated: "The Atlantic Alliance is the main factor of political and military stability of our continent. For Poland it constitutes a real base for security and defence". The 2003 Strategy had a different formula: "Poland is a part of an allied defense system. NATO and bilateral political and military cooperation with the USA and other main states-members of the alliance constitute the most important guarantee of external security and peaceful development of our country. Our bilateral relationship with the USA is a crucial chain of the transatlantic link." See Rzeczpospolita Polska, "Strategia Bezpieczeństwa Narodowego Rzeczpospolitej Polskie" (National Security Strategy of the Polish Republic), Biuro Bezpieczeństwa Narodowego, 2003 www.bbn.ogv.pl/pl/dokument/strategia_bezpieczenstwa.html, accessed March 18, 2004.

19 The realist "internal" balancing logic within NATO has been noticed by scholars, most notably Thompson (2004) and Michta (2006). The dictum that NATO's function is to "Keep Americans in, the Russians out and the Germans down" still held in this respect.

20 Aleksander Kwaśniewski, "Wystąpienie Prezydenta RP Aleksandra Kwaśniewskiego podczas uroczystości pożegnania żołnierzy sił głównych PKW udających się do Iraku" (Address by President Kwaśniwski to Troops Departing to Iraq) *Gazeta Wyborcza* July 31, 2003, www2.gazeta.pl, accessed March 18, 2004.

21 Aleksander Kwaśniewski, "Wykład Prezydenta RP Aleksandra Kwaśniewskiego Pt. 'Bezpieczeństwo transatlatyckie u progu 2003r' wygłoszony na Narodowym Uniwersytecie Obrony w Waszyngtonie,

w dniu 13 stycznia 2003 Roku" (A Lecture by President of the Polish Republic Aleksander Kwaśniewski Entitled "Trans-Atlantic Security at the Threshold of 2003" Delivered on January 13, 2003) Biuro Bezpieczeństwa Narodowego, www.bbn.ogv.pl/pl/kronika/2003/01/wyklad.html, accessed March 18, 2004.

22 Włodzimierz Cimoszewicz, "Poland's Raison d'Etat and the New International Environment," *Sprawy Miedzynarodowe – Yearbook*, no. 2003 (2003), www.sprawymiedzynarodowe.pl/yearbook/2003/druk/cimo szewicz.html, accessed March 20, 2004.

23 See various CBOS (Center for the Study of Public Opinion) surveys of Polish public opinion 2003–17, www.cbos.pl. For instance Centrum Badania Opinii Spolecznej. "O udziale polskich zolnierzy w operacjach za granica, tarczy antyrakietowej i zagrozeniu terroryzmem." February 2008. *Center for the Study of Public Opinion (CBOS)*, www.cbos.pl, accessed October 3, 2008. Also, while Poland remains one of the most pro-American countries in the world, the 2003–17 period was characterized by a substantial growth in negative views of the US and its policies, clearly as the result of the Polish deployments on NATO or US-allied missions.

24 For instance, an incident in the Afghan village of Nanghar Khel (actually, Sha Mardan close to Nanghar Khel) called "Polish My Lai" was widely reported and shook the country. Briefly, the story involved the Polish troops deployed to the Pakitka province, who, after a Taliban attack against a US convoy, deliberately mortared a neighboring village, killing six and severely injuring three civilians, mostly women and children. See Górka, Marcin, and Marcin Kacki, Zadworny. "Cztery szybkie w wioskę." *Gazeta Wyborcza* 29/07 2007, http://Wyborcza.pl/2029020,84763,5500609, accessed November 31, 2008, and Kulish, Nicholas. "An Afghanistan War-Crimes Case Tests Poland's Commitment to Foreign Missions." *New York Times* No. 29, November 29, 2007.

25 Polska Zbrojna, "Podziały" (Divisions) *Polska Zbrojna – Żolniez Polski*, February 19, 2003, www.zolnierz-polski.pl, accessed March 20, 2004.

26 Janusz Onyszkiewicz, "Egzamin z solidarności" (A Test of Solidarity) *Polska Zbrojna – Żolnierz Polski, February* 26, 2003, www.zolnierz-polski. pl, accessed March 20, 2004.

27 Jerzy Jastrzebowski, "Zgwalcona Ameryka" (America Violated) *Rzeczpospolita* March 14, 2003.

28 Krzysztof Wojna, "Sojusznicza nierównowaga" (Allied Unbalance) *Polska Zbrojna – Żolnierz Polski* February 13, 2002, www.zolnierz-polski.pl, accessed March 20, 2004.

29 Rzeczpospolita Polska, "Security Strategy of the Republic of Poland" (National Security Strategy of the Polish Republic) *Zbiór Dokumentow – Dokumenty z zakresu polityki zagranicznej Polski i stosunkow międzynarodowych*, no. 1 (2000), www.zbiordokumentow.pl/2000/18. html, accessed March 24, 2004.

30 Rzeczpospolita Polska, "Strategia Bezpieczeństwa Narodowego

Rzeczpospolitej Polskie" (National Security Strategy of the Polish Republic) Biuro Bezpieczeństwa Narodowego, 2003www.bbn.ogv.pl/pl/dokument/ strategia_bezpieczenstwa.html, accessed March 24, 2004.

31 Zdzisław Najder, "Polska wobec wspólnej polityki zagranicznej: Propozycja nowego stanowiska" (Poland's Position on the Common Foreign Policy: A Proposal for Adoption of a New Position), *Instytut Spraw Publicznych Biuletyn* 8 (April 2003).

32 Janusz Reiter, "Kontrolowane trzęsienie ziemi" (A Controlled Earthquake) *Rzeczpospolita*, March 19, 2003.

33 Kuźniar, *Droga do wolności*, 230.

34 The 2004 novelization of the 2001 statute required that procurement spending had to represent at least 16% of the military budget, and had to grow to reach at least 20% of the budget by 2006. Indeed, by 2006 this goal was reached and then exceeded in 2007 and 2008.

35 See Michał Fiszer, Jerzy Gruszczyński, "F-16 Jastrząb pięć lat na polskim niebie" in *Lotnictwo* no, 11/2011 s.38–45.

36 Anuszkiewicz, Janusz. "Ukraina a NATO (Ukraine and NATO)." October 1, 2003. www.cms.org.pl, accessed September 4, 2006.

37 Pomianowski, Jerzy. "Gra Nad Urwiskiem." *Rzeczypospolita* (Warszawa), August 19, 2005, 5–10.

38 Pomianowski, Jerzy. "Gra Nad Urwiskiem." *Rzeczypospolita* (Warszawa), August 19, 2005, 5–10; Copsey, Nathaniel. "Europe and the Ukrainian Presidential Elections of 2004." 2004. *Sussex European Institute*. www.suss ex.ac.uk/sei/1-4-2.html, accessed 14 April, 2006; Wikipedia. "Pomaranczowa Rewolucja." 2006. pl/wikipedia.org/wiki/, accessed April 20, 2007.

39 See Krzysztof Nałęcz, "Wczoraj polski rząd podpisał z USA porozumienie w sprawie budowy tarczy antyrakietowej," August 20, 2008, in www.gp24. pl/, accessed May 27, 2017; www.gp24.pl/serwisy/tarcza-antyrakietowa/ art/4358029,wczoraj-polski-rzad-podpisal-z-usa-porozumienie-w-sprawie-budowy-tarczy-antyrakietowej,id,t.html, accessed May 27, 2017.

40 See Tomasz Smura, "Rozmieszczenie systemów SM-3 w Polsce: skutki porozumienia w sprawie irańskiego programu nuklearnego," https://pulaski.pl/ rozmieszczenie-systemow-sm-3-w-polsce-skutki-porozumienia-w-sprawie-iranskiego-programu-nuklearnego/, Pulaski Foundation policy paper, 2016, accessed May 27, 2017.

41 See "Strategia Bezpieczeństwa Narodowego Rzeczypospolitej Polskiej," http://koziej.pl/wp-content/uploads/2015/09/Strategia-BN-pol.pdf, accessed April 2, 2017.

42 See "The Defence Concept of the Republic of Poland" www.mon.gov. pl/d/pliki/dokumenty/rozne/2017/05/KORP_web_mn_2017_05_31.pdf, accessed May 31, 2017.

43 See, "Byli ministrowie obrony narodowej piszą o Antonim Macierewiczu. "Stanowczy sprzeciw wobec takich metod i takiego postępowania," https:// wiadomosci.wp.pl/byli-ministrowie-obrony-narodowej-pisza-o-antonim-macierewiczu-stanowczy-sprzeciw-wobec-takich-metod-i-takiego-postepow

ania-6027401121535105a, accessed May 31, 2017. The letter was signed by seven prior Polish Ministers of Defense.

44 Instead of gray and boring formatting typical of official documents, the "Concept" was a glossy, snazzy publication, interspersed with dramatic pictures of Polish soldiers and modern equipment in action.

45 See NATO Public Diplomacy Division "Defence Expenditure of NATO Countries (2009–2016)" www.nato.int/nato_static_fl2014/assets/pdf/pdf _2017_03/20170313_170313-pr2017–045.pdf, accessed May 2, 2017.

46 These forces are being created at a furious pace and their two brigades are already in place. The cadre officers tend to come from Polish Special Forces, which gives the new formation a specific ethos and character. Polish partisan and media controversies around these forces tend to be ideological and focused on whether Macierewicz and PiS are not building a "private army" for internal repression. Experts are more concerned about the cost of these forces taking away and diluting modernization efforts of regular operational forces.

47 This idea would eerily return Poland to the Cold War era, when Soviet 180 tactical nuclear weapons were indeed stationed in Poland to be used by Polish troops in the event of an all-out nuclear conformation with NATO. See "Polska miała arsenał broni nuklearnej," June 10, 2016, *Wiadomości Dziennik*, http://wiadomosci.dziennik.pl/polityka/artykuly/198972,polska-miala-arsenal-broni-nuklearnej.html, accessed April 27, 2017. Heinrich Böll Stiftung Warszawa, "Reakcje krajów Grupy Wyszehradzkiej na konflikt rosyjsko-ukraiński," https://pl.boell.org/pl/2016/02/26/reakcje-krajow-gru py-wyszehradzkiej-na-konflikt-rosyjsko-ukrainski, accessed April 27, 2017.

# 7

## Slovakia: politics from the periphery

The national security situation of Slovakia is a unique one, for its entire foreign policy approach was subsumed under the framework of the Czechoslovak state for the better part of seventy-five years in the twentieth century. The one exception was the Second World War period, when it had a separate status under Nazi rule. In terms of defense policy, its leaders had to create the world anew after the separation of 1993. The newness of its experience had historical roots that penetrated deep into the past, for Budapest and the Hungarian Empire had governed the entity in the years prior to the creation of Czechoslovakia in 1918. Thus, its general orientation towards defense policy in the ensuing years was a fresh one but still parallel in many ways to that of its former Czech partner. Defense budgets increased prior to joining NATO in 2004, but a major factor was its need to wait five years after Czech accession to obtain full membership. Following accession, it was difficult to maintain the alliance target of defense budgets that constituted 2% of GDP. Attention to the size of the Armed Forces is also meaningful, for they needed to be ample enough to underpin the new obligations that came with NATO membership as well as the EU responsibilities that they acquired after joining in 2004. Deployments of their forces to Bosnia, Kosovo, Afghanistan, and Iraq paralleled the decisions made by Czech leaders, but the Slovak numbers of personnel were understandably much lower. Matters of concern beyond the deployments included the topic of absorption of refugees from the Middle East and pressures on that topic from the EU. Defense policy for this nation on the periphery of Europe was critical in light of regional and global threats from terrorists and civil wars. Its focused decisions made it a small but important segment of the Western alliance.

## General orientations to defense policy

Slovaks had been subordinate to Hungary in the long period that led up to the First World War. Budapest never really put much emphasis on the socio-economic development of the Slovak-speaking region. Industrialization was not a priority, and thus their areas maintained a concentration principally on agriculture. By the same token, education of Slovak youth received very little attention, the consequences being that the Slovak regions were ill prepared for the nationalist movements and transformations that occurred in the late nineteenth and early twentieth centuries. The Hungarian Empire itself achieved greater visibility and status with creation of the Dual Monarchy in 1867. Although the Magyars achieved a kind of co-equal status with the Austrians, they never accorded more rights to, or took concrete steps in overall development with, their minorities such as the Slovaks. Thus, Magyar–Slovak hostility continued to grow.

Such inattention by Budapest made the Slovaks ill-prepared to take-up a co-equal status with the Czechs in their new state in 1918. In contrast to the Slovaks, Czechs had benefitted from the freedom to develop their own industrial base using the natural resources that were part of their geographic inheritance, and educational levels were higher in the Czech areas of the Austrian Empire than were Slovak levels in the Hungarian Empire. The experiences of Slovaks in the Czechoslovak state from 1918 until 1993 were very mixed. On the one hand, President Masaryk promised them co-equal status and a chance for considerable development opportunities within the new state. However, the Slovaks often perceived the policy of national leaders as benefitting Czechs at the expense of Slovaks. The promise from Prague for more of a focus on economic and educational development of the Slovak areas never really came to fruition. During the Scond World War, the Nazi occupiers divided the Czech and Slovak areas into two geographic units. In the West, they formed the Protectorate of Bohemia and Moravia. In the East, they created "The First Slovak Republic." Technically, the latter geographical entity was an independent state, but in reality it persisted during the war under German protection. Some Slovaks perceived this experience as one that equalized them with Czechs, but the outcome overall was quite different.

Following the communist take-over of the federation in 1948, the experience of being Slovaks continued to be a mixed blessing. For the first twenty years after the communist take-over, their status remained as it had been in pre-communist times. There was lip service paid to their allegedly co-equal status, but the reality was quite different. Ironically, there was an upgrade to their position during and after the 1968 "Prague Spring." Alexander Dubček, First Secretary of the Czechoslovak Communist Party, was a Slovak, and his position during the brief reform period was a symbolic step towards better representation for that ethnic group in the state. A high number of Slovaks also took part in crafting the reform proposals, some of which would have empowered them to a greater degree within the state. Following the invasion by the WTO, another Slovak emerged at the peak of power in the top party position within the state. Gustav Husák remained in power for nearly two decades, and Slovakia did benefit from an infusion of resources that they had not experienced before.

Following the anti-communist revolutions of 1989, most observers expected that the Czechoslovak federation would hold together. The ability of both main groups to co-exist looked to be higher than the capacity of republics in Yugoslavia and the Soviet Union. However, constitutional arrangements were nearly unworkable in terms of the role of both groups. Basically, for any key legislative proposal to pass, it was necessary to gather three separate majorities, one from the Slovak delegation, a second from the Czech legislators, and the third from the combined delegations within the all-Czechoslovak legislative body. This basically gave the Slovak unit veto power over undesirable Czech legislative proposals. There also were difficulties between leaders such as the Slovak Vladimír Mečiar and Czechs such as Václav Klaus. As the result, the "Velvet Divorce" occurred in 1993 and it was necessary for both nation-states to set up their own defense policies.

The emerging Slovak strategic culture was linked to the shared Czechoslovak culture of the period of the federation's life. Like the Czechs, Slovaks had experienced exploitation and repression by larger powers in the neighborhood during both World Wars (Lefebvre 2010, 335). During the Great War, they were under the control of the Austro-Hungarian Empire and were forced to join them against the Western powers and Russia. Some Slovaks joined the Czechoslovak Legion, a move that only occurred after the soldiers broke away from their controlling empire. Slovaks had more control under their separate Protectorate during the Second World War, but it would be hard to conclude that their citizens benefitted from this Nazi set of controls. Given the betrayal of Czechoslovakia through the 1938 Munich Agreement, there was a natural leaning toward the Soviet Union, especially in the Slovak areas that were closer geographically to that great power than were Bohemia and Moravia.

The experience of Slovakia in the 1990s differed from that of the Czechs in one major respect. They did not gain admission to NATO in 1999 but had to wait until 2004. Partly, this delay was related to their controversial leader Mečiar and his very nationalistic policies towards minorities such as the Hungarians. As a result, Europeanization was a stronger force in their defense calculations than it was for the Czechs. EU projects such as the ESDP had a more central role in their calculations than for the Czechs. For Slovaks, the 2003 European Security Strategy was more central in their calculations and overshadowed NATO objectives to a certain extent (Kříž and Chovančík 2013, 50–8). At the same time, the November 2002 Prague NATO Summit was crucial, for it resulted in an invitation to Slovakia and seven other PfP powers to formally join the alliance (Simon 2004, 251). This was a tribute to their progress in creating a defense force and program after the 1993 separation into two states, as well as to their willingness to reach out to both Western alliances, in spite of the coolness of the West to them during the Mečiar period of governance. Czechs were able to make faster progress towards Western organizations in part because they inherited the defense structure of the larger federation in 1993.

## Slovak defense policy reforms after 1993

One of the first items of business for the new state in 1993 was establishment of a Ministry of Defense, for the broader Czechoslovak organization had handled their national security needs in the past. With NATO membership on the horizon, they pursued a radical reform in 2001. It included a constitutional amendment that permitted deployment of Slovak troops outside the nation, for which outreach from NATO had set the stage. Alliance membership in 2004 brought with it a number of other changes. Professionalization of the military commenced, coupled with abolition of mandatory military service. Draftees would not have had the same incentive to perform and move up at a high level as would volunteers. Even though the size of the military continued to decline in a purposeful way, there was a new focus on the creation of specialized units that could contribute in meaningful ways to the collective action of the two alliances that they would join in 2004 (Kříž and Chovančík 2013, 53–6).

## Changing Slovak defense budgets

At the time of the break-up of the Czechoslovak state, Slovak defense expenditures were at a respectable level that accorded with the residue spending levels of the Cold War period and its immediate aftermath. However, there was a gradual decline through the year 2000. In the first few years, this paralleled a similar downturn in the Czech defense budget. A major difference, though, lay in the fact that the Czech figures increased

**Table 7.1** Slovak defense expenditures as a percentage of GDP prior to admission to NATO

| Year | % GDP | Year | % GDP | Year | % GDP |
|------|-------|------|-------|------|-------|
| 1993 | 2.2   | 2001 | 1.8   | 2009 |       |
| 1994 | 2.18  | 2002 | 1.9   | 2010 |       |
| 1995 | 2.5   | 2003 | 1.9   | 2011 | 0.97  |
| 1996 | 2.33  | 2004 |       | 2012 |       |
| 1997 | 2.17  | 2005 |       | 2013 |       |
| 1998 | 1.9   | 2006 |       | 2014 |       |
| 1999 | 1.7   | 2007 |       | 2015 |       |
| 2000 | 1.7   | 2008 |       | 2016 |       |

*Source*: Simon 2004, 169; Kříž and Chovančík 2013, 57.

in the 1998–2000 period, which coincided with their entry into NATO in 1999. Slovaks suffered from a delay in joining that alliance as a formal member, and there was a decline in defense spending in 1998, 1999, and 2000. Interestingly, the upturn began for Slovaks in 2001, as the expectation for membership became more real. The figures continued to increase somewhat in 2002, the year of the Prague Summit, which formally issued the invitation to Slovakia to become a member. However, by 2011 the proportion of GDP dedicated to defense had sunk below 1%. The corresponding figure for the Czech defense sector had followed a similar pattern but one that was not so extreme. In the end, Slovak defense planners had endeavored to close the gap between capabilities and NATO expectations, but their success was confined purely to a short period of years surrounding alliance accession (Kříž and Chovančík 2013, 56).

### Size of the military over time

In the first five years after independence, there was a sharp reduction of the total force in tune with the lack of major regional hostilities and the post-Cold War wind-down. The number of career military personnel remained stable within the period, jumping only in the year 1996. This period coincided with the Mečiar years, and it is apparent that the military force structure remained stable throughout those years. However, it is also true that NATO did not extend an invitation for formal membership to Slovakia, due to the newness of the nation-state as well as the uncertainly about the direction of Mečiar's domestic policy. Had those conditions not existed, and had Slovakia entered the alliance in 1999 with the Czech Republic, Poland, and Hungary, a strengthening of the size of the Armed Forces would have made sense.

**Table 7.2** Changes in the composition of the Slovak Defense Forces, 1993–98

| Year | Career soldiers | Total force |
|------|-----------------|-------------|
| 1993 | N/A | 58,346 |
| 1994 | N/A | 54,223 |
| 1995 | 19,721 | 52,015 |
| 1996 | 25,175 | 45,832 |
| 1997 | 20,816 | 45,483 |
| 1998 | 19,187 | 45,483 |

*Source*: Simon 2004, 161.

**Table 7.3** Changes in the composition of the Slovak Armed Forces, 1999–2003

| Year | Career soldiers | Total force |
|------|-----------------|-------------|
| 1999 | 20,370 | 44,880 |
| 2000 | 15,700 | 38,500 |
| 2001 | 15,200 | 39,000 |
| 2002 | 14,000 | 30,000 |
| 2003 | 14,200 | 30,000 |

*Source*: Simon 2004, 161.

Surprisingly, troop size entailed a sharp reduction in the five years that preceded admission to NATO in 2004. Of course, this pertained to both the total force numbers and the number of careerists. It may be that Slovak leaders did not think they had to prove their credentials to NATO planners, since admission was inevitable after the Prague Summit, at which there was an invitation to a number of formerly communist nations. The 9/11 attacks on the US did not evoke a change in Slovak defense patterns, for there was a sharp reduction in the total force during the following year. Data are available on the number of civilians who worked for the Slovak Armed Forces in 2002 only, and reveal a phenomenon of nearly equal numbers with the careerists. Such a finding reinforces the picture of a nation and its leadership that were seriously committed to reduction of the military and probably the accompanying cost reductions as well.

## Deployments outside Slovakia

Slovak troops, despite smaller numbers than their Czech counterparts, contributed to the regional and global missions in Bosnia, Kosovo, Afghanistan, and Iraq. In light of the small size of their military, they maximized impact by joining, in 2001, the Czech-Polish-Slovak multi-national brigade. This enabled them to partner with very similar Central European defense forces in an effort to combat global terrorism within their own region (Kříž and Chovančík 2013, 56). In light of the delay in their entry to NATO, contributions to the ESDP of the EU bore equal importance to partnership with the Western military alliance. In general, they specialized in expeditionary forces with a special focus on engineering groups and helicopter units.

### Former Yugoslavia

In the collapsed Yugoslavia, the Slovaks were willing to provide assistance within their sphere of capabilities. In the 1992–98 period, 2,600 Slovak soldiers contributed to UN projects in the former Yugoslavia. An engineering group of 400 served in Croatia under UN command in 1995. After the Bosnian War ended in 1995, Slovakia later transferred 120 of these troops from Eastern Slavonia to Bosnia as part of the SFOR operation there. In addition to contributions to the UN, Slovakia also made contributions to NATO. For example, they permitted transit rights to the alliance, and the group of 400 engineers was under their command prior to the transfer to UN jurisdiction. In addition, at the June 1995 meeting of the NATO Cooperation Council, Slovakia made a promise of a 600-soldier battalion as well as six MIG-29 aircraft that were deployable within ten days of their request (Simon 2004, 163–78). Slovakia thus fulfilled Western expectations that nations close to the Balkans share in the responsibility of bringing order to that troubled region.

### Bosnia

Slovak contributions to Bosnia included a 150-man engineering unit in March 1999 (Simon 2004), 194). Their 600-soldier engineering battalion also became part of the United Nations Protection Force, the individuals in it working on road repair and refugee camp construction in 1998. One of their helicopter units operated there as well in an effort to enhance security (Peterson 2011, 66). As late as August 2002, Slovakia sent another helicopter unit with 5 pilots and 16 support staff, who reported to the Dutch (Simon 2004, 224). That unit continued on through the next year.

### Kosovo

Commitments to the KFOR peacekeeping mission in Kosovo after the NATO bombing campaign were part of their contributions to a number of related missions. For example, in 1999, they sent 40 soldiers to

Kosovo, 40 to Macedonia, and 40 to Albania. By January 2001, 127 Slovak soldiers had served in Kosovo under KFOR, as part of the joint engineering battalion "Tisa." In that unit, they cooperated with troops from Hungary, Romania, and Ukraine in a group that helped cope with natural disasters (Simon 2004, 204–24). Attention shifted to the Kosovo capital city Priština by March 2002. A Czech-Slovak battalion worked under the leadership of the UK, as 100 Slovak troops cooperated in that framework with 400 Czechs (Peterson 2011, 72). In the 2002–3 period, they worked on road repair, communications, mine clearance, and construction of civil structures for local residents. Their base in the 1999–2003 time frame was Casablanca camp near Suva Reka in the German sector (Ministry of Defense of the Slovak Republic 2016). By 2008, a Slovak unit of 134 troops had the mandate of projects that protected the Serb minority through a variety of humanitarian organizations (Peterson 2011, 73). In sum, the Slovaks worked with the units of other nations to gain experience and also to maximize the contributions that the military of a new, small nation was able to offer.

*Afghanistan*
Slovak contributions to Operation Enduring Freedom galvanized on August 19, 2002. Again, a Slovak engineering group arrived, as well as a number of airport experts. Their job was restoration of the damaged Bagram Airport. Utilizing equipment that they had brought in with them, they worked with both American and Italian troops in repairing takeoff and landing areas (Ministry of Defense of the Slovak Republic 2016). At the end of 2005, 40 Slovak troops switched over from the US-led Operation Enduring Freedom to NATO-led International Security Assistance Force. At that point, most troops in Afghanistan on the allied side were under the umbrella of the alliance, but many still remained solely under American command. Near the end of the war, all troops technically came under NATO command. Slovak troops linked up with an engineer-mine clearance unit that was part of an engineering company of the Kabul Multinational Brigade (Ministry of Defense of the Slovak Republic 2016). In addition, Slovakia sent 17 engineers to assist with construction projects at Kabul Airport.

Activity continued apace in the 2007–9 period in a variety of locations. They dispatched health specialists to work with the Czechs in their field hospital in Kabul in 2007. In the same year, they sent 47 troops to work with the Dutch in Uruzgan Province, increasing that number to 125 during the following year. Involvement in that province centered on work at Camp Hadrian. Slovakia sent 50 troops to that location in 2009, increasing to 240 by the end of the year (Peterson 2011, 98–9).

Clearly, Slovakia found a niche area of specialization that blended well with the efforts of other allied forces.

### Iraq

Operation Iraqi Freedom was a magnet for Slovak troops, as well as many others from the Western allies. In fact, their troops had assisted in UN efforts for a dozen years before the American-led invasion in 2003. Slovaks participated in a Guard Contingent that gave protection to humanitarian workers with a specific responsibility for creating a stable environment for Kurds and Shiites (Ministry of Defense of the Slovak Republic 2016). After March 2003, a Slovak Engineering Company of 150 operated in the Polish sector between Basra and Baghdad. Poland managed a group of troops from 21 countries, and the Slovak engineers contributed to mine clearance, pyrotechnics, and weapons disposal (Ministry of Defense of the Slovak Republic 2016). In the 2003–4 period, the Slovak group consisted of 70 soldiers, 4 of whom were assigned to surveillance patrols. Additional duties consisted of monitoring chemical, radiation, and biological risks (Peterson 2011, 124). In spite of the multiple challenges in Iraq, Slovak specialists and engineers continued to work there and produce helpful results.

## Concluding matters of concern

It is clear that Slovak defense plans converged with those of its Central European partners as well as with NATO and the EU. Their recent emergence as a nation-state in 1993 made this a remarkable occurrence, for they had a huge agenda in establishing the parameters for their political life in independence. They also experienced the challenge of having a problematic leader whom much of the West and local public opinion rejected, due to his hardline stance against the Hungarian minority. For example, there was a proposal that street names in the Hungarian section of Slovakia bear Slavic-style names and also that report cards in that region be in the Slovak language only. The tradition had been dual reports in both Slovak and Hungarian. In spite of those twin impediments, Slovakia pursued the path to both EU and NATO membership, contributed to the UN humanitarian mission in the former Yugoslavia after it broke apart into several pieces, sent soldiers to monitor the situation in Iraq before the American-led invasion, and provided military forces to the four troubled nations that preoccupied the West in the two decades from 1995–2016. In all of these respects, Slovak defense policy was one of convergence.

Divergence was a minor theme but one that occasionally appeared and became a relevant factor in their own policy and in the coordinated strategies with the West. Given their small size, they could not contribute the number of troops to NATO and the EU that their Visegrád partners could. Poland, Hungary, and the Czech Republic had larger populations, but the Slovaks often compensated by participating in military units that included the other Central European nations. Like the Czechs, they also identified certain unique specializations that differed from those of other partner nations and in which they had expertise of value to the allies, including mainly engineering battalions but also helicopter units. Airport security was another priority to which the engineers often contributed in positive ways.

Historically, the Slovaks had also developed a reputation of being more pro-Russian than the other three Visegrád nations. Partly, this was based on their geographic location in the East, but was also rooted in a long period of unhappiness with their experience in the Czechoslovak federation. This special linkage to Russia reappeared in the immediate aftermath of the Ukrainian Crisis of 2014. For example, Prime Minister Robert Fico attended Victory Day in Moscow in May 2015, a step that the Slovak President was unwilling to take. In turn, Russian Foreign Minister Sergei Lavrov came to Bratislava to help celebrate the 70th Anniversary of its liberation from Nazi controls. In the 1990s, it was apparent that Russia owed a financial debt to Slovakia, and the "deal" was that Russia would repay part of it through provision of military equipment. Subsequently, they sent the Slovaks MIG-29 fighters, Mi-17 helicopters, and equipment for their air defense system. This pattern continued through the Ukrainian Crisis of 2014.

Eventually, those conflictual events led to a partial erosion of divergence. Slovakia reaffirmed continuation of Western sanctions against Russia at the June 2015 meeting of EU Foreign Ministers. The Crimea-centered events also led to a Slovak decision to rely on American and Swedish military equipment rather than Russian (Groszkowski July 1, 2015). By early 2017, the earlier expression of divergence from the other Central European nations abated even further when the Obama Administration sent 3,000 troops to Central Europe in late January. Initially, there was considerable anxiety in Slovakia about Russian responses to the introduction of those troops. There was also concern, however, that President Trump might back off from the commitment, leaving Slovakia in the lurch along with other neighborhood nations (*SME* 2017a, *SME* 2017b). Such a development would lengthen the shadow of the bear and perhaps result in increasing convergence among the four Central European defense policies.

# 8

# Recapitulation: from convergence to divergence and back?

## Historical patterns

The themes of convergence and divergence resound and re-echo throughout both the earlier and more recent political history of the four East-Central European states. As such, they constitute important legacies to defense planning in the twenty-first century. Each country had a common historical experience during the imperial period prior to 1918. However, there were major divergences as well, for Hungarians had their own empire, while the other three were mainly in subordinate status. The 1848 Revolutions awakened a common body of nationalistic and even democratic expectations in each, and the follow through of national independence occurred at the same time in 1918. However, divergence existed in the sense that Czechs and Poles finally achieved their national dreams while Hungarians had to deal with a truncated state. Slovaks were part of a federation but had qualms about whether their status would be an equal one to Czechs. During the interwar period, each began with a democratic or semi-democractic (Hungary) structure, but only the Czechs maintained it until 1938. All succumbed to Nazism and communism, and that meant that forced convergence had taken hold.

Following the Second World War, the forced convergence of high Stalinism followed. However, after 1956 the countries stared diverging again, and in very important ways. Paradoxically, and perhaps surpisingly, Hungary started its path towards the demilitarization of its culture after 1956, while still under communism. In the meantime, Poland and Czechoslovakia persisted as well-militarized communist states, but with a dramatic difference. In 1968 communist Czechoslovakia was invaded by Warsaw Pact countries, in the alliance's one and only true military operation, while the country's military totally stood down, offering no resistance. This was very different from the cases of Poland and Hungary, in which the actual armed resistance (Hungary) or the threat of armed resistance (Poland) were an important part of the events of 1956. In Poland, also, the communist military actually nominally assumed power in December 1981, which was a unique event in the entire universe of Marxist-Leninist countries. All in all, the communist era was very important in the formation of the distinct and different strategic and political cultures of the countries in question, explaining the persistence of military prestige and importance in the Polish system of values, and devaluation of both military spending and military institutions in the Czechoslovak and Hungarian cases.

A period of convergence that focused on liberal values and institutions followed after 1989. In 1989, there was also clear convergence in the elimination of communist controls. Poland accomplished it through the electoral process in mid-1989, and Hungary by the mid-1990s. In Czechoslovakia, a week of popular demonstrations rather quickly brought down the weakened communist regime. Following the collapse of communism in the region, there was a chance for each state to take an independent path with direction from Moscow ended. Czechs and Slovaks parted ways in 1993, as the problematic nation-state created for both in 1918 was no longer sustainable. Three of the four became NATO members in 1999, while the Slovaks had to wait until 2004. All four became EU members in 2004. From then on, convergence probably dominated divergence as a guiding theme until 2012. All four became "loyal" members of NATO, focusing on adjusting their defense policies to the requirements of the "war on terror." For example, all contributed, allbeit in dramatically different degrees, to the American-led missions in both Afghanistan and Iraq. To each of them, that seemed to be the right thing to do after gaining admission to key Western institutions.

## Impact of ideology

Insight provided by liberalism, constructivism, and realism all explain defense policies of post-communist of East-Central Europe. The importance of constructivist and liberal frameworks in explaining convergence in the countries' post-communist defense policies is undeniable: the institutional convergence of post-communist defense reforms and, then, the adjustment of the countries' militaries to the realities of the "war on terror" all followed very similar paths. The countries' respective defense strategies were similar, and based on liberal internationalist premises and goals. The roles of "loyal allies" that the countries assumed were also similar, and came to define their defense policies in the decade between 2002 and 2012.

Underneath the appearance of convergence, though, signs of divergence abounded, only to burst into the open with dramatically different policy responses to the Russian takeover of Crimea and the Ukrainian Crisis of 2014. Poland's uniquely robust, focused and militarized response to the heightened perception of the Russian threat after 2014 could not contrast more with the other V4 members' lukewarm/borderline pro-Russian policy responses (albeit still "loyal" in practice) and, essentially, continuation of the same defense policies that focus on "minimum" loyalty functions in NATO. This difference has suddenly highlighted the fact that Poland and the other V4 countries had really been following different paths ever since 1989: the former with its continuous emphasis and relatively high spending on the military, the latter with pretty much systematically falling military spending and a commitment to a minimal defense posture.

Today, we understand historical roots of divergence in Visegrád countries defense policies, while the concept of strategic culture describes the causal mechanism of divergence. Within the narrow scope of the book's comparative framework, Poland and Hungary stand at opposite ends: one as a country with a strategic culture with a high degree of threat perception from Russia, and an emphasis on military preparedness, the other with behaviorally manifested little perception of threat from any state party (except from unarmed refugees, perhaps) and a political culture in which military preparedness comes last in the hierarchy of priorities. The fact that the countries otherwise converge in patterns of political development (recently, both of them have had populist nationalist governments) makes the difference all the more paradoxical and puzzling, and highlights the importance of a rigorous comparison of actual patterns of countries' behavior – as contrary to rhetoric and grand-standing – as a focus of inquiry. Of course, if we are to believe in Hungary's recent and uncertain commitment to a military buildup, backed by incoherent motivation and unclear planning, a different conclusion can be reached, but our notion of strategic culture makes us skeptical about these pronouncements. After all, this is not the first time Hungary has made loud promises to increase its military spending and even engaged in some increases, only to revert to what seems to be a culturally embedded and long-standing pattern of behavior that actually corresponds to Hungarians' political values and preferences.

In the broader comparative framework, however, there is nothing exceptional about the defense policy behavior of Hungary, the Czech Republic, and Slovakia on the one hand, and Poland on the other. The other V4 countries have behaved like "normal" European liberal countries, skeptical about the value of defense spending in a world that seems to be free of conventional threats, and where social, economic, or environmental concerns and threats appear much higher on the hierarchy of concerns and values. Poland, in turn, has behaved precisely like other "frontier" countries bordering Russia – Georgia, the Baltic countries, and Romania, most prominently. In this comparison, the importance of geopolitics, and therefore realism, in conjuction with a role of strategic cultures in which a fear of subjugation by Russia is prominent, is manifest. Lovers of geopolitics, in turn would respond that the strategic cultures themselves have been created by a specific political geography, and that the insights of geostrategic factors in explaining any country's foreign and policy behavior are decisive. In this respect, Robert Kaplan's predictions about the increasing future importance of geopolitics might be prophetic (Kaplan 2012).

## Current and future dynamics

### EU as a whirlpool of convergence

One EU-related pressure for convergence is the V4, consisting of the Czech Republic, Hungary, Poland, and the Slovak Republic. In November 2017, the Defense Ministers of the V4 met during a broader official session of the EU in Brussels. They agreed that there was a need for them to deepen their own internal patterns of cooperation (Ministry of Defence of Hungary 2017a). Their intentions included the establishment of a joint battle group by 2019, which would enable partnership with both NATO and the EU. Related goals also included achievement of the objective of spending at least 2% of GDP on defense as well as 20% of their defense budgets on development by 2024 (Ministry of Defence of Hungary 2017b). As this group of four states coordinated more fully on defense questions, convergence in the region would come closer to being a reality.

However, the EU by itself made serious efforts to supplement NATO initiatives, and their endeavors often bore the potential to pull nations together more fully than had the Western military alliance. NATO pressures to meet the 2% GDP goal often put undue pressure on the economics of the member states, while its involvement in life-threatening situations such as Afghanistan had led to caveats that guaranteed that individual member states would assist in relatively peaceful areas of the region. In contrast, EU initiatives set goals for member states with less pressure and typically operated in areas in which the conflict had abated. Thus, NATO operations often included a mix of convergence and divergence, while EU missions usually bore a more unifying character.

In the 1990s, the EU had developed the Common Foreign and Security Policy, which looked ahead to some cooperation among the members on joint missions. After the 9/11 attacks, it was renamed the Common

Security and Defense Policy (CSDP), whose name bore a stronger military thrust. In June 2016, the EU adopted a new Global Strategy that included three components. First, they called for member states to develop capabilities that would permit them to be more self-sufficient and responsible for their own defense needs. Second, they promised new financial tools that would assist members in injecting up-to-date defense research and technology into their respective defense industries. Third, they underlined forty-two action points that linked EU and NATO efforts, although the signatories admitted that both organizations possessed different "tool boxes" (European Union 2017a). Such goals pulled EU member states together and pointed in the direction of greater organizational coherence and independence in planning.

One of the clearest illustrations of the coherent pull of EU projects was Operation EUFOR ALTHEA in Bosnia-Herzegovina. After the 1995 Dayton Accord that ended the civil war in that country, NATO had been the principal force for management and conflict prevention under Implementation Force and SFOR. However, the EU took over that project from the military alliance on December 2, 2004, and their involvement has continued under changing conditions since that date. The size of their military forces was 7,000 personnel in 2004 but by 2017 had dropped to 600. Funding for the project came from 17 of the 28 EU members and five partner nations that had not yet achieved full membership status. Goals of the operation were still in tune with the stipulations of the Dayton Agreement, centering on control of weapons as well as demining efforts (European Union 2017b). Member state Poland completed its main activity there at the end of 2010 but still maintains a force of 50 soldiers. Their duties entail training of the local Armed Forces, monitoring of security situations, and joint projects with local authorities (Ministry of Defence of Poland 2017a). After 2010, the Czech Republic stationed two officers at Butmir Base in Sarajevo. One Czech officer worked with the Management Storage Group, while the other completed tasks connected with destruction of weapons (Ministry of Defence of the Czech Republic 2017a). The fact that widespread conflict had not broken out since the Dayton Accord made the accomplishments of the EU more compelling as well as unifying.

At the beginning of 2011, the EU established its European External Action Service (EEAS), which supervised a number of additional peacekeeping missions of importance. Its development had occurred in stages, initiated by the Treaty of Lisbon in 2007. It entered into force in 2009, two years before its official launch. EU High Representative Frederica Mogherini appointed Helga Schmidt to be Secretary General of EEAS and to be responsible for its management (European Union 2017c).

A key EU peacekeeping mission was the European Union Monitoring Mission in Georgia, in the wake of the war with Russia in 2008. In the middle of November 2017, the Polish Foreign Minister accompanied the Swedish Foreign Minister on a visit to that troubled nation, as both had "many qualified women and men" in the mission. They boldly visited the border with South Ossetia and observed the Russian border guards in operation on the other side (European Union 2017d). Hungary was an engaged member of the mission in Georgia, and their Defense Minister paid a visit to the small but divided nation in late July 2017. His discussions centered in part on the interest of Georgia in Euro-Atlantic Integration as well as the Eastern Partnership Program of the V4. Under the auspices of NATO, Hungary also provided one logistics expert to the nation (Ministry of Defence of Hungary 2017c). Thereby, the EU was able to supplement NATO operations in the Black Sea that sought to counter the extension of Russian influence in the region.

In July 2017, Helga Schmidt had also visited Operation European Union Rule of Law Mission (EULEX) in Kosovo in a commemoration of its Justice Agreement and first round of local elections. She emphasized the links between Kosovo and Europe as well as the EU. This was a diplomatic visit of importance, for EULEX was the biggest civilian operation of the EU's CSDP (European Union 2017d). Specifically, EULEX worked with families affected by the earlier turbulence in Kosovo. Since 2008, they had conducted 576 field operations that successfully identified 423 missing persons from the earlier civil war (European Union 2017e). Poland was particularly involved with its Polish Military Contingent Kosovo Force, which consisted of 200 soldiers. They worked to contain organized criminal activity and smuggling, but also assisted local officials in the preservation of order (Ministry of Defence Poland 2017b). Like Bosnia-Herzegovina, Kosovo provided a scenario in which the EU could combine member capabilities in efforts to contain conflict as well as to cope with the lingering challenges from the wars of the 1990s.

The EU pulled together the capabilities of its members in joint contributions to additional areas of conflict in the world. Under the heading of European Union Navel Force Mediterranean, the organization promised a commitment at least until the end of 2018. Under that heading, they would conduct anti-smuggling operations and also train the Libyan Coast Guard (European Union 2017f). In addition, there had been a number of EU missions in Somalia. One was EUCAP Somalia, which helped to build civilian maritime capacity as well as Naval Force Atalanta, which helped to protect transport of foreign products that traveled off the coast and near the mainland. An additional mission was EU Training Mission Somalia, which provided training to the Somalian

Army (European Union 2017g). At the end of November 2017, the EU brought an Advisory Mission (EUAM) into Iraq, whose work centered in Baghdad (European Union 2017h). There was also EU activity through its European Neighborhood Policy (ENP), which focused on sixteen nations to its south and east (European Union 2017i). In light of the 2014 Crisis in Ukraine/Crimea, the EU was willing to dispatch short-term contingents on an air policing mission in the Baltics. They also provided a non-combat operation to Mali, to which Poland contributed twenty soldiers (Ministry of Defence Poland 2017c).

Soldiers from the Czech Republic were involved in a number of these missions and cooperated with military personnel from other EU members. For instance, they provided five military officers to the EU Mediterranean operations, whose focus was containment of illegal African migration to Europe. They also provided a rotation of military personnel to Mali that began in 2013. The operation was labelled MINERVA, and included twenty-five Czech soldiers from the 601st Special Forces Group. They stopped their activities at the end of 2016, but left one soldier there untill 2017. Czechs also engaged in their first naval operation, which pertained to the mission in Somalia. This operation had its headquarters in the UK. The rotations lasted six months and continued through 2017 (Ministry of Defence of the Czech Republic 2017b). This engagement by representatives of the Czech military was symbolic of the commitment to integrating EU missions by the other three members of the V4. The divergences persisted in the nations under supervisions, but there was consensus within the EU about the need to help stabilize these situations.

The EU also worked for several years to set up the Permanent Structured Cooperation on security and defense (PESCO). That organization came into effect at the end of 2017, its goal being assurance to members that the EU had the capacity to act either by itself or in cooperation with other organizations. Its central feature would be work with the member states to develop joint defense capacities (European Union 2017a). Hungary confirmed its engagement with this new program in the middle of November by underlining the way in which it would enhance both Hungarian and European security. Minister of Defence István Simicskó pointed out that reliance on NATO for protection was still primary but that the new organization would be useful in confronting "Illegal migration and terrorism" (Ministry of Defence of Hungary 2017a).

Concrete application of the concepts of PESCO would in part be through the European Union Battle Groups, which had been operation since 2007. Deployment of them had not yet occurred and was contingent on a supportive unanimous vote of the European Council.

Approval by the UN Security Council was probably also a necessity for deployment of these units. In June 2017, the European Council had cited the Lisbon Treaty in its effort to broaden the base of the costs that members incurred in support of the program. Specifically, the BGs would consist of 1,500 personnel who would be prepared for 30-day missions that could be extended to 120 days. The aim would be the establishment of two such units at a time, and they would be in standby for six months. Overall, the BGs would strengthen the existing rapid response capability of the EU, and they could operate in a stand-alone way or in a "spearhead" role that might lead to more widespread operations. Although the goal was clearly the strengthening of the EU's capacity to act alone, they would also make NATO more effective in related operations (European Union 2017a). Czech planners in 2017 explicitly stated that they would maintain a battalion size task force that could support either an EU Battle Group or the NATO Response Force, as both centered on rapid reaction capabilities (Ministry of Defence of the Czech Republic 2017c).

It is probable that the Ukrainian-Crimean Crisis of 2014 and after prompted increased EU awareness of the value of affirming both PESCO and the BGs. Planners were also careful to mention that increasing EU military capacities would not undermine or conflict with existing and long-standing NATO projects and commitments. Both alliances met in Warsaw in July 2016, resulting in a joint declaration that enumerated the common threats that each confronted. Common work in three pilot countries would center on Bosnia-Herzegovina, Moldova, and Tunisia. The first had experienced a tragic civil war in the early 1990s, while the second faced occasional Russian provocations, and the last was perhaps the most successful Middle East nation to have weathered the Arab Spring revolts. The first joint exercises were held in October 2017, while communication improvements included improved dialogue between the NATO Defence Planning Process and the EU Capability Development Plan (European Union 2017j). The 2012 Hungarian National Military Strategy also made NATO-EU cooperation into an explicit goal, for membership in both together made it possible for Hungary to possess capabilities that they could not afford by themselves (Ministry of Defence of Hungary 2017a). Similarly, Czechs underlined the importance of con-tributing to both alliances in order to help stabilize "volatile regions," a label that made increasing sense after the events of 2014 (Ministry of Defence of the Czech Republic 2017c). Even in their 2015 "Long-Term Perspective," the Czechs had highlighted the need for "greater NATO and EU responsiveness" in order to accomplish twelve important goals (Ministry of Defence of the Czech Republic 2017d). In the earlier 2012

Czech Defence Strategy, there was a sense that America's pivot to Asia made reliance on solely European resources a greater need in the future (Ministry of Defence of the Czech Republic 2017e). The EU would need to upgrade capabilities but still preserve its strong role in tandem with NATO.

In conclusion, the sharply increased attention of the EU to security and defense questions after 2014 added an additional component of convergence to the V4 states and their neighbors. Pre-existing alliance commitments to NATO were still overwhelmingly important, but supplementary commitments within the EU framework would strengthen the collective spirit of the twenty-two states that belonged to both organizations.

### Nationalism as a waterfall of divergence

A searing crisis of identity in Europe has recently produced intense and, at times, extreme nationalist movements and political parties. The long lines of refugees seeking entry into the more developed European states generated in part a "return of the politics of fear," while the extremist nationalist leaders rode "the wave of instability." Targets of the nationalist wrath included both the classical political parties and "the abstract bureaucracy of Brussels" (Postelnicescu 2016, 203–7). Further, these destabilizing dynamics brought important questions of security to the surface. In effect, there was a triple crisis of "migration-security-identity," and many perceived the weakened sense of national identity as a threat to state security. In the Copenhagen School, "securitization" entailed perceptions by elites and the public that unchecked migration undermined national identity in a way that made security problematic (Bogdan, Mera, and Oroian 2014, 111–16). In the end, the combination of a huge refugee influx, eruptions of nationalism, and threats to national identity and security became a volatile mix that infected the V4 nations in continuously disruptive ways.

Events in wider Europe also impinged on attitudes within the four East-Central European states. For example, the UK held a referendum on withdrawal from the EU on June 23, 2016: there was irony in this vote in light of the fact that they had joined the pan-European structure over forty years earlier after rejection by the organization through two vetoes of their membership. This Brexit movement sparked even more activity among a number of far-right movements in Europe. None of these groups understood refugees to be a part of the nations into which they had entered, joined, or attained citizenship (Howard 2016, 3). Importantly, the German nation that had admitted so many refugees in 2015 and after, experienced the emergence of sharp domestic resistance to the massive admission of so many persons from countries whose populations were principally Muslim in belief. In 2013, the AfD entered the political fray as a party that resisted the official governmental policy of open borders to so many. Their anti-immigrant emphasis led to their election and entry into 14 of 16 state parliaments just prior to the 2017 national elections. In those national elections, they garnered 94 seats out of a national total of 709. Even though Chancellor Merkel had considerable difficulty negotiating with smaller political parties to form a governing coalition, there was no prospect that the AfD would receive an invitation to enter a coalition. Some observers concluded that there was a blue/red division that paralleled the same divide within the American political system. In the eastern part of Europe, the "red" nationalist parties were "lurching to the right" (USATODAY 2017). As such, the affected nations became enormously problematic for the EU, especially in light of the Brexit withdrawal and the rise of an ultra-nationalist political party in Germany.

In 2014–17, each of the four Visegrád states held critical elections, all characterized by powerful nationalist movements that paralleled Brexit in the UK and the AfD in Germany. In each of the elections, strong undercurrents of nationalism played a role in the election process and outcome: the policy impact was probably greatest in Hungary and Poland. This evidence makes clear that expressions of nationalist extremism characterized the entirety of Europe.

In 2014, Hungary held general elections that reinstated Fidesz as the dominant parliamentary party and its leader Viktor Orbán as, once again, Prime Minster. Fidesz won 133 of the 199 seats in the legislature; other parties winning seats included Unity with 38, Jobbik with 23, and LMP with 5. Orbán had already developed a reputation for his strong nationalist views, and made a follow-up decision during the next year to build a wall that would keep the huge refugee flow out of his nation. This move was in sharp contrast to the German decision: many refugees who had been blocked in the Budapest train station were released and then made their way across the open border into the Munich train station. János Áder had been elected President of Hungary by the National Assembly in 2012 and won re-election in 2017. Ironically, one charge against him in his re-election campaign was that he had demonstrated too much passivity on the refugee issue when the EU called for national quotas on numbers of refugees in 2016. Clearly, the refugee issue had become the touchstone of political controversy for Hungarian voters.

In Poland, the Law and Justice Party (PiS) became the centerpiece of nationalist viewpoints as well as resistance to refugees. Its Chair was Jarosław Kaczyński, the key player behind the scenes, with a powerful impact on the elected officials. He ensured with his personal force that the party leaders would remain "conservative and Euroskeptic." His comments about the personal habits of the migrants were very demeaning, and he did not think they could bring anything of value into Poland (BBC 2015). Thus, reassertion of national control as well as identity were the primary values incorporated as a means of resistance against the liberalism of other Polish political parties and the pressure from EU bureaucracy (*Politico* 2017). In the 2015 elections, PiS won 235 of the 460 seats and thus was able to govern by itself. PO had been the governing party but was able to win only 138 seats in 2015. The new Prime Minister was Beata Szydło, who replaced Ewa Kopacz. Poles elected a new President also in 2015, Andrzej Duda of PiS. He gave up party membership after his election but stayed consistent with his resistance to the EU quota on immigrants. Clearly the nationalist movement had acquired considerable power in Poland.

Slovak elections were held in 2015, and a four-party coalition emerged as a result. Smer-SD continued in power with Prime Minister Robert Fico, winning 49 seats out of 150. Coalition partners included SNS with 15 seats, Most-Hid with 11, and # Network with 10. Thus, the governing coalition controlled 85 of the 150 seats in the national legislature. During the election campaign, Smer-SD assumed an anti-immigrant stance, but it was a moderate approach in contrast with the prevailing attitudes in Hungary and Poland. During the previous year, Andrej Kiska had won the election as the Slovak President, but was independent of the political party system and essentially had come into politics from a business background.

In October 2017, the Czech political system endured a major upheaval, with the previously governing Czech Social Democratic Party (ČSSD) garnering only 7.3% of the popular vote and 15 seats out of a total of 200 in the legislature. Action of Dissatisfied Citizens and its leader Andrej Babiš won 29.6% of the vote and earned 78 seats. Babiš had created that political party in 2012 and had served as Finance Minister in the government for the previous four years. His personal wealth was based on holdings of important industries as well as two newspapers, a radio station, and a TV network. His attitudes included resistance to refugees, unwillingness to embrace the euro, and a clear "no" on continued sanctions against Russia (*The New York Times* 2017). The Czech President was Miloš Zeman, who appointed Babiš as Premier in December, even though the Action of Dissatisfied Citizens leader had not yet put together a governing coalition with other political partners. It was then imperative that the new leader would be successful in forging a working coalition after his own personal appointment (*iDnes*, December 6, 2017). Zeman himself had proven to be unpredictable in a number of other ways. For example, he recognized Jerusalem as the capital of Israel shortly after the announcement by President Trump of the US that he would do the same. In doing so, Zeman accused the other EU states of being "cowards." However, the Czech Foreign Ministry responded by saying that the Czech President could only make that kind of decision after consultation with other "regional partners" (*The Times of Israel* 2017). Would these Czech election results push the nation towards the Polish and Hungarian example, or would the eventual coalition force a moderation in such views? Most importantly, as the drift towards nationalist populism is not just limited to V4 countries, but Europe-wide, should we see it as a force of divergence, or, paradoxically, convergence? The rise of nationalist-populism certainly brings a prospect of upsetting defense policies based on Western-Europe-oriented liberal-internationalist principles and institutions, which have dominated V4 countries since the end of the Cold War.

## Conclusion

Will the whirlpool of convergence or the waterfall of divergence prove to be the stronger force in future defense policy for the East-Central European nations? One answer might be that it would depend on the country. Poland and Hungary appeared to be characterized by more powerful nationalist forces of divergence than did either the Slovak Republic or the Czech Republic. However, as the detailed analysis of Polish and Hungarian defense policies has shown, one has to carefully distinguish between rhetorical and actual behavioral realities in the most recent Hungarian and Polish defense policies. Indeed all V4 countries show signs of continuity of policies based on persistence of strategic cultures and institutional routines created on the basis of post-Cold War liberal internationalism. Still, untrammeled forces of nationalism have become so powerful a factor on both sides of the Atlantic that their explosive development threatens to undermine the key institutions of trans-Atlantic and European cooperation, without which liberal internationalism is unimaginable. Alternatively, the answer might also center on the temporal nature both of the refugee issue and of the related disenchantment with the EU, which would point towards more convergence. Convergent forces such as NATO, the EU, and Visegrád might take the lead in intertwining nations of East and West Europe in ways that would overcome the strong divisive forces. A security crisis that affected all might be a force that pushed them in the same direction, but the experience of working together each day on mutual defense challenges and issues might have the same result!

# References

Aggestam, Lisbeth. 2004. *A European Foreign Policy? Role Conception and the Politics of Identity in Britain, France, and Germany.* Stockholm Studies in Politics, vol. 106. Stockholm: Stockholm University Department of Political Science.

Agnew, Hugh. 2004. *The Czechs and the Lands of the Bohemian Crowns.* Stanford, California: Hoover Institution Press.

Allen, Paul. 2010. *Katyn: Stalin's Massacre and the Triumph of Truth.* Dekalb, IL: Northern Illinois University Press.

Bak, János. 1990. "The Late Medieval Period 1382–1526." In: *A History of Hungary,* edited by Peter Sugar, Pétér Hanák, and Tibor Frank. Bloomington and Indianapolis: Indiana University Press.

Baka, Igor. 2006. *Slovenská Republika a nacistická agresia proti Pol'sku.* Bratislava: Vojenský historcký ústav.

Barany, Zoltan. 1993. *Soldiers and Politics in Eastern Europe 1945–90: The Case of Hungary.* New York: St. Martin's Press.

—. 1995. "The Military and Security Legacies of Communism." In: *The Legacies of Communism in Eastern Europe,* edited by Zoltan Barany and Ivan Volgyes. Baltimore: The Johns Hopkins University Press.

Bažant, Jan, Nina Bažantová, and Frances Starn. 2010. *The Czech Reader.* Durham: Duke University Press.

BBC. 2015. "Poland Elections: Conservatives Secure Decisive Win." October 26. www.bbc.com (Accessed May 2, 2017).

Békés, Csaba. 2010. "The 'Prague Spring,' Hungary and the Warsaw Pact." In: *The Prague Spring and the Warsaw Pact Invasion of Czechoslovakia, 1968: Forty Years Later,* compiled and edited by M. Mark Stolarik. Mundelein, Illinois: Bolchazy-Carducci Publishers, Inc.

Beneš, Václav. 1973. "Czechoslovak Democracy and its Problems, 1918–1920." In: *A History of the Czechoslovak Republic, 1918–1948,* edited by Victor S. Mamatey and Radomír Luža. Princeton, New Jersey: Princeton University Press.

Bernád, Dénes, and Charles Kliment. 2015. *Magyar Warriors: The History of Royal Hungarian Armed Forces, Vol. 1,* Warwick: Helion & Company.

Beschloss, Michael, and Strobe Talbott. 1993. *At The Highest Levels: The*

*Inside Story of the End of the Cold War*. Boston, MA: Little, Brown, and Company.

Biró, István. 2005, March 18. "The National Security Strategy and Transformation of the Hungarian Defense Forces," USAWC Strategy Research Project http://handle.dtic.mil/100.2/ADA432740 (Accessed July 14, 2017).

Bischof, Gunter, Stefan Karner, and Peter Ruggenthaler. 2010. "Introduction and Historical Context." In: *The Prague Spring and the Warsaw Pact Invasion of Czechoslovakia*, edited by Gunter Bischof and Stefan Karner, Ruggenthaler. Lanham, Maryland: Lexington Books.

Bogdan, Ioan, Maria Claudia Mera, and Florin Ioan Oroian. 2014. "Determinations and Conditionality in the Context of the Migration in the European Union." *Eurolines*, 18: 111–26.

Braham, Randolph. 2000. *The Politics of Genocide: The Holocaust in Hungary*. Condensed edition. Detroit: Wayne State University Press.

*The Budapest Beacon*. 2017. "Hungary to Increase Military Spending in 2018," http://budapestbeacon.com/news-in-brief/hungary-increase-military-spend ing-2018/46796 (Accessed July 25, 2017).

Bursztyński, Andrzej. 2009. " Charaksterstyka budżetu MON latach 2001–2008." *Zeszyty naukowe Akademii Marynarki Wojennej*, 50: 57–86.

Calka, Marek. 1998. "Polska-Rosja-Ukraina: Perspektywy, Szanse i Zagrozenia." In: *Polska i Rosja. Strategiczne sprzecznosci i możliwości dialogu*, edited by Agnieszka Magdziak-Miszewska. Warszawa: Centrum Stosunków Miedzynarodowych. Instytut Spraw Publicznych.

Calopareanu, Gheorghe. 2011. "The Visegrád Gorup Security Policy During the Euro-Atlantic Structrures Pre-Accession Period." *Buletin Stiinfic*, 2: 93–9.

Chodakiewicz, Jan Marek. 2012. *Intermarium: The Land Between the Black and Baltic Seas*. New Brunswick, NJ: Transaction Books.

Crane, Keith. 1987. "Military Spending in Czechoslovakia, Hungary and Poland." Rand Paper Series, vol. P-73161. 35.

Csiki, Tamás. 2015. "Lessons Learnt and Unlearnt. Hungary's 15 Years in NATO." In: *Newcomers No More? Contemporary NATO and the Future of Enlargement from the Perspective of "Post-Cold War" Members*, edited by Robert Czulda and Marek Madej. Warsaw-Prague-Brussels: Nato public diplomacy division.

Ćwieluc, Juliusz, and Grzegorz Rzeczkowski. 2017. "Nato nie ma zgody." *Polityka* (Warszawa) 03/29–04/04, 10–13.

Davies, Norman. 1982. *God's Playground: A History of Poland*. New York: Columbia University Press.

—. (2005), *Rising '44: The Battle for Warsaw*. London: Penguin Books.

Deák, István. 1990. "The Revolution and the War of Independence." In: *A History of Hungary*, edited by Peter Sugar, Pétér Hanák, and Tibor Frank. Bloomington and Indianapolis: Indiana University Press.

Dmowski, Roman. 1991 [1908]. *Niemcy, Rosja a kwestia polska*. Warszawa: Instytut Wydawniczy "Pax."

—. 2009 [1925]. *Polityka polska i odbudwanie państwa*. Warszawa: Neriton.

Domber, Gregory. 2014. *Empowering Revolution: America, Poland and the End of the Cold War*. The New History of the Cold War. Chapel Hill: University of North Carolina, Chapel Hill.

Doyle, Michael. 1986. "Liberalism and World Politics." *American Political Science Review*, 80, no. 4, December: 1151–69.

Dreisziger, N.F. 1972. "New Twist to an Old Riddle: The Bombing of Kassa (Košice), June 26, 1941". *The Journal of Modern History*, 44, no. 2: 232–59.

Dudek, Antoni. 2003. *Stan Wojenny w Polsce 1981–83*. Warszawa: Instytut Pamięci Narodowej.

European Union 2017a. "EU Security and Defence Package." December 2. www.eeas.europa.eu(Accessed 2017).

—. 2017b. "EU Military Operation in Bosnia and Herzegovina (Operation EUFOR ALTHEA)." December 3. www.eeas.europa.eu (Accessed 2017).

—. 2017c. "About the European External Action Service (EEAS)." December 3. www.eeas.europa.eu (Accessed 2017).

—. 2017d. "EU Monitoring Missions." December 2. www.eumm.eu (Accessed 2017).

—. 2017e. "Ending the Agony of Uncertainty in Kosovo: EU Leads the Efforts in Identifying the Missing." December 3. www.eeas.europa.eu (Accessed 2017).

—. 2017f. "EU extends and enhances mandate of Mediterranean anti-smuggling operation." December 2. www.eeas.europa.eu (Accessed 2017).

—. 2017g. "Three EU Missions in Somalia." December 3. www.eeas.europa.eu (Accessed 2017).

—. 2017h. "Civilian CSDP Missions: EUAM Iraq." December 3. www.eeas.europa.eu (Accessed 2017).

—. 2017i. "ENP (European Neighborhood Policy." December 3. www.eeas.europa.eu (Accessed 2017).

—. 2017j. "EU-NATO Cooperation." December 2. www.eeas.europa.eu (Accessed 2017).

Felkay, Andrew. 1997. *Out of Russian Orbit: Hungary Gravitates to the West*. Westport, CT: Greenwood Press.

Fried, Marvin Benjamin. 2014. *Austro-Hungarian War Aims in the Balkans*. London: Palgrave-Macmillan.

Fryer, Peter. 1956. *Hungarian Tragedy* (London: Dobson Books Ltd).

Gati, Charles. 2006. *Failed Illusions: Moscow, Washington, Budapest, and the 1956 Hungarian Revolt* (Cold War International History Project Series). Stanford: Stanford University Press.

Gazdag, Ferenc. 1994. "The New Security and Defense Policies of Hungary." *European Security*, 3, no. 2, 19 October: 350.

Germuska, Pál. 2015. *Unified Military Industries of the Soviet Bloc: Hungary and the Division of Labor in Military Production*. The Harvard Cold War Studies Book Series. Lanham, Maryland: Lexington Books.

Goldgeier, James. 1999. *Not Whether but When. The US Decision to Enlarge NATO*. Washington, D.C.: Brookings Institution Press.

Gray, Colin. 1999. "Strategic Culture as Context: The First Generation of Theory Strikes Back." *International Affairs*, 7, no. 1: 46–69.

Gross, Jan. 1988. *Revolution From Abroad: The Soviet Conquest of Polish Western Ukraine and Western Belarussia*. Princeton: Princeton University Press.

Groszkowski, Jakub. 2015. "Prime Minister Fico's Russian Card." *Ośrodek Studiów Wschodnich, im Marka Karpia*. July 1. www.osw.waw.pl/en/publikacje/osw-commentary/2015-07-01/prime-minister-ficos-russian-card (Accessed January 5, 2016).

Gyulá, Razsó. 1982. "The Mercenary Army of King Matthias Corvinus." In: *From Hunyadi to Rakoczi: War and Society in Late Medieval and Early Modern Hungary*, edited by János Bak and Béla Király. New York: Brooklyn College Press.

Hajdú, Tibor, and Zsuzsa Nagy. 1990. "Revolution, Counter-Revolution; Consolidation." In: *A History of Hungary*, edited by Peter Sugar, Pétér Hanák, and Tibor Frank. Bloomington and Indianapolis: Indiana University Press.

Hanebrink, Paul. 2005. "'Christian Europe' and National Identity in Interwar Hungary." In: *Constructing Nationalities in East-Central Europe*, edited by Pieter Judson, and Marsha Rozenblit. New York: Berghahn Books.

Harna, Josef. 2009. "First Czechoslovak Republic." In: *A History of the Czech Lands*, edited by Jaroslav Pánek and Oldřich Tůma, 395–415. Prague: Karolinum Press.

Havel, Václav, and John Keane. 1985. *The Power of the Powerless: Citizens Against the State in Central and Eastern Europe*. Abingon: Routledge.

Hendrickson, Ryan. 2000. "NATO's Višegrad Allies: The First Test in Kosovo." *The Journal of Slavic Military Studies*, 13, no. 2, June: 25–38.

Hetherington, Peter. 2012. *Unvanquished: Joseph Piłsudski, Resurrected Poland, and the Struggle for Eastern Europe*. Houston: Pingora Press.

Hey, Jeanne. 2003. "Introducing Small State Foreign Policy." In: *Small States in World Politics: Explaining Foreign Policy*, edited by Jeanne Hey. Boulder, London: Lynne Rienner Publishers.

Howard, Duncan. 2016. "Editorial." *International Migration*, 54, no 4.

Hungarian Republic Ministry of Defense. 2009. "2009 Magyarország Nemzeti Katonai Stratégiája" mhtt.eu/hadtudomany/2009/1_2/033-046.pdf (Accessed January 7, 2017).

—. 2012. "2012 Magyarország Nemzeti Katonai Stratégiája" www.kormany.hu/download/a/40/00000/nemzeti_katonai_strategia.pdf (Accessed March 7, 2017), translated as "Hungarian National Military Strategy." http://2010-2014.kormany.hu/download/b/ae/e0000/national_military_strategy.pdf. (Accessed March 7, 2017).

*iDnes*. 2017. "Babišův Velký Den: Stal se Premiérem, Zeman ho Podpoří ve Sněmovně." www.idnes.cz. (Accessed December 6, 2017).

Interview with Michael Žantovský. 2016. "On the Role of the Višegrad Group and Havel's Legacy," *New Eastern Europe*. August 4.

Janowski, Maciej. 2002. *Polish Liberal Thought Before 1918*. Budapest: Central European University Press.

Jaszay, Béla, Péter Fodor, and Zoltán Lakner. 2009. "Hungarian Military Economy in the Twentieth Century: Lessons and Experience." *AARMS*, 8, no. 2: 231–48.

Jeszenszky, Géza. 1990. "Hungary Through World War I and the End of Dual Monarchy." In: *A History of Hungary*, edited by Peter Sugar, Pétér Hanák, and Tibor Frank. Bloomington and Indianapolis: Indiana University Press.

—. 1996. "Hungary's Bilateral Treaties with the Neighbours," *Ethnos-Nation. Eine europäische Zeitschrift* (1–2) www.hungarianhistory.com/lib/jeszenszky/jesz5.pdf (Accessed August 7, 2017).

Jones, Christopher. 1981. *Soviet Influence in Eastern Europe: Political Autonomy and the Warsaw Pact*. Santa Barbara, CA: Praeger.

Jones, Nate. 2016. *Able Archer*. New York: The New Press.

Jowitt, Ken. 1993. *The New World Disorder: The Leninist Extinction*. Berkeley: University of California Press.

Kajetanowicz, Jerzy. 2013. *Wojsko polskie w systemie bezpieczeństwa państwa 1945–2010*. Częstochowa: Wydawnictwo im. Stanisława Podobińskiego Akademii im. Jana Długosza.

Kalan, Dariusz. 2012. "The End of a 'Beautiful Friendship?' US Relations with the Viŝegrad Countries Under Barack Obama (2009–2013)." *The Polish Quarterly of International Affairs*, 4: 83–100.

Kamiński, Łukasz. 2010. "The 'Prague Spring' and the Warsaw Pact Invasion." In: *The Prague Spring and the Warsaw Pact Invasion of Czechoslovakia, 1968: Forty Years Later*, compiled and edited by M. Mark Stolarik. Mundelein, Illinois: Bolchazy-Carducci Publishers, Inc.

Kaplan, Robert. 2012. *The Revenge of Geography: What the Map Tells Us About Coming Conflicts and the Battle Against Fate*. New York: Random House.

Kenez, Peter. 2006. *Hungary: From the Nazis to the Soviets: The Establishment of the Communist Regime in Hungary, 1944–1948*. Cambridge: Cambridge University Press.

Király, Béla. 2003. "The Battle of Nagykovacsi." In:*The Art of Survival*, edited by Béla Király. War and Society in East Central Europe, vol. 38. Boulder, Colorado: Columbia University Press.

Kirschbaum, Stanislav. 1995. *A History of Slovakia: The Struggle for Survival*. New York: St. Martin's Griffin.

Kochanski, Halik. 2012. *The Eagle Unbowed*. New Haven and London: Harvard University Press.

Konrád Györgi. 1984. *Antipolitics*. San Diego: Harcourt.

Kovrig, Bennett. 2006. "Stalin's Legacy: The Soviet Dominated Regimes in Hungary and East-Central Europe 1953–59." In: *1956: The Hungarian Revolution and War for Independence*, edited by Béla Király. War and Society in East Central Europe, vol. 40. Boulder, Colorado: Columbia University Press.

Koziej, Stanisław, and Adam Brzozowski. 2015. "Strategie Bezpieczeństwa Narodowego RP 1990–2014. Refleksja Na ćwierćwiecze." In: *Strategia bezpieczeństwa narodowego Rzeczypospolitej Polskiej. pierwsze 25 lat*, edited by Robert Kupiecki. Warszawa: Wojskowe Centrum Edukacji Obywatelskiej im. płk. dypl. Mariana Porwita.

Kramer, Mark. 2010. "The Prague Spring and the Soviet Invasion in Historical Perspective." In: *The Prague Spring and the Warsaw Pact invasion of Czechoslovakia in 1968*, edited by Günter Bischoff, Stefan Karner, and Peter Ruggenthaler. Boulder: Rowman & Littlefield Publishers, Inc.

Kříž, Zdeněk, and Martin Chovančík. 2013. "Czech and Slovak Defense Policies Since 1999: The Impact of Europeanization." *Problems of Post-Communism* 60, no. 3: 49–62.

Kucharczy, Jacek, and Grigorij Meseznikov. 2016, February 26. "Reakcje krajów Grupy Wyszehradzkiej na konflikt rosyjsko-ukrainski" https://pl.boell.org/pl/2016/02/26/reakcjekrajowgrupywyszehradzkiejnakonfliktros yjskoukrainski. (Accessed April 5, 2017).

Kufčak, Jakub. 2014. "The V4 Countries and the Impact of the Austerity Cuts on their Defence Spending and Armed Forces." *Obrana a Strategie* (60) 2: 35–48.

Kuźniar, Roman. 2008. *Droga do Wolności: Polityka Zagranicza III Rzeczypospolitej*. Warszawa: Wydawnictwo Naukowe "Scholar."

Laqueur, Walter. 1997. *Guerrilla Warfare: A Historical and Critical Study*. New Brunswick: Transaction Publishers.

Latysh, Mikhail V. 2010. "The Czechoslovak Crisis of 1968 in the Context of Soviet Geopolitics." In: *The Prague Spring and the Warsaw Pact Invasion of Czechoslovakia, 1968: Forty Years Later*, compiled and edited by M. Mark Stolarik. Mundelein, Illinois: Bolchazy-Carducci Publishers, Inc.

Lefebvre, Stéphane. 2010. "The Czech Republic and National Security, 1993–1998: The Emergence of a Strategic Culture." *Journal of Slavic Military Studies* 23: 328–69.

Leff Carol Skalnik. 1997. *The Czech and Slovak Republics: Nation Versus State*. Boulder, Colorado: Westview Press.

Lepianka, Paweł. 2004. "Determinants of Defense Budget Process in Post-Communist Poland: From the Warsaw Pact to the 21st Century." MA Thesis, Naval Post-Graduate School, Monterrey.

Levy, Jonathan. 2006. *The Intermarium: Wilson, Madison, & East Central European Federalism*. Boca Raton: Dissertation.Com.

Lewis, William. 1982. *Warsaw Pact: Arms, Doctrine and Strategy*. Cambridge: Institute for Foreign Policy Analysis.

Likowski, Michal. 2017. "Kontrowersyjna Obrona Terytorialna." *Raport Wojsko Technika Obronnosc*, March: 40–8.

Lis, Tomasz. 1999. *Wielki Final: Kulisy Wstępowania Polski Do NATO*. Kraków: Wydawnictwo "Znak."

Lubecki, Jacek. 2005. "Poland in Iraq: The Politics of the Decision." *The Polish Review*, 50, no. 1, Spring: 69–92.

—. 2011. "Piłsudski's Influence on the Polish Armed Forces of the Interwar Period." *The Polish Review*, 56, no. 1–2, Spring: 23–45.

Luetzow, Count 1914. *The Hussite Wars*. London and New York: J.M. Dent & Sons and E.P. Dutton & Co.

Lukowski, Jerzy, and Hubert Zawadzki. 2006. *A Concise History of Poland*. Cambridge: Cambridge University Press.

Lunák, Petr. 2006. "War Plans from Stalin to Brezhnev: The Czechoslovak Pivot." In: *War Plans and Alliances in the Cold War: Threat Perceptions in the East and West*, edited by Vojtech Mastny, Sven Holstmark, and Andreas Wenger. New York: Routledge.

Magdziak-Miszewska, Agnieszka. 1998. "Zapis dyskusji." In: *Polska i Rosja: strategiczne sprzeczności i możliwosci dialogu*, edited by Agnieszka Magdziak-Miszewska. Warszawa: Centrum Stosunków Miedzynarodowych. Instytut Spraw Publicznych.

Magyarics, T. 2013. "Hungary in NATO: The Case of Half Empty Glass." In: *NATO's European Allies. Military Capabilities and Political Will*, edited by Janne Haaland Mattlary, and Magnus Petersson. London: Palgrave Macmillan.

Makkai, László. 1990a. "Transformation Into a Western-Type State, 1196–1301." In: *A History of Hungary*, edited by Peter Sugar, Pétér Hanák, and Tibor Frank. Bloomington and Indianapolis: Indiana University Press.

—. 1990b. "The Foundation of the Hungarian Christian State." In: *A History of Hungary*, edited by Peter Sugar, Pétér Hanák, and Tibor Frank. Bloomington and Indianapolis: Indiana University Press.

—. 1990c. "The Hungarian Pre-History, Their Conquest of Hungary, and Their Raids to the West to 955." In: *A History of Hungary*, edited by Peter Sugar, Pétér Hanák, and Tibor Frank. Bloomington and Indianapolis: Indiana University Press.

Mastny, Vojtech, and Malcolm Byrne. 2005. *A Cardborad Castle? An Inside History of the Warsaw Pact, 1955–1991*. Budapest: Central European University Press.

Matei, Florina Cristiana. 2013. "The Impact of NATO Membership on Military Effectiveness: Hungary." In: *Routledge Handbook of Civil-Military Relations*, edited by Thomas Bruneau, and Cristiana Florina Matei. London and New York: Routledge.

May, Arthur J. 1951. *The Habsburg Monarchy, 1867–1914*. New York: W.W. Norton & Company, Inc.

Mearsheimer, John. 1990. "Back to the Future." *International Security*, 15, no. 1, Spring: 5–52.

Merlingen, Michael. 2012. *EU Security Policy: What It Is, How It Works and Why It Matters*. Boulder and London: Lynn Rienner Publishers.

Michnik, Adam. 1987. *Letters from Prison and Other Essays*. Berkeley, CA: University of California Press.

Michta, Andrew. 1990. *Red Eagle: The Army in Polish Politics, 1944–1988*. Stanford: Hoover Institute Press.

—. 1997. *Soldier-Citizen: The Politics of the Polish Army after Communism*, Basingstoke, Macmillan, 1997.

—. 2006. *The Limits of Alliance: The United States, NATO, and the EU, in North and Central Europe*. Lanham, Maryland: Rowman and Littlefield.

Ministerstwo Obrony Narodowej. 2017. "Koncepcja obronna Rzeczypospolitej Polskiej." http://mon.gov.pl/d/pliki/dokumenty/rozne/2017/06/korp_web_13_06_2017.pdf (Accessed July 15 2017).

Ministry of Defense of the Czech Republic. 2016a. "History of the Czech Military Participation in Operations Abroad (1990–2016)" www.army.cz (Accessed December 22, 2017).

—. 2016b. "Personnel Size of the Defence Department in 1992–2015." www.army.cz (Accessed December 22, 2017).

—. 2017a. "ALTHEA-EUFOR in BIH." September 14. www.army.cz (Accessed 2017).

—. 2017b. "EU-NAVFOR-SOMALIA-ATALANTA Operation." September 14. www.army.cz (Accessed 2017).

—. 2017c. "The Defence Strategy of the Czech Republic." September 14. www.army.cz (Accessed 2017).

—. 2017d. "The Long-Term Perspective for Defense 2030." September 14. www.army.cz (Accessed 2017).

—. 2017e. "The Defence Strategy of the Czech Republic 2012." September 14. www.army.cz (Accessed 2017).

Ministry of Defence of Hungary. 2017a. "EU Ministers Sign Joint Notification on Strengthening the EU's Defence Dimension." December 4. www.kormany.hu (Accessed July 15, 2017).

—. 2017b. "The V4 Supports Initiatives Aimed at Protecting Europe's External Borders." December 4. www.kormany.hu (Accessed July 15, 2017).

—. 2017c. "Hungary is Committed to Georgia's Europe-Atlantic Integration." December 4. www.kormany.hu (Accessed July 15, 2017).

Ministry of Defence of Poland 2017a. "Polish Military Contingent /MTT." December 3. www.mon.gov.pl (Accessed May 15, 2017).

—. 2017b. "Polish Military Contingent KFOR." December 3. www.mon.gov.pl (Accessed May 15, 2017).

—. 2017c. "Missions." December 3. www.mon.gov.pl (Accessed May 15, 2017).

Ministry of Defense of the Slovak Republic. 2016. "Foreign Operations." www.med.gov.sk (Accessed December 28, 2016).

Misiło, Eugeniusz. 2013. *Akcja Wisła 1947: dokumenty i materiały*. Warszawa: Archiwum Ukraińskie.

Mizokami, Kyle. 2016. "Revealed: How the Warsaw Pact Planned to Win World War Three in Europe," *National Interest*, July 2, http://nationalinterest.org/feature/revealed-how-the-warsaw-pact-planned-win-world-war-three-16822, accessed April 17, 2017.

MTI. 2014. "Sovereign Hungary Needs Strong Armed Forces, Says Defence Minister." June 18. www.politics.hu/20140618/sovereign-hungary-needs-strong-armed-forces-says-defence-minister/ (Accessed 2014).

Nagy, Boldizsár. 1997, March. "Hungary-Romania: Treaty on Understanding Cooperation and Good Neighborliness," in J-stor, *International Legal Matters* 36(2) https://www.jstor.org/stable/20698661?seq=1#page_scan_tab_contents (Accessed August 7 2017).

Nedelsky, Nadya. 2009. *Defining a Sovereign Community: The Czech and Slovak Republics*. Philadelphia: University of Pennsylvania Press.

*The New York Times*. 2017. "Czech Election, a New Threat to European Unity." October 17, www.nytimes. (Accessed December 12, 2018).

North Atlantic Council. 1957. "Report on Hungarian Refugees." Paris: North Atlantic Council, https://www.nato.int/nato_static/assets/pdf/pdf_archives_hungarian_revolution/20130904_C-M_57_65-ENG.PDF (Accessed April 7, 2017)

Nosek, Vladimir. 1926. *The Spirit of Bohemia: A Survey of Czechoslovak History, Music, and Literature*. London: George Allen & Unwin, Ltd.

Okulewicz, Piotr. 2001. *Koncepcja "Międzymorza" w myśli i praktyce politycznej obozu Józefa Piłsudskiego w latach 1918–1926*. Poznań: Wydawnictwo Poznańskie.

Omitruk, Tomasz. 2015. "Realizacja planu Modernizacji Technicznej Sil Zbrojnych RP (The Implementation of the Polish Armed Forces Technical Modernizaton Plan)." Special issue of *Nowa technika wojskowa*, 1230–655.

Onuf, Nicholas. 1989. *The World of Our Making*. Chapell Hill; NC: University of North Carolina Press.

Onyszkiewicz, Janusz. 1999. *Ze Szczytów do NATO. Z Ministrem Obrony Narodowej Januszem Onyszkiewiczem rozmawiaja Witold Bereś i Krzysztof Burnetko*. Warszawa: Dom Wydawniczy Bellona.

Orbán, Viktor. 2014. "Full text of Viktor Orbán's speech at Baile Tusnad (Tusnádfürdo) of 26 July 2014." http://budapestbeacon.com/public-policy/full-text-of-viktor-orbans-speech-at-baile-tusnad-tusnadfurdo-of-26-july-2014/10592 (Accessed July 27, 2017).

—. 2017. "Will Europe Belong to Europeans?" July 24. https://Višegradpost.com/en/2017/07/24/full-speech-of-v-orban-will-europe-belong-to-europeans/ (Accessed July 26, 2017).

Ormos, Mária. 1990. "The Early Interwar Years." In: *A History of Hungary*, edited by Peter Sugar, Pétér Hanák, and Tibor Frank. Bloomington and Indianapolis: Indiana University Press.

Orvis, Stephen, and Carol Ann Drogus. 2015. *Introducing Comparative Politics: Concepts and Cases in Action*. Los Angeles: Sage/CQ Press.

Ouimet, Mathew J. 2010. "Reconsidering the Soviet Role in the Invasion of Czechoslovakia." In: *The Prague Spring and the Warsaw Pact Invasion of Czechoslovakia, 1968: Forty Years Later*, compiled and edited by M. Mark Stolarik. Mundelein, Illinois: Bolchazy-Carducci Publishers, Inc.

Paces, Cynthia. 2009. *Prague Panoramas: National Memory and Sacred Space in the Twentieth Century*. Pittsburgh: University of Pittsburgh Press.

Paczkowski, Andrzej, and Malcom Byrne. 2008. *From Solidarity to Martial Law. The Polish Crisis of 1980–1981: A Documentery History*. Budapest: Central European University Press.

Palak, Jerzy, and Jerzy Telep. 2002. *Kierunek armia zawodowa? Aspekty ekonomiczne przebudowy i modernizacji sił zbrojnych Rzeczypospolitej Polskiej*. Warszawa: Dom Wydawniczy Bellona.

Pałka, Jarosław. 2008. *Generał Stefan Mossor (1896–1957), Biografia wojskowa*. Warszawa: Oficyna Wydawnicza "Rytm."

Pecsvarady, Szabolcs. 2010. "Special Operations Forces of Hungary: Is a Transformation Necessary?" MA Thesis. Army Command and General Staff College Fort Leavenworth Ks., http://www.dtic.mil/dtic/tr/fulltext/u2/a536818.pdf (Accessed July 12, 2017).

Peterson, James. 2011. *NATO and Terrorism: Organizational Expansion and Mission Transformation*. Cambridge: Continuum.

—. Forthcoming. "Czech National Security: Balancing NATO and EU Responsibilities." In: *Co-Dependency, Globalization, and Regime Change*, edited by Robert Evanson. Rowman and Littlefield.

Petrov, Nikita. 2010. "The KGB and the Czechoslovak Crisis of 1968: Preconditions for the Soviet Invasion and Occupation of Czechoslovakia." In: *The Prague Spring and the Warsaw Pact Invasion of Czechoslovakia in 1968*, edited by Günter Bischoff, Stefan Karner, and Peter Ruggenthaler. Boulder: Rowman & Littlefield Publishers, Inc.

Piahanau, Aliaksandr. 2014. "Hungarian War Aims During WWI: Between Expansionism and Separatism." *Central European Papers*, 2, no. 2: 95–107.

*Politico*. 2017. "Jarosław Jaczyński: The Backbench Driver." December 10.

Porter-Szucs, Brian. 2002. *When Nationalism Began to Hate: Imagining Modern Politics in Nineteenth-Century Poland*. Oxford: Oxford University Press.

—. 2014. *Poland in the Modern World: Beyond Martyrdom*. Hobboken: Wiley-Blackwell.

Postelnicescu, Claudia. 2016. Europe's New Identity: The Refugee Crisis and the Rise of Nationalism." *Europe's Journal of Psychology* (ejop.psychopen. eu), 12, no. 2: 203–9.

Quimet, Matthew. 2003. *The Rise and Fall of the Brezhnev Doctrine in Soviet Foreign Policy*. Chapel Hill and London: University of North Carolina Press.

Racz, András. 2012. "As Afghanistan Exits Loom, Let's not forget Hungary's contribution." February 16. www.paprikapolitik.com/2012/02/as-afghanistan-exits-loom-let-s-not-forget-hungary-s-contribution/ (Accessed July 11 2014).

Racz, András, and Erzsebet, Rozsa. 2012. "The Democratic Soldier in Hungary." In: *Democratic Civil-Military Relations: Soldiering in 21st Century Europe*, edited by Sabine Mannitz, Cass Military Studies, London and New York: 146–66.

Rees, H. Louis. 1992. *The Czechs During World War I: The Path to Independence*. Boulder: East European Monographs. Distributed by Columbia University Press.

Republic of Hungary. 2002. "National Security Strategy of the Republic of Hungary." http://www.mfa.gov.hu/NR/rdonlyres/61FB6933-AE67-47F8-BD D3-ECB1D9ADA7A1/0/national_security_strategy.pdf (Accessed July 15, 2018).

—. 2004. "National Security Strategy of the Republic of Hungary" https:// www.files.ethz.ch/isn/157029/Hungary_English-2004.pdf (Accessed July 13, 2017).

—. 2012. "National Security Strategy of the Republic of Hungary." https:// www.eda.europa.eu/docs/default-source/documents/hungary-national-secu rity-strategy-2012.pdf (Accessed July 14, 2018).

Ross Johnson, A. 1977. "Soviet-East European Military Relations." Rand Paper Series, vol. 374.

Rothenberg, Gunther. 1981. *The Army of Francis Joseph*. Lafayette: Purdue University Press.

Rothschild, Joseph. 1974. *East Central Europe Between the Two World Wars*. Seattle: University of Washington Press.

Ruggenthaler, Peter, and Harald Knoll. 2010. "The Moscow 'Negotiations': 'Normalizing Relations" Between the Soviet Leadership and the Czechoslovak Delegation after the Invasion." In: *The Prague Spring and the Warsaw Pact Invasion of Czechoslovakia in 1968*, edited by Günter Bischoff, Stefan Karner, and Peter Ruggenthaler. Boulder: Rowman & Littlefield Publishers, Inc.

Rychlík, Jan. 2010. "The 'Prague Spring' and the Warsaw Pact Invasion as Seen from Prague." In: *The Prague Spring and the Warsaw Pact Invasion of Czechoslovakia, 1968: Forty Years Later*, compiled and edited by M. Mark Stolarik. Mundelein, Illinois: Bolchazy-Carducci Publishers, Inc.

Rzeczpospolita Polska. 2014. "Strategia bezpieczeństwa narodowego Rzeczpospolitej Polskiej." (National Security Strategy of the Republic of Poland). https://www.bbn.gov.pl/ftp/dok/NSS_RP.pdf (Accessed June 15, 2017).

Sanecka-Tyczyńska, Joanna. 2011. "Modele bezpieczeństwa zewnętrznego państwa w myśli politycznej Prawa i Sprawiedliwości." *Zeszyty Naukowe WSOWL* (161) 3: 218–31.

Seton-Watson, Hugh. 1962. *Eastern Europe Between the Wars 1918–1941*. New York: Harper Torchbooks.

Sherr, James. 2000. "Nato's New Members: A Model for Ukraine? The Example of Hungary" https://www.files.ethz.ch/isn/97634/00_Sep_3.pdf (Accessed July 14, 2017).

Simon, Jeffrey. 2002. *Hungary and NATO: Problems in Civil-Military Relations*. Lanham, Maryland: Rowman and Littlefield.

—. 2003. *NATO and the Czech and Slovak Republics: A Comparative Study in Civil-Military Relations*. New York: Rowman & Littlefield Publishers, Inc.

—. 2004. *Poland and NATO: A Study in Civil-Military Relations*. Lanham, Boulder, New York: Rowman and Littlefield.

Skálová, Ivana. 2010. "Bulgarian Participation in Suppressing the 'Prague Spring' of 1968." In: *The Prague Spring and the Warsaw Pact Invasion of*

*Czechoslovakia, 1968: Forty Years Later*, compiled and edited by M. Mark Stolarik. Mundelein, Illinois: Bolchazy-Carducci Publishers, Inc.

*SME*. 2017a. "Američania už posilňujú Poľsko aj Pobaltie. Trump-Netrump." www.sme.sk (Accessed January 12, 2017).

—. 2017b. "Lotyšský analytik: Rusko neohrozuje len Pobaltie, ale aj Slovensko." www.sme.sk (Accessed January 12, 2017).

Smoliński, Józef. 2016. "Wstęp." In: *Polskie Siły Zbrojne na Zachodzie po II Wojnie Światowej. Klęska zwycięzców*, edited by Jozef Smoliński. Kraków: Drukarnia Wydawnicza im. W.L. Anczyca SA w Krakowie.

Snyder, Timothy. 2010. *Bloodlands: Europe Between Stalin and Hitler*. New York: Basic Books.

Staff. 2017. "Hungary to increase military spending in 2018". http://budapest-beacon.com/news-in-brief/hungary-increase-military-spending-2018/46796 (Accessed July 25, 2017).

Staniszkis, Jadwiga. 1984. *Poland's Self-Limiting Revolution*. Princeton: Princeton University Press.

Szabo, Miklós. 2001. "The Development of the Hungarian Aircraft Industry, 1938-1944." *The Journal of Military History*, 65, no. 1983, January: 53–76.

Szenesz, Zoltan. 2007. "Peacekeeping in the Hungarian Armed Forces." *AARMS: Academic and Applied Research in Military Science*, 6, no. 1: 121–33.

Szilagyi, Zsofia. 1997. "Hungary. A Year of Optimism." In: *The Challenge of Integration*, edited by Peter Rutland. Annual Survey of Eastern Europe and the Former Soviet Union, 103–23.

Talas, Péter, and Tamás Csiki. 2013. "Hungary." In: *Strategic Cultures in Europe: Security and Defense Policies Across the Continent*. Biehl, Heiko; Giegerich, Bastian; Jonas, Alexandra: Springer-Verlag.

Taylor, A.J.P. 1970. *The Habsburg Monarchy*. London: Penguin Books.

Than, Krisztina, and Gergely Szakacs. 2017. "Hungary to boost defence spending to 2% of GDP – minister" www.reuters.com/article/uk-hungary-defence-minister-idUKKBN14W2D1 (Accessed July 18, 2017).

Thompson, James. 2004. "History's Rhyme," paper presented at Mid-Western Political Science Association Annual Conference, April 15, Chicago.

Tibor, Frank. 1990. "Hungary and the Dual Monarchy 1867–1890." In: *A History of Hungary*, edited by Peter Sugar, Pétér Hanák and Tibor Frank. Bloomington and Indianapolis: Indiana University Press.

Tilkovszky, Loránd. 1990. "The Later Interwar Years and World War II." In: *A History of Hungary*, edited by Peter Sugar, Pétér Hanák, and Tibor Frank. Bloomington and Indianapolis: Indiana University Press.

*The Times of Israel*. 2017. "Zeman followed Trump by recognizing Jerusalem as Israel's Capital." December 10.

Törö, Csaba. 2001. "Hungary: Building a National Consensus." In: *Enlarging NATO: National Debates*, edited by Gale A Mattox and Arthur Rachwald. Boulder, London: Lynne Rienner Publishers.

Ungváry, Krisztiám. 2006. *The Siege of Budapest: One Hundred Days in World War II*. Yale: Yale University Press.

*USATODAY* 2017. "EU divided along U.S.-style blue state, red state lines." October 19. www.usatoday.com. (Accessed October 19, 2017).

Vegh, Zsusanne. 2015. "Hungary's 'Eastern Opening' Policy Towards Russia: Ties That Bind?" *International Issues and Slovak Foreign Policy Affairs*, 24, no. 1–2: 47–65.

Wagner, Peter, and Peter Marton. 2014. "Hungarian Military and the War on Terror." *The Polish Quarterly of International Affairs*, 2014, no. 2: 107–20.

Wandycz, Piotr. 1974. *The Lands of Partitioned Poland, 1795-1918*. A History of East-Central Europe v. 7. Seattle and London: University of Washington Press.

—. 1990. "Poland's Place in Europe in the Concepts of Piłsudski and Dmowski." *Eastern European Politics and Societies*, 4, no. 3: 451–68.

—. 2001. *The Price of Freedom. A History of East-Central Europe from the Middle Ages to the Present*, 2nd edition. London and New York: Routledge.

Wedgewood, C.V. 1961 [1938]. *The Thirty Years War*. New York: Anchor Books. Doubleday & Company, Inc.

Wendt, Alexander. 1999. *Social Theory of International Politics*. Cambridge: Cambridge University Press.

Wenzke, Rüdiger. 2010. "The Role and Accessories of the SED, the East German State and its Military During the 'Prague Spring' of 1968." In: *The Prague Spring and the Warsaw Pact Invasion of Czechoslovakia, 1968: Forty Years Later*, compiled and edited by M. Mark Stolarik. Mundelein, Illinois: Bolchazy-Carducci Publishers, Inc.

Wiesel, Elie. 1982. *Night*. New York: Bantam Books.

Wolpiuk, Waldemar. 1998. *Sily zbrojne w regulacjach konstytucji RP*. Warszawa: Wydawnictwo "Scholar."

Wróbel, Piotr. 2010. "The 'Prague Spring,' Poland and the Warsaw Pact Invasion." In: *The Prague Spring and the Warsaw Pact Invasion of Czechoslovakia, 1968: Forty Years Later*, compiled and edited by M. Mark Stolarik. Mundelein, Illinois: Bolchazy-Carducci Publishers, Inc.

Wyszczelski, Lech. 2005. *Wojsko Piłsudskiego: Wojsko Polskie w latach 1926–1935*. Warszawa: Wydawnictwo NERITON.

Zgórniak, Marian. 1993. *Europa w przededniu wojny. Sytuacja militarna w latach 1938–1939*. Kraków: Wydawnictwo Księgarni Akademickiej Adam Roliński.

Zychowicz, Piotr. 2012. *Pakt Ribbentrop-Beck czyli jak Polacy mogli u boku III Rzeszy pokonać Związek Radziecki*. Poznań: Dom Wydawnicz Rebis.

—. 2013. *Obłęd '44. Czyli jak Polacy zrobili prezent Stalinowi wywołując Powstanie Warszawskie*. Poznań: Dom Wydawniczy Rebis.

# Index

EU authorised representative for GPSR:
Easy Access System Europe, Mustamäe tee 50,
10621 Tallinn, Estonia
gpsr.requests@easproject.com

www.ingramcontent.com/pod-product-compliance
Lightning Source LLC
Chambersburg PA
CBHW031136270326
41929CB00011B/1643